SOCIAL ATTITUDES ... GATHERING

‖‖‖‖‖‖‖‖‖‖‖‖‖‖‖‖‖‖‖‖
D1434569

# SOCIAL ATTITUDES IN NORTHERN IRELAND
## The Eighth Report

Edited by
Ann Marie Gray, Katrina Lloyd,
Paula Devine, Gillian Robinson
and Deirdre Heenan

Pluto Press

LONDON · STERLING, VIRGINIA

First published 2002 by Pluto Press
345 Archway Road, London N6 5AA
and 22883 Quicksilver Drive, Sterling, VA 20166–2012, USA

www.plutobooks.com

British Library Cataloguing in Publication Data
A catalogue record for this book is available from the British Library

Library of Congress Cataloging in Publication Data
A catalogue record for this book is available

ISBN 0 7453 1912 2 hardback
ISBN 0 7453 1911 4 paperback

10   9   8   7   6   5   4   3   2   1

Designed and produced for Pluto Press by
Chase Publishing Services, Fortescue, Sidmouth EX10 9QG
Typeset by Stanford DTP Services, Towcester
Printed in the European Union by Antony Rowe, Chippenham, England

# Contents

# List of Figures and Tables

## Figures

## Tables

# Introduction

*Ann Marie Gray, Katrina Lloyd, Paula Devine,*
*Gillian Robinson and Deirdre Heenan*

This volume is the eighth in a series on social attitudes in Northern Ireland. The previous editions (Stringer and Robinson, 1991; 1992; 1993; Breen, Devine and Robinson, 1995; Breen, Devine and Dowds, 1996; Dowds, Devine and Breen, 1997; Robinson, Heenan, Gray and Thompson, 1998) were based on data from the Northern Ireland Social Attitudes (NISA) survey series. This volume is based on the successor to that survey – the Northern Ireland Life and Times survey.

Since 1989, these attitudinal surveys and the output from them – both in the edited volumes and the more recently available on-line Research Updates <http://www.ark.ac.uk/nilt/publications.html> – have become an acknowledged source of information on contemporary values in Northern Ireland. This volume, drawing largely on data collected in the 1998 and 1999 Life and Times surveys, includes a broad spectrum of policy relevant chapters from an authoritative list of Northern Ireland commentators. Three themes are explored in the chapters in this volume. The first, addressed in many of the earlier volumes, is the extent of change in values centred on religion, politics and community relations. This theme is, of course, omnipresent in any debate on Northern Ireland and the Life and Times survey is committed to ensuring reliable monitoring of these issues, especially in the current volatile political environment. The second theme is a new one to the series and concentrates on public attitudes to science and to genetic information. Both of these issues have increasingly come into the spotlight in recent years and show high levels of uncertainty among the public. It will be interesting to compare this base-line data in future years as medical and scientific advances continue. The third cluster of chapters concentrates on what might be called core social policy issues: education, housing, pensions, transport, social inequality and the rights of the child. In all these chapters the distinctive features of Northern Ireland social policy form a backdrop to a detailed examination of the issues. In some cases comparisons are made with Britain, as well as with findings from earlier years of NISA.

The Life and Times survey was launched in the autumn of 1998. Its mission is to monitor the attitudes and behaviour of people in Northern Ireland to a range of social policy issues. By running annually, the survey provides a time series and a public record of how our attitudes and behaviour develop.

In particular, the survey aims to provide:

- a local resource for use by the general public, and
- a data source for a more theoretical academic debate.

The Life and Times survey is a direct descendent of the NISA survey which ran from 1989 to 1996. NISA was a sister survey to the British Social Attitudes (BSA) survey, and, by running the same modules as BSA, it provided a time series of social attitudes, and allowed comparisons with Britain. When funding for NISA ended in 1996, the opportunity was taken to develop a new survey that would continue to record attitudes to social policy issues in Northern Ireland, but would cut the close link to BSA to allow for a more specific Northern Ireland focus. The Life and Times survey is largely Northern Ireland focused, it is social policy focused, and it is designed to be used by the wider public in Northern Ireland. Nonetheless, each year's survey includes a substantial component which either continues an old NISA time series, or replicates a BSA module.

Every year 38 countries participate in the International Social Survey Programme (ISSP) in which the same module of questions is asked cross-nationally. Northern Ireland has taken part in this exercise since 1989, originally via NISA, and now via the Life and Times survey. Individual datasets for all the member countries can be obtained from the Zentralarchiv für Empirische Sozialforschung (Central Archive for Empirical Social Research) at the University of Cologne, Germany, which is the official archive of the ISSP. The Zentralarchiv also produces a merged datafile for each year, containing data from all countries. Information on the ISSP can be found at its web site at <http://www.issp.org>, while the English version of the Zentralarchiv web site is at <http://www.gesis.org/en/za/index.htm>.

The fact that this volume is possible is due to the many generous funders who have supported the Life and Times survey since its inception. We are particularly grateful to those who came in at the beginning of the new survey without whom this valuable time series could have been lost. Among them, the Central Community Relations Unit (now the Equality Unit Research Branch within the Office of the First Minister and Deputy First Minister) has supported a module focusing on community relations each year since 1989. The chapter by Hughes and Donnelly in this volume shows the benefits of such a time series. The Nuffield Foundation has also provided continuous support both through its ongoing interest in education in Northern

Ireland and also in its support for the detailed work on pensions. The Pensions and Pensioners module was also boosted by funding from the Department for Social Development, the Social Security Agency and the Training and Employment Agency. The Wellcome Foundation funded the Attitudes to Genetics Research module, and the Royal Irish Academy (through its Social Science Research Council) supported the work on social inequality by funding the inclusion of the ISSP module in the 1999 survey. The Northern Ireland Housing Executive (NIHE) provided generous support for the Housing module and has itself prepared a report from the data (NIHE, 2000). The Economic and Social Research Council has demonstrated its interest in Northern Ireland matters through support for the Political Attitudes module in 1999 (Award Number: L327253045). It continues its support through the Devolution Programme funding for nationwide attitudes surveys on devolution and constitutional change in 2001 and 2003 (Award Number: L219252024). The Rights of the Child module was supported by a portfolio of funders including the Calouste Gulbenkian Foundation, Save the Children and the Department of Health and Social Security.

Finally, this survey is quite unique in that it is a genuine collaboration between the two universities in Northern Ireland – the University of Ulster and Queen's University Belfast. Both of these have provided invaluable financial and practical support to the survey, and the editors and survey team wish to record their sincere appreciation of this support.

The Life and Times series is, of course, a team effort. In particular, the survey coordinator Lizanne Dowds deserves special mention for her vision and enterprise in establishing and continuing to develop the survey. The survey team is also supported by Research and Evaluation Services, who have conducted the fieldwork in these first years. We are grateful to Peter Ward and his team for their efficient service.

The Life and Times survey is conducted each year in the hope that its findings may impact positively upon policy-making in the region. We reserve our warmest appreciation for all of those anonymous respondents to the survey who give freely of their time. Without them, no research of this kind is possible. We hope you will find the results of interest and may indeed benefit in some small way from the findings. For more information on all aspects of the series please visit our web site at <http://www.ark.ac.uk/nilt>.

### References

Breen, R., Devine, P. and Dowds, L. (eds) (1996) *Social Attitudes in Northern Ireland: The Fifth Report, 1995–1996* (Belfast: Appletree Press).

Breen, R., Devine, P. and Robinson, G. (eds) (1995) *Social Attitudes in Northern Ireland: The Fourth Report, 1994–1995* (Belfast: Appletree Press).

Dowds, L., Devine, P. and Breen, R. (eds) (1997) *Social Attitudes in Northern Ireland: The Sixth Report, 1996–1997* (Belfast: Appletree Press).

Northern Ireland Housing Executive (NIHE) (2000) *Public Attitudes Survey 1998* (Belfast: Northern Ireland Housing Executive).

Robinson, G., Heenan, D., Gray, A.M. and Thompson, K. (eds) (1998) *Social Attitudes in Northern Ireland: The Seventh Report* (Aldershot: Ashgate).

Stringer, P. and Robinson, G. (eds) (1991) *Social Attitudes in Northern Ireland, 1990–91 Edition* (Belfast: Blackstaff Press).

Stringer, P. and Robinson, G. (eds) (1992) *Social Attitudes in Northern Ireland: The Second Report, 1991–92* (Belfast: Blackstaff Press).

Stringer, P. and Robinson, G. (eds) (1993) *Social Attitudes in Northern Ireland: The Third Report, 1992–1993* (Belfast: Blackstaff Press).

# 1 More Knowing than Knowledgeable: Attitudes Towards Devolution

*Roger MacGinty and Rick Wilford*

The protracted delay in the initial implementation of the 1998 Good Friday Agreement and its fitful outworking thereafter tends to confirm the axiom that peace processes are fragile affairs, rarely prospering over the long term without active public support. Between 1989 and 1999, for instance, just 21 of 110 armed conflicts were ended by peace agreements, and only a minority of those agreements survive (Wallensteen and Sollenberg, 2000).

Public understanding of peace processes and/or political transitions is critical, particularly where a peace accord relies on formal public approval through a referendum. Similarly, the satisfaction of the public expectations attached to a peace process seems important. Peace accords are often accompanied – and justified – by promises of an end to violence, demonstrably better living standards, and the improved provision of public goods and services. This chapter discusses public knowledge of, and expectations about, Northern Ireland's newly devolved institutions and the significance of the consent principle to the forging of the new political dispensation. The data come from the 1999 Northern Ireland Life and Times survey, which was undertaken during the critical period when powers were first transferred to Northern Ireland (late October 1999 to mid-January 2000). As such, the chapter provides a compelling and contemporary insight into public attitudes when the, as it turned out, fitful process of restoring devolution to Northern Ireland got underway. The chapter also explores whether the consent principle, a cornerstone of both the Good Friday Agreement and the political process that produced it, found broad acceptance across both communities.

## Consent

The consent principle has a long association with Northern Ireland. Yet, for most of Northern Ireland's history, the principle has been a formal legal mechanism, strictly in the hands of parliaments (Westminster and Stormont), and somewhat removed from the people of Northern Ireland. The Good Friday Agreement marked a *political* rejuvenation of the consent principle by empowering the electorate of Northern Ireland to decide their own constitutional future. The Agreement insisted that the territory's constitutional status could only be changed with the consent of a majority of its citizens. As explored by the authors elsewhere (MacGinty, Wilford, Dowds and Robinson, 2001) the acceptance of the principle by the Irish government, nationalists and – albeit implicitly – by republicans, was of immense significance. The endorsement of the principle in the 1998 referenda also helped draw it further into the public political sphere.

With the renewed immediacy of the consent principle in mind, the Life and Times survey sought to gauge its public acceptance. Put starkly: would unionists be prepared to come quietly if a majority of Northern Ireland's citizens voted to accept a united Ireland? As a starting point, the survey measured constitutional preferences of all respondents. A majority (56 per cent) favour continued union with the United Kingdom and less than a quarter (21 per cent) favour Irish unity (Table 1.1).[1] From this evidence, it would seem that Northern Ireland's constitutional status is unlikely to change, at least in anything but the long term. Yet the survey shows that public uncertainty about Northern Ireland's constitutional future is high. Responses to the question, 'at any time in the next 20 years, do you think it is likely or unlikely that there will be a united Ireland?', reveal that 40 per cent think this scenario to be quite or very likely. A similar proportion (45 per cent) thinks that a united Ireland is unlikely or very unlikely within 20 years. Interestingly, the levels of constitutional uncertainty are broadly similar (and significant) in both the Catholic and Protestant communities. This uncertainty is noteworthy in the context of the Good Friday Agreement – a purposively comprehensive peace accord that attempted to place constitutional issues to rest, at least for the medium term.

Table 1.1  What should the long-term policy for Northern Ireland be? (%)

| | |
|---|---|
| To remain part of the United Kingdom | 56 |
| To reunify with the rest of Ireland | 21 |
| Independent state | 11 |
| Other answer | 3 |
| Don't know | 9 |

The key to consent is the idea that a minority (or minorities) will accept the wishes of the majority: a potentially risky assumption in a deeply divided society. In the Northern Ireland case, with increasingly finely balanced Catholic–Protestant demographics, any minority has the potential to be significant in number. Bearing in mind that asking respondents to anticipate their reactions to possible future events is inevitably an inexact science – not least because the prevailing political context will be unknown – the survey asked those who *do not* want a united Ireland for their response to a majority vote for Irish unification. As Table 1.2 shows, 77 per cent say that they would accept a united Ireland either happily or resignedly. In other words, the results indicate a strong acceptance of the consent principle.

However, a significant minority (19 per cent) say that they would find a majority vote for a united Ireland 'almost impossible to accept', although whether this unacceptability would endorse political violence as a mode of opposition is not recorded. Certainly the 19 per cent by far exceeds recent electoral support for parties associated with loyalist paramilitarism, suggesting that some current voters for constitutional unionist parties would find the prospect of a united Ireland an intolerable option.

Table 1.2 How would you feel if the majority of people in Northern Ireland ever voted to become part of a united Ireland? (%)

| | |
|---|---|
| Would find this almost impossible to accept | 19 |
| Would not like it but could live with it if you had to | 35 |
| Would happily accept the wishes of the majority | 42 |
| Don't know | 5 |

When disaggregated by religion (Table 1.3) it becomes clear that 69 per cent of Protestants would accept Irish unity by consent, a remarkable figure given that the survey also found that 87 per cent of Protestants favour continued union with the UK. This points to a sophisticated internalisation of the consent principle among Protestants. On the one hand, many unionists champion consent as a safeguard for their continued place within the Union. On the other hand, many also see consent as a double-edged sword that can also act as a mechanism to take them out of the Union.

Table 1.3 How would you feel if the majority of people in Northern Ireland ever voted to become part of a united Ireland? (%)

| | Catholic | Protestant | No religion |
|---|---|---|---|
| Would find this almost impossible to accept | 1 | 29 | 15 |
| Would not like it but would live with it if you had to | 13 | 44 | 40 |
| Would happily accept the wishes of the majority | 80 | 25 | 42 |
| Don't know | 6 | 4 | 4 |

But what if consent worked to permanently reject a united Ireland? After all, the Irish Republican Army's (IRA) long war had been ostensibly justified by the denial of their constitutional objective. Respondents who had indicated that they did not want Northern Ireland to remain within the UK were asked for their reaction if a majority of people in Northern Ireland *never* voted for a united Ireland. The survey found that only 2 per cent of this group find the permanent rejection of a united Ireland 'almost impossible to accept' (Table 1.4). In particular, only 2 per cent of Catholics who were asked this question would find the rejection of a united Ireland 'almost impossible to accept', indicating that the vast majority of both nationalists and republicans are willing to accept the wishes of the majority. Although the republican movement has shied away from an explicit embrace of the consent principle, these findings suggest that much of their support base is willing to accept options short of a united Ireland.

Table 1.4    How would you feel if the majority of people in Northern Ireland never voted to become part of a united Ireland? (%)

| | |
|---|---|
| Would find this almost impossible to accept | 2 |
| Would not like it but could live with it if you had to | 24 |
| Would happily accept the wishes of the majority | 68 |
| Don't know | 6 |

Given that Northern Ireland's recent political history has been dominated by violent attempts by various groups to force their constitutional will on others, the survey findings are significant. They suggest that consent to the will of the majority has gained widespread acceptance in both communities. Potentially, this has profound implications for the operation of politics in a devolved Northern Ireland. The broad acceptance that constitutional issues can be dealt with politically, rather than militarily, and that the people of Northern Ireland will be the final arbiters of the territory's constitutional fate is a potentially stabilising force.

### A Difficult Birth for Devolution

Despite the acceptance of the consent principle by pro-Agreement forces within Northern Ireland, there was a sharp division of opinion within the unionist electorate towards the Agreement, one that contrasted sharply with overwhelming support from nationalist and republican voters. At first sight, the balance of pro- and anti-Agreement forces within the Assembly was – and is – heavily tilted to the former: nominally, 80 of the 108 Members of the Legislative Assembly (MLAs) were drawn from pro-Agreement parties, and just

28 from their opponents. However, the ostensibly narrow majority of the 30 pro-Agreement unionists (comprising 28 Ulster Unionist Party (UUP) and two Progressive Unionist Party (PUP) members) over their 28 anti-Agreement opponents (including 20 from the Democratic Unionist Party (DUP), five from the United Kingdom Unionist Party (UKUP) and three Independent unionists) was somewhat misleading. A number of the UUP's MLAs had in fact voted against the Agreement at the referendum and could not be relied upon to provide unequivocal support to the party's leader, David Trimble, as subsequent events have borne out. Indeed, shortly after the Assembly first convened, one of their number – Peter Weir – had the whip withdrawn and thereafter sat in the chamber alongside Dr Ian Paisley's DUP. This left an exact split of 29:29 pro- and anti-Agreement unionists in the Assembly, adding to the existing uncertainty surrounding the outworking of Northern Ireland's devolution project.

These uncertainties were compounded by the fact that a further six months elapsed between the June 1998 Assembly elections and interparty agreement on the size and shape of the devolved Executive Committee. The eventual outcome of the negotiations was that there were to be eleven devolved departments, instead of the six local departments that had administered direct rule. This reconfiguration was the result of a political bargain rather than a careful exercise in administrative rationality. Given that there were to be two co-equal ministers (David Trimble, UUP and, initially, Seamus Mallon, Social Democratic and Labour Party (SDLP)) in the Office of the First Minister and Deputy First Minister, the bargain created parity of ministerial numbers (if not esteem) around the Executive Committee table. Through the application of the D'Hondt formula (for details see Wilford, 1999, p. 314) there would be six unionists and six nationalists in the Executive, although the DUP's two ministers refused to participate in Executive meetings because of the inclusion of two Sinn Féin ministers.

Despite agreement on the size and shape of the Executive Committee, further interparty disagreement meant that power was not formally transferred until 2 December 1999, almost 18 months after the Assembly elections. Indeed, it was only three days earlier that the electorate was to discover which of the devolved departments would be selected by the four major parties (UUP, DUP, SDLP and Sinn Féin) and the identities of the newly nominated ministers. Thus, the fieldwork for the Life and Times survey reported here coincided with the realisation of devolution and the first phase of its implementation.

The undeniably subtle and complex design of the Agreement's political institutions, together with the processes of change it set in train – including the reform of both the Royal Ulster Constabulary (RUC) and the criminal justice system, a new Human Rights

Commission and a new equality regime – meant that there was much for politicians and the public alike to digest. In addition, there was a key issue that remained unresolved: the decommissioning of all para-military weapons. This particularly wicked issue, coupled with the early release on licence of scheduled offenders and the looming reform of the RUC, did occasion unease within the wider population. For Protestants, in particular, the failure to make tangible progress on decommissioning jarred uncomfortably with the realisation that, from 2 December 1999, not only were there to be two Sinn Féin ministers in the devolved Executive, but they would lead the two biggest spending departments: Health, Social Services and Public Safety, and Education.

The lengthy delay in transferring powers might be conjectured to have created the time and space for the wider population to gain some clearer understanding of the nature of the devolved structures, yet this appears not to be the case. However, with the 'cushion' of the consent principle in place, the time lapse did little to dampen public expecta-tions about the capacity of devolution to make a difference, as the survey results disclose.

### Knowledge and Awareness

The survey findings reveal a widespread perception that levels of public awareness about the devolved institutions are low. Overall, just 14 per cent of respondents *perceive* that most people in Northern Ireland understand how the new Assembly and other new governing institu-tions are supposed to work, whereas 81 per cent perceive that most people do not understand the new Assembly. What is especially compelling is that respondents are emphatic in stating whether or not they believe that most people grasp the way in which devolution operates: only 4 per cent don't know whether their fellow citizens understand how the new institutions will work. Perhaps reflecting the more enthusiastic reception they accorded to the Agreement, slightly more Catholics (18 per cent) believe that their fellow citizens are aware of the workings of the new institutions than Protestants (13 per cent) (Table 1.5).

Table 1.5 Do most people understand how the new Assembly and other government bodies are supposed to work? (%)

|  | Catholic | Protestant | No religion | All |
| --- | --- | --- | --- | --- |
| Yes | 18 | 13 | 10 | 14 |
| No | 78 | 83 | 87 | 81 |
| Don't know | 4 | 5 | 3 | 4 |

Those who answered 'no' or 'don't know' to this question were asked if *they* understand how the new Assembly and other new government bodies are supposed to operate. As Table 1.6 shows, only one in four (28 per cent) say that they do, while the remainder – an overwhelming 72 per cent – say they do not. The differential between Catholics and Protestants on this item is relatively modest (69 per cent of Catholics and 74 per cent of Protestants state that they do not grasp how the devolved bodies are supposed to work), but the gender difference is significant. Men, whether through hubris or self-delusion – or some combination of both – are twice as likely as women (39 per cent compared to 20 per cent) to assert that they understand the mysteries of devolution.

Table 1.6 Do you understand how the new Assembly and the other government bodies are supposed to work? (%)

|     | Men | Women | Catholics | Protestants | No religion | All |
|-----|-----|-------|-----------|-------------|-------------|-----|
| Yes | 39  | 20    | 31        | 26          | 32          | 28  |
| No  | 61  | 80    | 69        | 74          | 68          | 72  |

Asked about the transparency of the political process leading to devolution, a narrow overall majority (52 per cent) thinks that the process should have been more open, whereas 39 per cent think that it was open enough and 8 per cent don't know. While roughly equal proportions of Catholics and Protestants believe that the process should have been more open, 45 per cent of Catholics believe that the process was sufficiently transparent as opposed to 36 per cent of Protestants (Table 1.7).

Table 1.7 Should the setting up of the Assembly and other government bodies have been more open? (%)

|                              | Catholic | Protestant | No religion | All |
|------------------------------|----------|------------|-------------|-----|
| Should have been more open   | 51       | 54         | 50          | 52  |
| Was open enough              | 45       | 36         | 34          | 39  |
| Other                        | 1        | <1         | 2           | 1   |
| Don't know                   | 4        | 10         | 14          | 8   |

How can this perceived lack of public understanding surrounding the introduction of devolution be explained? At the outset, it is worth noting that the process leading up to the Agreement, the 10,000 word text itself, and the cross-cutting constitutionalism that it heralded were indeed complex. New layers of governance would sit alongside existing institutions. The advent of interlocking and interdependent institutions, a restructuring of government departments and powers, the concept of power-sharing between parties who held diametrically opposed views of the same Agreement, and a confusing transitional interregnum between Good Friday 1998 and the eventual operation of the Agreement was, for a society long used to the blunt simplicities of direct rule, a somewhat bewildering prospect.

Furthermore, the high levels of secrecy maintained throughout much of the peace process may have contributed to a low level of public awareness. Secrecy has long been regarded as a key element in the negotiation of peace accords (Egeland, 1999), and much of the Northern Ireland peace process was restricted to the political elites. Negotiations between prime ministers, party leaders and nominated delegations occurred *in camera*. Although the broad outline of an agreement – notably its three-stranded nature – had long been in the public domain, many of the details of the Agreement were only finalised in the hothouse atmosphere of Castle Buildings in the 72 hours leading up to the release of the final text. New ideas and drafts were introduced in the terminal hours of the negotiations, and there were few plenary sessions of the talks in which ideas could be aired among all of the parties. Instead, much of the business of the talks was conducted in corridors.[2]

Another possible factor limiting public awareness and understanding of devolution was that by the time the Agreement was reached, political discourse, mindful of an impending referendum, was already in election mode. There was little space for dispassionate, educative or informative analysis of the Agreement. The nature of the referendum campaign, necessarily dividing arguments into the pros and cons of the Agreement, meant that conflicting interpretations of the text filled the newspaper columns and dominated the airwaves. The DUP regarded the Agreement as 'a staging post to a united Ireland', whereas the leadership of the UUP portrayed the Agreement as 'securing Northern Ireland's place within the United Kingdom'.[3] The fact that the UUP did not speak with an unequivocally pro-Agreement voice also meant that the minutiae of the devolution scheme were largely unaddressed. Six of the party's ten MPs declared themselves as anti-Agreement, in part because of conflicting opinions about its constitutional significance and also because of a lack of certainty about decommissioning and RUC reform, allied to the very real prospect of having what they regarded as 'unreconstructed terrorists' in a devolved government.

The withdrawal of the DUP and UKUP from the multi-party negotiations in September 1997 may also have added to public confusion on the details of devolution. Their exit meant that a substantial section of the unionist population was not represented at the talks and this helped to fan the flames of suspicion that 'Ulster' was to be 'sold out' by an unholy alliance of London, Dublin and local pro-Agreement parties. Indeed, the abrupt departure of a number of the UUP's delegates to the talks – notably the (youngish) pretender to the party's leadership, Jeffrey Donaldson MP – immediately before the Agreement was unveiled added further fuel to the flames. Institutional detail was simply crowded out of the debate.

While a copy of the Good Friday Agreement was sent to every household in Northern Ireland, much of the text was less than pellucid. Moreover, the Northern Ireland Office did not supply supplementary and explanatory information as an aid to popular understanding. Instead, Tony Blair was drawn onto the moral high ground, territory on which he revels, and issued a handwritten note to the plain people of Ulster setting out the consequences of a failure by paramilitaries to decommission their arsenals, thereby seeking to allay widespread (especially unionist) anxieties about the imminent arrival of 'gunmen in government'.

Deadlines for the start of devolution passed unmet and, amid scenes of high farce, an exclusively SDLP–Sinn Féin Executive was nominated on 15 July 1999. Since it failed to meet the Agreement's cross-community criteria and the hastily issued standing order by the then Secretary of State, Mo Mowlam, that the Executive must contain at least three unionists and three nationalists, it was immediately deemed invalid. Disillusioned with what he saw as UUP prevarication, Seamus Mallon resigned as Deputy First Minister, triggering the lengthy Mitchell review of the implementation of the Agreement during the autumn of 1999. The successful, albeit as it proved interim, outcome was a package that included the appointment by the IRA of an 'interlocutor' to liaise with John de Chastelain's Independent International Commission on Decommissioning and the establishment of an Executive with SDLP, UUP, DUP and Sinn Féin members.

Given this convoluted process of post-Agreement bargaining and negotiation, it is not surprising that the Life and Times survey reports relatively low levels of public understanding of how the Assembly and new government bodies were supposed to work. The reinstatement of Seamus Mallon as Deputy First Minister, via the political intervention of the Secretary of State, rather than due process, may have also muddied public understanding of how the Assembly was meant to operate (*Irish Times*, 1999).

The professed lack of knowledge and understanding of the devolved institutions was not a deterrent to support for the Agreement, nor to the expectations it had generated. In that respect, there appears to have been a certain consistency of opinion between the electorate and the leaderships of three of the four parties that were to constitute the Executive Committee – UUP, SDLP and Sinn Féin – as well as the other pro-Agreement parties. That is, most voters and the leaders of these parties were prepared to take a political risk in creating and implementing the devolved institutions, even though voters in particular had an imperfect understanding of their *modus operandi*. The disarmingly frank admission on the part of most of the electorate, whether Catholic or Protestant, that they don't understand the prospective workings of devolution renders their preparedness to embark on this voyage of discovery to be even more arresting. It was almost as if the pro-Agreement electorate was saying, in effect, 'better the devil we don't know than the devil we do'.

There is something of a puzzle here. The lengthy run-in to the negotiations that led to the Agreement, together with traditionally high levels of electoral mobilisation in Northern Ireland, might be assumed to imply the existence of a politically sophisticated electorate. What the survey results suggest, however, is that the electorate is more *knowing* than knowledgeable, at least in relation to the intricate model of devolution engineered during the talks process. Such 'knowingness', structured by perceptions of the mutually exclusive constitutional preferences of the two dominant ethno-nationalist blocs, meant that the debate about the pros and cons of the Agreement was swiftly elevated to the high ground of constitutional politics. For unionists, the argument turned on whether the Agreement safeguarded or threatened the Union; for nationalists, on whether it consolidated partition or created the opportunity for a transition to a united Ireland. The (terrible) beauty of the Agreement was that, via the entrenchment of the consent principle, each of these mutually exclusive futures could be canvassed by their supporters.

After 30 years of the Troubles it is no surprise that the terms of the debate during both the referendum and election campaigns focused upon the alleged threat or, conversely, the opportunity posed by the Agreement. The constitutional open-endedness of the Agreement, allied with controversy over decommissioning, police reform, prisoner releases and, latterly, the scaling down of the British Army's presence in Northern Ireland, dominated the debate. This top-heavy agenda squeezed out reflective arguments about the detail of the devolution scheme, and instead led to a focus on the bigger picture: did it copperfasten the Union or subvert it?

In this bifurcated context it is no surprise that voters were at the least unclear about the devolved institutions. The absence of a coherent, multi-party pro-Agreement campaign, despite a government-backed 'Yes' campaign, meant that each party operated within its own bailiwick, seeking to mobilise its own voters in terms that accorded with their own interpretation of the Agreement and the alternative futures it conjured up. This was no easy task, even in the best of all possible worlds.

## Expectations

Northern Ireland has long been identified with a 'democratic deficit', direct rule leaving locally elected representatives politically emasculated – or, rather, in a position to exercise veto power without responsibility, the prerogative of the political harlot. Direct rule also created something of a policy deficit: the preoccupation with constitutional and security matters meant that discussion and debate about 'bread and butter' issues within the parties was conspicuously absent. Hailed by its supporters as a truly historic opportunity for a new beginning, the Agreement created the occasion to bridge both deficits. Yet the low levels of public comprehension of the working of the new institutions did not augur well – or at least implied that both the politicians and the public at large would be confronted with a sharp learning curve in relation to both democratic practice and policy-making.

The Life and Times survey questioned respondents about a range of policy matters and their expectations about what the new institutions should deliver, including the scope of the Assembly's agenda. Whether, for instance, it was preferable for the new Assembly to spend its time dealing with 'day-to-day' issues, such as health or education, or with 'political' issues, such as Northern Ireland's constitutional future.

Although there was nothing in the Agreement to prevent members of the Assembly from debating 'high policy' matters, the legislative and executive powers enjoyed by the devolved institutions within Northern Ireland were limited to transferred matters, that is those previously administered by the six direct rule departments. Powers in relation to reserved and excepted matters remained within the remit of the Secretary of State and the Northern Ireland Office, although the Secretary of State could consult with local politicians on reserved matters, including policing issues.

On the broad question of day-to-day versus political issues, almost half of all respondents (48 per cent) say that the Assembly should prioritise the former, but a substantial minority (39 per cent) say that it should deal with both equally. Just 11 per cent state that it should concentrate on political issues (Table 1.8).

Table 1.8 Should the Assembly deal with day-to-day or political issues? (%)

|  | Catholic | Protestant | No religion | All |
|---|---|---|---|---|
| Day-to-day issues | 52 | 43 | 50 | 48 |
| Political issues | 9 | 13 | 9 | 11 |
| Both equally | 37 | 42 | 39 | 39 |
| Don't know | 2 | 3 | 2 | 3 |

While a majority of Catholics (52 per cent) believe that the Assembly should concentrate on day-to-day issues, a minority of Protestants (43 per cent) agree, perhaps reflecting greater Protestant dissatisfaction with the Agreement and a sense that the Assembly could, or should, be used as a forum for the redress of Protestant political grievances. However, the proportion of Protestants prioritising high policy issues is low (13 per cent), and only slightly higher than among Catholic respondents (9 per cent). The results suggest that many respondents anticipate that the Assembly would be a serious working chamber rather than a venue for the sectarian struggle to be conducted by other means. They also suggest a certain fatigue with the already protracted peace process and a desire to move on to more prosaic, but immediately relevant, issues of governance and the delivery of services by local politicians.

Invited to identify which day-to-day issues are the most important for the Assembly to deal with, improving the health service is ranked first, attracting 41 per cent support from all respondents, followed by improving the economy (29 per cent) and, relatedly, increasing job opportunities (20 per cent). Other matters – including education (6 per cent), transport (1 per cent), the environment (1 per cent) – fared much less well as agenda-topping issues (Table 1.9).

Table 1.9 Which of these is the most important for the Assembly to deal with? (%)

|  | Catholic | Protestant | No religion | All |
| --- | --- | --- | --- | --- |
| Improving the health service | 42 | 42 | 32 | 41 |
| Improving the economy | 25 | 32 | 30 | 29 |
| Increasing employment opportunities | 23 | 18 | 21 | 20 |
| Improving education | 7 | 6 | 11 | 6 |
| Improving transport | 1 | 1 | 1 | 1 |
| Improving the environment | 1 | 1 | 1 | 1 |
| None of these | 1 | <1 | 2 | 1 |
| Don't know | 1 | 1 | 2 | 1 |

There is a marked convergence between Protestants and Catholics in terms of the rank ordering of the preferred priorities for the Assembly. Improving the health service is jointly preferred by each cohort as the first priority, although a rather higher proportion of Protestants favour economic improvement while Catholics give this item and improving employment opportunities equivalent levels of support.

The finding that respondents are four times more likely to prefer an Assembly dominated by day-to-day rather than divisive political issues suggests that the population harbours the aspiration for the realisation of a more 'normal' political system than one disfigured by the Troubles. However, there is no overwhelming sentiment that devolution will generate the more *efficient* delivery of public services. Asked if they think that day-to-day services such as health or education will become more or less efficient when under Assembly control, 56 per cent think that they will become a lot or a little more efficient, as against 13 per cent who think they will become less efficient. Perhaps reflecting *their* general lack of knowledge about the operation of devolution noted earlier, almost a third (31 per cent) of respondents say either that service provision will remain the same or that they don't know whether or not there will be efficiency gains (Table 1.10).

Table 1.10 Will day-to-day services like health and education become more or less efficient if the Assembly takes control? (%)

|  | Catholic | Protestant | No religion | All |
|---|---|---|---|---|
| More efficient (a lot or a little) | 68 | 49 | 51 | 56 |
| Just the same | 14 | 18 | 17 | 16 |
| Less efficient (a lot or a little) | 7 | 17 | 14 | 13 |
| Don't know | 11 | 17 | 17 | 15 |

What is apparent, though, is the existence of a significant communal division in relation to expectations of service delivery. Catholics (68 per cent) are much more likely to believe that devolved services would prove to be more efficient when placed in the hands of local politicians, compared to 49 per cent of Protestants. However, only 17 per cent of the latter feel that the delivery of day-to-day services will deteriorate with the ending of direct rule. Interestingly, almost exactly the same proportions of Catholics (55 per cent) and Protestants (56 per cent) feel that local services will become more expensive under local devolved government, even though the revenue raising powers available to the devolved administration will be restricted to (modest) income derived from the district and regional rates. Overall, 55 per cent of respondents believe that day-to-day services would cost more under devolution, 10 per cent that they would cost less, with 35 per cent believing they would either remain the same (19 per cent) or saying that they don't know (16 per cent).

While devolution was an almost wholly untested project at the time of the survey, there is a surprising preparedness among respondents to entertain an extension to the Assembly's capacity to raise revenue. Asked whether the Assembly should, like the Scottish parliament, enjoy a tax varying power, overall 57 per cent agree, 30 per cent disagree and 13 per cent don't know. The 2:1 ratio in favour of the power to either increase or reduce taxation levels does, however, conceal a communal difference. More than two thirds of Catholics

(68 per cent) support this proposition compared to half (49 per cent) of Protestants. The latter are twice as likely to oppose this extension of power than Catholics, and emerge as much more evenly split on the issue (Table 1.11).

Table 1.11 Should the Assembly have the power to raise or lower income tax? (%)

|            | Catholic | Protestant | No religion | All |
|------------|----------|------------|-------------|-----|
| Yes        | 68       | 49         | 55          | 57  |
| No         | 20       | 38         | 35          | 30  |
| Don't know | 12       | 14         | 10          | 13  |

One other policy area explored by the survey, and which lay beyond the immediate scope of devolved powers, was policing. Respondents were asked whether the Assembly should assume responsibility for policing, an aspiration that was signalled by the report of the Patten Commission on the future of the RUC published in the autumn of 1999 (Independent Commission on Policing for Northern Ireland, 1999). Overall, more than half of respondents (55 per cent) agree that the Assembly should be responsible for policing, 34 per cent disagree and 11 per cent don't know, although there is a significant disparity of view between Catholics and Protestants (Table 1.12).

Table 1.12 Should the Assembly be responsible for policing in Northern Ireland? (%)

|            | Catholic | Protestant | No religion | All |
|------------|----------|------------|-------------|-----|
| Yes        | 67       | 48         | 44          | 55  |
| No         | 22       | 41         | 46          | 34  |
| Don't know | 11       | 11         | 10          | 11  |

The prospect of local responsibility for the governance of a new police service is more appealing to Catholics than Protestants. The latter are much more evenly divided, with only a narrow plurality in favour of the restoration of policing matters to a local Assembly. The latter part of 1999, during the run-up to devolution and the conduct of the survey, was characterised by the intense controversy surrounding the reform of the RUC. On this matter, unionists – whether pro- or anti-Agreement – were united in their criticisms of many of the Patten Report's recommendations. David Trimble for instance described it as a 'gratuitous insult' to both past and serving officers and their families, especially those families who had lost an officer during the course of the Troubles. While the question itself did not establish the views of the respondents towards the Patten Report, the hostile reception accorded to it by unionists generally is likely to have influenced the expressed reluctance of Protestants towards the proposition that the Assembly should assume responsibility for its implementation. It is also plausible that among the 48 per cent of Protestants who agree that policing powers be devolved, a number would regard such a development as an opportunity to temper what they regard as the most objectionable aspects of the reform package.

The generally more positive attitudes among Catholics towards the devolution settlement, as compared with the decidedly ambivalent views among Protestants, sustained the asymmetry that had prevailed at the referendum of May 1998. Protestants were deeply divided about the Good Friday Agreement in principle, a division that has widened since then. The evident difficulties of implementing devolution, more particularly the failure finally to resolve the decommissioning issue, coupled with the root and branch reform of the RUC and the early release of prisoners, served to generate a great deal of scepticism – if not cynicism – within the Protestant community.

By the time devolution actually took effect – and its first phase was to prove short-lived – a majority of Protestants had come to the view that there was a fundamental imbalance in Northern Ireland's model of devolution. While exactly half of the respondents (50 per cent) believe that the Agreement has benefited unionists and nationalists equally, one in four (27 per cent) believe nationalists have benefited a lot more, a view shared by a plurality of Protestants (46 per cent). Indeed, well over half of Protestant respondents (59 per cent) believe that nationalists have benefited either a lot or a little more than unionists from the Agreement, a view shared by 11 per cent of Catholics (Table 1.13).

Table 1.13 Who has the Good Friday Agreement benefited most? (%)

|  | Catholic | Protestant | No religion | All |
|---|---|---|---|---|
| Unionists benefited a lot more than nationalists | 2 | <1 | – | 1 |
| Unionists benefited a little more than nationalists | 3 | 1 | 1 | 2 |
| Nationalists benefited a lot more than unionists | 3 | 46 | 30 | 27 |
| Nationalists benefited a little more than unionists | 8 | 13 | 14 | 11 |
| Unionists and nationalists benefited equally | 74 | 32 | 43 | 50 |
| Don't know | 10 | 8 | 13 | 9 |

Catholics are more than twice as likely to perceive the Agreement as having bestowed equal benefits on both communities than Protestants, while the proportions believing unionists had emerged as its beneficiaries are negligible. In a divided society within which zero-sum politics had prevailed, the sense of 'loss' among Protestants is evident from these results. It was the 'ancillary' issues – police reform, prisoner releases, decommissioning – rather than the outworking of devolution *per se* that is likely to have nourished the perception among Protestants that they had 'lost' and that Catholics had 'won' from processes that in key respects had only begun on Good Friday 1998.

The mutuality and inclusiveness of the Agreement that had been paraded as its underlying philosophy by its proponents, whether in Northern Ireland, Britain, Ireland or the international community, had, by the time the Life and Times survey was undertaken, fallen on many more deaf ears among Protestants than Catholics. The comprehensive nature of the political and peace processes made the idea of an Assembly more attractive to Catholics. Overall the survey findings reveal that Catholics are more optimistic about the Assembly's future. Perhaps reflecting the extent of significant unfinished business left in the wake of the Agreement, less than one half of Protestants (46 per cent) think that the Assembly will still be in place in three years time, compared to two thirds (64 per cent) of Catholics.

Protestant pessimism about the future of the Assembly, and their more muted willingness to see the Assembly assume greater powers, can be regarded as a reflection of unionist dissatisfaction with the Agreement and the peace process. The nationalist–unionist debate was framed in different terms. For many unionists, issues were discussed defensively, such as keeping Sinn Féin out of the new Executive, or preserving the RUC intact. Nationalist and republican arguments were framed more positively, in terms of securing the implementation of 'gains' already made in the negotiations. The political fragmentation of unionism, with the DUP and UKUP opposed to the Agreement and substantial sections of the UUP coming to similar conclusions, is also reflected in Protestant pessimism. The nature of nationalist and unionist compromises that made the Agreement possible may also help explain the stronger Protestant than Catholic political pessimism. Many nationalist and republican compromises were aspirational and academic, for example, the recognition of a Northern Ireland state that was already in existence anyway. Many unionist compromises were of a different order; reform of the police force and prisoner releases had visible manifestations, reinforcing a sense of loss and compromise that was not wholly offset by the entrenchment of the consent principle, even in the Republic of Ireland's reformed constitution. In effect, the fate of the Agreement was – and still remains – finely poised. The delicacy of Protestant opinion at the outset of devolution was evident: it is all the more remarkable that in such unpropitious circumstances, David Trimble was able to carry a sufficient body of opinion within his party to enable devolution to occur. As the subsequent fitful outworking of the (thrice-suspended) new political architecture has already threatened, and despite a series of reprieves, devolution in Northern Ireland may yet turn out to have been an event rather than a process.

### Notes

This research has been supported by Economic and Social Research Council, Award Number L327253045.

1. It is worth noting that the percentage favouring a continued union has experienced a steady drop since the late 1980s. In 1989, the figure was 69 per cent.
2. Author interview with a senior member of the Ulster Unionist Party (18 May 1998).
3. Both quotations are from the DUP and UUP referendum communications (1998).

### References

Egeland, Jan (1999) 'The Oslo Accord: multiparty facilitation through the Norwegian channel' in Chester A. Crocker, Fen Osler Hampson and Pamela Aall (eds), *Herding Cats: Multiparty Mediation in a Complex World* (Washington DC: USIP Press) pp. 529–46.

Independent Commission for Policing in Northern Ireland (1999) *A New Beginning: Policing in Northern Ireland: The Report of the Independent Commission for Policing in Northern Ireland* (Belfast: HMSO).

*Irish Times* (1999) 'DUP pledges to fight on after Mallon election', 30 November.

MacGinty, R., Wilford, R., Dowds, L. and Robinson, G. (2001) 'Consenting adults: the principle of consent and Northern Ireland's constitutional future', *Government and Opposition*, Vol. 36, No. 4, pp. 472–92.

Wallensteen, Peter and Sollenberg, Margareta (2000) 'Armed conflict, 1989–99', *Journal of Peace Research*, Vol. 37, No. 5, pp. 635–49.

Wilford, R. (1999) 'Epilogue' in P. Mitchell and R. Wilford (eds), *Politics in Northern Ireland* (Boulder, CO: Westview Press) pp. 285–303.

# 2 Are There Any Christians in Northern Ireland?

*John D. Brewer*

It might be thought that little more could be written about religion in Northern Ireland. Actually there is quite a lot. This society is well known for its high levels of religiosity, the importance that religion still retains in many aspects of everyday life, and the link that exists between religion and ethno-national conflict. The number of people attending Mass, the number of active Protestant communicants and the level of Protestant church membership are the highest within all the regions of the United Kingdom. Morever, while these figures are declining, they are doing so at a much slower rate than elsewhere (Brierley, 1999). Figures in the Annual Reports of the Registrar General for the four regions of the United Kingdom, for example, show the number of marriages celebrated religiously is highest in Northern Ireland, being almost double that of the rate in England (Rosie, 2001). The normal explanation for this is that religiosity is a surrogate for ethno-national identity, so that it is Northern Irish politics that keeps religion alive. This being so, it is interesting to examine recent patterns in religious belief and observance to see if levels of religiosity have declined during the period of the ceasefires (which began in 1994), and leading up to the Good Friday Agreement in 1998. Social surveys are single snapshots at one point in time, but comparisons between the 1991 Northern Ireland Social Attitudes survey and the 1998 Northern Ireland Life and Times survey permit an examination over time.

## Religiosity

In order to inform the forthcoming discussion, it is first necessary to identify the religious breakdown of the samples, as shown in Table 2.1. Put starkly, while the proportion of Catholics has risen, the proportion of Protestants has fallen. Demographic factors can explain the rise in the proportion of Catholics, but the fall in the percentage of Protestants is not as simple as it seems. While the Mainstream Protestant churches (Church of Ireland, Presbyterian and Methodist) have experienced a decline, the increase in the number of Other Christians masks two different trends within Protestantism. The first is the growth of conservative evangelical churches, like the Baptists and Free Presbyterians, and the second is the increase in more liberal charismatic and independent house churches. Overall, Protestantism is still the majority faith, but it is declining.

Table 2.1 Religion of respondents, 1991 and 1998 (%)

|  | 1991 | 1998 |
| --- | --- | --- |
| None | 8 | 9 |
| Catholic | 35 | 38 |
| Mainstream Protestant | 47 | 39 |
|    Church of Ireland | 19 | 15 |
|    Presbyterian | 24 | 21 |
|    Methodist | 4 | 3 |
| Other Christian | 8 | 12 |
| Non-Christian | <1 | <1 |
| Don't know | <1 | 2 |
| Refused | 1 | 1 |

Due to the small number of respondents in the non-Christian, refused and don't know categories, analysis and discussion in this chapter will focus on four main categories: those with no religion, Catholics, Mainstream Protestants and Other Christians.

Religiosity is a many-sided process and four issues will now be addressed: what people believe, what they practise, who the religious are, and what impact belief has on their life.

*Belief*

Surveys always throw up odd things. When asked which of six statements comes closest to expressing what they believe about God, some Christians choose 'I don't believe in God', including 2 per cent of Catholics, 2 per cent of Mainstream Protestants and 5 per cent of Other Christians. Interestingly, 21 per cent of those who claim that they have no religion indicate 'I know God really exists and I have no doubts about it'. A further 16 per cent of this group endorse the statement 'while I have doubts I feel I do believe in God'. The latter scenario is less strange than it appears, for the no religion category contains two sorts of people: those who have rejected God and those who have rejected institutionalised religion. The latter does not involve denial of belief in God, and represents the phenomenon that Grace Davie calls 'believing without belonging' (Davie, 1990a, 1990b). Not surprisingly, belief in God is strong among those who identify themselves as belonging to any of the Christian denominations (that is, Catholic, Mainstream Protestant, or Other Christian). More than three quarters (77 per cent) of Christians say they believe in God and always have. In response to a further question on belief, 54 per cent of Christians say they have no doubts about the existence of God.

Of more interest, however, are other trends in belief among Christians. Respondents within the Mainstream Protestant category appear to have undergone the most liberalisation and, as shown in Table 2.2, are expressing the greatest doubts, which is consistent with trends in Britain (Bruce and Alderdice, 1993).

Table 2.2 Certainty of belief in God (%)

|  | No religion | Catholic | Mainstream Protestant | Other Christian |
|---|---|---|---|---|
| I don't believe in God | 18 | 2 | 2 | 5 |
| I don't know whether there is a God and I don't believe there is any way to find out | 14 | <1 | 5 | 5 |
| I don't believe in a personal God, but I do believe in a Higher Power of some kind | 26 | 3 | 5 | 6 |
| I find myself believing in God some of the time but not at other times | 3 | 12 | 10 | 6 |
| While I have doubts, I feel I do believe in God | 16 | 25 | 28 | 19 |
| I know God really exists and I have no doubts about it | 21 | 58 | 49 | 59 |

It cannot be said of religious belief that it permits no ambiguity, for other tenets of Christian faith reveal similar uncertainty among a good proportion of believers, as well as diversity across the categories. Interestingly, some respondents who have no religion – some of whom believe without belonging – share many beliefs with Christians. However, as Table 2.3 indicates, these are the more central beliefs, such as life after death.

Among Christians, the Mainstream Protestant group again appear the least definite, while the Other Christians are more certain. This may well reflect the impact of conservative evangelicalism in the Other Christian category, which tends to admit no ambiguity in the Christian faith. But what is also clear from these figures is that, contrary to Bruce and Alderdice's (1993) observation based on the 1991 Northern

Ireland Social Attitudes survey, the Mainstream Protestant churches do not now contain a large theologically conservative element.

Table 2.3 Belief in Christian tenets (% of respondents who definitely believe)

|  | No religion | Catholic | Mainstream Protestant | Other Christian |
|---|---|---|---|---|
| Life after death | 14 | 42 | 38 | 59 |
| Heaven | 12 | 53 | 47 | 60 |
| Hell | 10 | 40 | 39 | 58 |
| Miracles | 3 | 36 | 19 | 37 |

A good way to demonstrate this is to examine the stress respondents place on a conversion experience in their personal commitment to God. The idea of 'being saved' as a turning point in coming to faith, which is so characteristic of the conservative evangelical tradition, is not common among respondents. When asked 'has there ever been a turning point in your life when you made a new and personal commitment to religion?', the proportion saying 'yes' has dropped for all categories between 1991 and 1998, but particularly so for the Other Christian category. Those replying in the affirmative among Other Christians has fallen from 73 per cent to 20 per cent, from 29 per cent to 12 per cent among Mainstream Protestants, and from 23 per cent to 7 per cent among Catholics. These are remarkable figures and show the reduced emphasis placed on the idea of 'being saved', which is perhaps a measure of growing theological liberalism in the intervening period.

Another dimension of theological conservatism is the conviction that there is but one true religion, normally one's own. Religion here can mean 'denomination' or 'world faith', and it is impossible to know how respondents interpret the term. Either way, denying the possibility of the equal value of other denominations or world faiths is normally a sign of conservative evangelicalism. In order to explore this, respondents were asked to identify which of three statements comes closest to their views, and what might be called 'liberal' and 'conservative' responses were offered. The liberal response – 'there are basic truths in many religions' – is supported by 77 per cent of Catholics, 64 per cent of Mainstream Protestants and 45 per cent of Other Christians. The conservative position – 'there is truth only in one religion' – is endorsed by 11 per cent of Catholics, 17 per cent of Mainstream Protestants and 29 per cent of Other Christians. Thus, even the Other Christians are overall not very conservative, but liberalism is most evident within the remaining categories. It is reasonable to conclude that conservative evangelical beliefs are not widely held by respondents. This is not to argue for a shift in belief among conservative evangelicals; rather, it reflects the small number of conservative evangelicals in the sample and the difficulty in isolating them within the Other Christian category.

Other beliefs are equally clear. The God in whom Christians believe is strongly interventionist in their personal lives. Respondents were asked if they agree or disagree that 'there is a God who concerns himself with every human being personally'. Looking at those who agree in some way with such a view, they make up 70 per cent of Catholics, 64 per cent of Mainstream Protestants and 69 per cent of Other Christians; 16 per cent of those with no religion also support this statement. Moreover, Christians strongly believe that God changes people's lives: very few strongly agree with the statement that 'we each make our own fate' or that 'life is only meaningful if you provide the meaning yourself', being less than one in ten in all categories. Not surprisingly, many more show some agreement with the statement that 'life is meaningful only because God exists', although the denominational differences are more marked. Just over one third of Catholics (35 per cent) and Mainstream Protestants (37 per cent) show agreement, compared with 53 per cent of Other Christians. Again the impact of conservative evangelicalism is apparent in the last category.

The depth of religious feeling within the Other Christian category is perhaps best captured by responses to a question asking how religious they are. As indicated in Table 2.4, it is worth noting the proportion of Christians, albeit small, describing themselves as extremely or very non-religious, especially among those in the Other Christian category. However, this may reflect an opposition to denominationalism rather than to religious belief, especially among those in this category who belong to independent house churches.

Table 2.4 Depth of religiosity (%)

|  | No religion | Catholic | Mainstream Protestant | Other Christian |
|---|---|---|---|---|
| Extremely religious | 1 | 2 | 2 | 6 |
| Very religious | 0 | 8 | 8 | 18 |
| Somewhat religious | 11 | 56 | 44 | 33 |
| Neither religious nor non-religious | 15 | 20 | 24 | 17 |
| Somewhat non-religious | 22 | 7 | 10 | 6 |
| Very non-religious | 22 | 4 | 5 | 4 |
| Extremely non-religious | 25 | 3 | 4 | 12 |
| Don't know | 4 | 1 | 3 | 5 |

Further analysis within this chapter includes levels of religiosity, which are determined by respondents' answers to the question about the depth of their religious belief, represented in Table 2.4. High religiosity amalgamates the extremely and very religious categories, medium refers to those who are somewhat religious, low means the respondent is neither religious nor non-religious, and the non-religious category amalgamates the somewhat, very and extremely non-religious responses. In order to make accurate comparisons, the small number of respondents belonging to non-Christian religions are excluded from the analysis.

*Observance*

Belief is one thing, practice another. Indeed, what has distinguished Northern Irish Christians from their British co-religionists in the past is the higher numbers of them who live out their faith in religious observance. The phenomenon of believing without belonging, of not practising what one believes, is much stronger among people in Britain. It has been noted that religious observance in Northern Ireland is something people do either very regularly or very irregularly (Bruce and Alderdice, 1993). Practice, unlike belief, permits little ambiguity – this is clear from Table 2.5.

Table 2.5 Patterns of religious observance (%)

|  | Catholic | Mainstream Protestant | Other Christian |
|---|---|---|---|
| *Church attendance* | | | |
| At least weekly | 67 | 29 | 49 |
| At least fortnightly | 7 | 9 | 4 |
| At least monthly | 7 | 10 | 5 |
| Less often | 8 | 23 | 12 |
| Varies too much | 5 | 8 | 2 |
| Practically never | 5 | 22 | 28 |
| *Prayer* | | | |
| Several times a day | 11 | 8 | 24 |
| Once a day | 34 | 22 | 16 |
| Several times a week | 13 | 12 | 13 |
| Every week | 18 | 6 | 6 |
| Less often | 19 | 37 | 21 |
| Never | 5 | 15 | 21 |
| *Participation in church activities* | | | |
| Several times a week | 2 | 5 | 8 |
| Every week | 10 | 3 | 13 |
| Nearly every week | 4 | 4 | 5 |
| Less often | 40 | 45 | 36 |
| Never | 44 | 43 | 37 |

What is noticeable is that while Catholics attend church more frequently on a regular basis, other respondents do as much 'out of church religion' on a regular basis, such as praying. However, Mainstream Protestants are less inclined to pray than Other Christians, reflecting their liberalisation. This is significant, for it is widely believed in popular perception that Catholics are more nominal in their belief and observance than Other Christians. Table 2.5 shows the reverse to be the case.

*Who Are the Religious?*

There are more Christians in Northern Ireland per head of population compared to the rest of the United Kingdom, and they are more devout and regular in their observance. However, in terms of their socio-demographic characteristics, they are much like their co-religionists in Britain (Bruce and Alderdice, 1993). Some general socio-demographic dimensions of respondents are outlined in Table 2.6, a few of which are particularly noteworthy.

Table 2.6 Socio-demographic profile (%)

|  | No religion | Catholic | Mainstream Protestant | Other Christian |
|---|---|---|---|---|
| *Location* | | | | |
| Urban | 78 | 62 | 73 | 75 |
| Rural | 22 | 38 | 28 | 25 |
| *Age* | | | | |
| 18–34 | 43 | 33 | 27 | 36 |
| 35–49 | 34 | 32 | 24 | 30 |
| 50–64 | 18 | 24 | 29 | 27 |
| 65 years and over | 5 | 12 | 19 | 7 |
| Don't know | 0 | 0 | <1 | 0 |
| No answer | 0 | 0 | 1 | 0 |
| *Gender* | | | | |
| Male | 54 | 43 | 46 | 57 |
| Female | 46 | 57 | 54 | 44 |
| *Social class* | | | | |
| Professional/managerial/technical | 32 | 40 | 23 | 36 |
| Skilled non-manual | 23 | 12 | 23 | 23 |
| Skilled manual | 16 | 21 | 14 | 26 |
| Partly skilled/unskilled | 22 | 22 | 33 | 12 |
| No answer | 7 | 5 | 6 | 3 |
| *Political identity* | | | | |
| Unionist | 27 | 1 | 74 | 66 |
| Nationalist | 8 | 63 | <1 | 2 |
| Neither | 63 | 33 | 24 | 30 |
| Don't know | 3 | 2 | 2 | 2 |

What is clear is that describing oneself as having no religion decreases with age: only 5 per cent of the no religion category are 65 years and over, with 43 per cent between 18 and 34 years. With respect to particular denominations, Catholicism is younger than Mainstream Protestantism, which has an ageing population. Put another way, Catholicism is maintaining its support among the young to a better extent than Mainstream Protestantism. So too are the Other Christian denominations.

Women dominate within Catholicism. The converse is worth stressing, in that the Other Christian category appeals more to men than other groups. This Other Christian category contains conservative evangelicals such as Baptists and Free Presbyterians, as well as those in the charismatic and Pentecostal traditions. When men do religion, they clearly prefer to do the conservative kind. The categories are classless in their general appeal, in that they have a spread from all classes, although at the level of individual congregations this is unlikely to apply. There is a slight tendency for respondents within the Mainstream Protestant category to be more working class than within the other categories, although it nonetheless contains a cross-section in class terms.

The political identities of the religious are noteworthy. The first point to note is that those with no religion not only seem to reject religion, but they also reject the political identities normally associated with religion in Northern Ireland. This suggests that a respondent within this category who believes without belonging might equally have rejected the politics associated with institutionalised religion as much as denominationalism itself. However, a good proportion of those belonging to a denomination also claims to eschew conventional political identities. The least likely to do this are Mainstream Protestants, although several processes are likely to be at work here. Exclusive Brethren – who tend to avoid political involvement – would show up within the Other Christian category, and are likely to express their political affiliation as neither. The small group of respondents saying that they don't know is likely to include those who, for reasons of sensitivity, decline to give their political affiliation; this response accounts for no more than 3 per cent of any category.

The final point to make is that the vast majority of respondents belonging to any of the Christian churches were brought up in families with some kind of religious affiliation. More than that, there is little church switching. Over 85 per cent of Christians in both the Catholic and Mainstream Protestant categories had both parents in the same grouping, demonstrating the power of early childhood socialisation in fixing lifelong church identity. Because both parents are overwhelmingly in the same category, it is impossible to discern the relative impact of fathers or mothers on imprinting church identity. What is more, approximately three fifths of respondents in the Other Christian category tend to come from Mainstream Protestant churches, with nearly two fifths from a background in the Other Christian tradition. This demonstrates that whatever shift there is in membership to the conservative evangelical and independent Protestant tradition comes from Mainstream Protestantism.

Not only is there some church switching from the Mainstream Protestant category, a substantial number of those brought up in these churches leave the faith outright. Just over half (56 per cent) of the respondents stating that they have no religion say that their mothers belonged to the Mainstream Protestant churches. For fathers, this figure is 46 per cent. This confirms the point that the main Protestant denominations are not maintaining the loyalty of the young. Conversely, about three in ten people who now state that they have no religion were brought up as Catholics. While it is not quite true to claim that once a Catholic, always a Catholic, becoming a lapsed Protestant is more common. The Other Christian category is best at maintaining the loyalty of the young, with only one in twenty of those with no religion coming from this background.

## The Impact of Belief

Beliefs impact on people's lives. It may be that people hold them because of what they confer on other parts of their lives, or holding them has unintended consequences in other areas of life. Either way, the beliefs people hold matter. Leaving aside the obvious impact religious beliefs in Northern Ireland have on political identity, one would expect sincerely held religious beliefs to influence other aspects of the lives of Christians. One possible impact is the development of social trust. The Life and Times survey permits analysis of the levels of confidence people have in social institutions like Westminster, business and industry, the legal system and the education system. Because some of these are highly contested politically, attitudes towards them are analysed according to denomination, as well as by levels of religiosity, in the hope of escaping the effect of Protestant and Catholic political identities. In fact, there is very little difference in confidence in these institutions between the categories, or among those with differing levels of religiosity, most of which have low to medium levels of confidence. The exception is the legal system, where Catholics show less confidence than Protestants. The most favoured social institution is the education system. Moreover, there is only a marginal difference in levels of confidence between respondents with high levels of religiosity and those who are non-religious. This strongly suggests that trust in social institutions – or the lack of it – is based on factors other than religious belief in Northern Ireland.

Religiosity does, however, impact on various social and moral issues, and this impact is more marked than denomination. The church has always been obsessed with sex, at least with the control of sexual matters, despite this seeming to be a matter of personal privacy. Thus, it is worth examining the extent to which people have absorbed the conservative attitudes of the church. Sex before marriage is always wrong for a fifth of Catholics and Mainstream Protestants, and for a third of Other Christians. However, it is always wrong for 62 per cent of those with high religiosity, although it is interesting that 15 per cent of this group say it is not wrong at all. As a sign of changing moral attitudes, double the number of Catholics and Mainstream Protestants think it is not wrong at all as think it is always wrong. Three quarters of the no religion category say there is nothing wrong with it either. Adultery, however, is not perceived as liberally: 70 per cent of Catholics and 74 per cent of Mainstream Protestants think it always wrong compared to two thirds of Other Christians and 48 per cent of the no religion category. This implies that disapproval of adultery is a general moral principle accepted irrespective of faith. For the highly religious, however, 99 per cent think it always wrong, as do 78 per cent of those with medium religiosity. Even 60 per cent of those with low religiosity condemn it as always wrong.

Homosexuality is only marginally less condemned as always wrong, although Catholics are slightly more liberal, with 50 per cent considering it always wrong, compared with 68 per cent of Mainstream Protestants and 65 per cent of Other Christians. Again, strength of religious belief impacts more than denominational category, with 86 per cent of the highly religious considering it always wrong and 54 per cent of those with low levels of religiosity. One third of people with no religion consider it always wrong. Clearly, the liberalisation on sexual matters does not extend very far.

The policing of sex by the church is not the only area of private life that historically it has tried to dictate. The Christian religion takes a position on such things as gender roles in the home, working mothers and marriage, holding a conservative view of the model family that is often incompatible with modern life. It is worth making an assessment of the impact these views have on religious believers in Northern Ireland.

Respondents were asked about their level of agreement with a range of statements that assess family policies. Table 2.7 shows the views of those who strongly agree with a range of statements, based on religious category and level of religiosity. The focus is only on those who strongly agree as this represents a measure of those for whom the church's position is most strongly followed or rejected.

Table 2.7 Support for statements on family issues (% of respondents who strongly agree)

|  | No religion | Religious category | | |
|---|---|---|---|---|
|  |  | Catholic | Mainstream Protestant | Other Christian |
| A husband's job is to earn money; a wife's job is to look after the home and family | 4 | 8 | 10 | 14 |
| All in all, family life suffers when the woman has a full-time job | 6 | 7 | 9 | 15 |
| It is alright for a couple to live together without intending to get married | 29 | 11 | 13 | 16 |
| It is a good idea for a couple who intend to get married to live together first | 33 | 14 | 15 | 14 |
|  | Level of religiosity | | | |
|  | High | Medium | Low | None |
| A husband's job is to earn money; a wife's job is to look after the home and family | 29 | 14 | 5 | 6 |
| All in all, family life suffers when the woman has a full-time job | 17 | 11 | 8 | 6 |
| It is alright for a couple to live together without intending to get married | 4 | 8 | 16 | 34 |
| It is a good idea for a couple who intend to get married to live together first | 5 | 11 | 23 | 32 |

One of the main points to emerge from this table is that not very many people agree without reservation with the Christian position, although the impact of religiosity is stronger than that of denominational category. This suggests that Northern Ireland has a large number of people who do not hold the church's most conservative theological position on family matters. This is not to say that conservative evangelicalism is losing sway, although one might claim thus. However, the realities of modern living have put even the most strongly committed believers in positions that are at odds with the conservative stance of the church on family issues. There is a powerful lesson here for modernisers in the church who wish to make it more relevant, as even a society like Northern Ireland, which has strong elements of tradition and religiosity, finds the conservative position unappealing.

Differences among Christians are slight, although in general, respondents within the Other Christian tradition are marginally more supportive of the conservative view. However, an interesting trend is for Catholics to take the more liberal position with respect to gender roles in the home, but the more conservative one with respect to marriage. This may reflect the reality of the working lives of women in Catholic homes, and the influence of the Catholic church's more trenchant teachings on marriage. Not surprisingly, those with no religiosity are the most liberal on all issues, although not excessively so in most cases. What is also noticeable in this respect is that there is a substantial difference between those with low and no religiosity in relation to cohabitation before marriage (but not to working wives). Clearly, being religious still counts for something in Northern Ireland, especially in relation to sexual mores.

These results show how the impact of religion on the lives of believers is mediated by a range of factors, to the extent that some tenets of faith impinge only on the highly religious, and even then, not on the majority of those with strong religious beliefs. Religious teachings, in other words, can be undercut by the circumstances pertaining to the believer's life or community. These noticeably affect attitudes towards working wives, but the point is demonstrated most clearly by attitudes towards two forms of illegal behaviour which are on the margins of social acceptability for some people: tax evasion and social security fraud. The media and politicians tend to treat them unequally, being obsessed with the latter, since it is a crime of the poor, rather than of the wealthy. Strictly speaking, however, both are crimes and thus beyond the pale as far as the church is concerned. The positive attitude some Christians take towards them, as shown in Table 2.8, reveals how faith does not dominate in comparison with other factors that make them socially acceptable.

Table 2.8 Attitudes towards tax evasion and social security fraud (%)

|  | Tax evasion | | Social security fraud | |
| --- | --- | --- | --- | --- |
|  | Not wrong | Seriously wrong | Not wrong | Seriously wrong |
| *Category* |  |  |  |  |
| No religion | 8 | 21 | 1 | 43 |
| Catholic | 10 | 14 | 5 | 28 |
| Mainstream Protestant | 4 | 22 | 1 | 50 |
| Other Christian | 2 | 29 | 1 | 45 |
| *Religiosity* |  |  |  |  |
| High | 1 | 35 | 0 | 45 |
| Medium | 4 | 20 | 2 | 42 |
| Low | 6 | 13 | 1 | 35 |
| None | 13 | 16 | 6 | 36 |

The figures speak volumes about many things. All groupings tend to consider social security fraud worse than tax evasion despite the fact that more is lost annually in tax fraud. This is testimony to the criminological argument that the crimes of the poor are deemed more serious than the crimes of the rich; it also reflects the impact of publicity campaigns against social security fraud, while there is no parallel focus on tax fraud. Broad denominational differences are interesting. Mainstream Protestants and those in the Other Christian category are much tougher than Catholics on social security fraud and tax evasion, but they are also more likely than Catholics to consider social security fraud a worse crime than tax evasion. After all, 'doing the double' in popular Loyalist misconception is thought to be rife in working-class Catholic areas. Protestants do not consider tax evasion, which has no such connotation, to be as bad. Levels of religiosity have the most profound effect, where there is a consistent pattern of worsening opprobrium as levels of religiosity increase. However, the final point to note is the number of believers who consider both crimes legitimate in unspecified circumstances. Clearly, attitudes towards some of the church's teachings are not shaped by faith.

### Changes in Religious Belief and Observance

With the exception of Northern Ireland, the story in the UK is of religious decline. Between 1950 and 2000, Mass attendance in England and Scotland declined by nearly half, and in Wales by 40 per cent, while in Northern Ireland it fell by only one tenth (Rosie, 2001). The number of active Protestant communicants in the Church of Scotland, the Church of England and the Anglican church in Wales fell by more than half in the same period, but only by 20 per cent in the Presbyterian church in Ireland (Brierley, 1999). The explanation proffered is that religion in Northern Ireland has not retreated to the private sphere, there to lose its significance in the face of competing leisure interests, family pursuits and personal identities, but has remained in the public sphere as a symbol for ethnic conflicts that have kept religion alive.

It is interesting, therefore, to speculate on what has been happening in Northern Ireland in the decade of the 1990s, leading up to the negotiation of the Good Friday Agreement. A comparison of survey results from 1991 and 1998 gives us a small glimpse. In fact, by 1998 Northern Ireland still remained a very religious society, with nearly nine out of every ten people considering themselves to belong to a church, although, as noted previously, there has been some decline for the Mainstream Protestant denominations. However, apart from identification with a church, changes are occurring. In virtually all measures of religious observance, practice and belief there is some decline, as shown in Table 2.9.

Those who describe themselves as religious now work out that faith by less strict observance. While the Catholic church has seen the biggest drop in regular attendance, from 82 per cent attending weekly in 1991 to 67 per cent in 1998, the Mainstream Protestant churches had the lowest regular attendance in 1998 at 29 per cent (down from 34 per cent in 1991). When this is combined with the drop in the number of people who say they belong to these churches, the haemorrhage for the main Protestant churches is severe. What is true for observance is also true for prayer, and while the number of people who participate regularly in church activities apart from the Sunday service is much the same, there is some growth in the number of those who never participate. Church is a way of life to the same small number of people, but the number for whom it means nothing more than routine Sunday attendance is growing.

Table 2.9 Religious observance, practice and belief, 1991 and 1998 (%)

|  | 1991 | 1998 |
| --- | --- | --- |
| *Attendance at church* | | |
| Weekly | 50 | 44 |
| Never | 15 | 22 |
| *Frequency of prayer* | | |
| Several times daily | 16 | 10 |
| Never | 10 | 16 |
| *Religiosity* | | |
| Extremely religious | 2 | 3 |
| Very religious | 11 | 8 |
| Somewhat religious | 53 | 45 |
| Extremely non-religious | 3 | 6 |
| *Participation outside church service* | | |
| Several times a week | 4 | 4 |
| Weekly | 9 | 7 |
| Never | 43 | 47 |
| *Belief* | | |
| I know God really exists and I have | | |
| no doubts about it | 61 | 51 |
| I don't believe in God | 2 | 4 |

These figures suggest that Northern Ireland people still identify with a church in larger numbers than in Britain, but with less certainty. This movement is reflected in the proportion of respondents who do not see their faith in terms of a moment of epiphany when they were 'saved', as discussed earlier. This drop – from 29 per cent in 1991 to 10 per cent in 1998 – is not the most significant move; it is that now many cannot choose. The uncertainty is reflected in a growth from 1 per cent who were unsure if they had been 'saved' in 1991 to 50 per cent in 1998. This uncertainty is also reflected elsewhere. While a similar number in the two surveys described themselves as extremely religious, the somewhat religious group grew in number, as did the number saying they are extremely non-religious. When these trends are combined with the growing liberalisation of belief that was noted earlier, we see Northern Ireland Christians slowly on the move. While the Northern Irish still have some way to travel to reach their secular neighbours in Britain, a journey of sorts has begun.

It would be best not to exaggerate the degree of change however, for the legacy of past patterns of religiosity is still evident in stable ethno-religious identities. Earlier it was noted that nearly one in three Northern Irish Christians refuse to identify themselves as nationalist or unionist, but this does not tap ethno-religious cultural identities. Some issues broached within the surveys come near to doing so. Mixed marriages are a case in point. Between 1991 and 1998, the proportion of respondents who were married or living with someone of the same religion dropped from 92 per cent to 83 per cent; religion clearly still matters in one's choice of partner. The drop is most pronounced in the Other Christian category, which might suggest that mixed denomination couples find it easier to manage their situation when not in one of the main Christian denominations. Nonetheless, eight out of ten people still marry or set up home with someone whose religious identity is the same. More than that, there is little intermarriage or cohabitation between denominations: 91 per cent of Catholics have partners who are Catholic, 68 per cent of Church of Ireland respondents have partners inside the denomination, as do 72 per cent of Presbyterians. Whatever dilution there is in the tenets of faith Northern Irish Christians hold, and no matter the change in their observance and practice, they have not opened up to accepting partners who are from a different denomination. A small majority of respondents (51 per cent) feel that most people in Northern Ireland would mind a lot or mind a little if a family member married someone from a different religion. Forty three per cent think that most people would not mind. However, as is usual in survey questions like this, people are more willing to attribute socially unacceptable views to others than to themselves, so only 26 per cent say that they personally would mind a lot or mind a little. It is worth noting that Catholics are the most open and liberal in response to these questions and Other Christians the least, something that completely belies the number of mixed marriages within each, since Catholics have the least and Other Christians the most (91 per cent of Catholics and 60 per cent of Other Christians have partners also within the same grouping). This is a good illustration of the sociological disjuncture between attitudes and behaviour.

The 1998 survey provides a second opportunity to assess the extent to which these changes in belief and practice are impacting on ethno-religious identity. Respondents were asked several questions with respect to 'community traditions' (something, however, which includes ethnic minority traditions as well as ethno-religious ones). Respondents were asked to record their level of agreement with the following statement: 'I have my own cultural tradition and see no need to take part in any others.' In all, 43 per cent agree or strongly agree with this, and only 4 per cent strongly disagree. Among those with a religious identification, levels of disagreement are lowest among Catholics. Significantly, 51 per cent of the highly religious agree, and none strongly disagree. Even 47 per cent of those with low levels of religiosity agree, with 3 per cent strongly disagreeing. Less than one in ten people expressing a religious identification strongly disagree with the statement 'my cultural tradition is always the underdog', irrespective of which church they identify with. That is, traditional ethno-religious identities are firmly rooted. There are no comparable figures for 1991, so it is impossible to assess whether the ethno-religious identities have weakened as religious observance becomes less strict and patterns of belief more liberal.

## Conclusion

There are two stories told by sociologists with respect to secularisation. The first is that an increasing number of people lose faith and end their identification with a church. The second is less stark. While many people stop going to church, they do not lose their faith. There are two versions of the latter story. The first is that people reject institutionalised religion but maintain belief – they believe without belonging. The second is that in circumstances where one denomination has a monopoly, people who have problems with that church have no alternative and thus stop going. They too can maintain faith and believe without belonging, but for different reasons. Northern Ireland has seen very little secularisation in the first sense, with virtually no diminution in the numbers identifying with a church over the last decade. However, if nominal identification has not declined, there have been other changes. Levels of observance are less strict, beliefs are held with more ambivalence and uncertainty than in the past, and attitudes are becoming more liberal. There is very little growth in non-belief however.

There is no evidence of secularisation in the second sense either. Northern Ireland does not have a monopoly by one denomination, so people can switch churches if they develop problems with their current loyalty rather than leave altogether. There is no evidence of church switching in Northern Ireland, except for the small growth in independent Protestant churches and charismatic groups. As we have seen, the overwhelming majority of respondents are in the denomination of their parents. However, there is evidence of 'believing without belonging' among respondents with no religion, some of whom have been shown to continue to hold religious beliefs and oblations. Given that this category is still quite small, secularisation has not stepped up a pace; Northern Ireland is hardly less religious now than it was in 1991.

The maintenance of these high levels of religious identification is normally explained by the role religion plays in ethno-national conflict. There is no evidence that events during the decade around the ceasefires and peace negotiations have weakened either religious identification or the impact of religion on ethno-national identities. Some Northern Irish Christians remain fixed in maintaining closed and exclusive ethno-religious identities. Time will tell whether the changes in observance, practice and belief evident during the period 1991 to 1998 will eventually impact on ethno-religious cultural identities and increase further the number of Christians in Northern Ireland who practise what Jesus preaches about neighbours and enemies.

## References

Brierley, P. (1999) *UK Christian Handbook, Religious Trends No. 2, 2000/01* (London: Harper Collins).

Bruce, S. and Alderdice, F. (1993) 'Religious belief and behaviour' in Peter Stringer and Gillian Robinson (eds), *Social Attitudes in Northern Ireland: The Third Report, 1992–1993* (Belfast: Blackstaff Press) pp. 5–20.

Davie, G. (1990a) '"An ordinary God": the paradox of religion in contemporary Britain', *British Journal of Sociology*, Vol. 41, No. 3, pp. 395–421.

Davie, G. (1990b) 'Believing without belonging: is this the future of religion in Britain?', *Social Compass*, Vol. 4, No. 4, pp. 455–69.

Rosie, M. (2001) *Religion and Sectarianism in Modern Scotland*, unpublished PhD thesis, University of Edinburgh.

# 3 Ten Years of Social Attitudes to Community Relations in Northern Ireland

*Joanne Hughes and Caitlin Donnelly*

The years between 1989 and 1999 have seen seismic changes in the political and policy landscape of Northern Ireland. The paramilitary ceasefires, new constitutional arrangements, and the establishment of a policy agenda and legal framework that uphold the principles of pluralism and equality for all, provide a context for community relations that is radically different to that which existed in 1989 at the time of data collection for the first Northern Ireland Social Attitudes (NISA) survey. This chapter begins with a brief background to the current state of community relations in Northern Ireland, thus setting the context for the presentation of time-series survey data that, over the last decade, indicate evidence of shifting patterns in attitudes towards community relations issues.

During the 1990s efforts by the British government in Northern Ireland focused on tackling systemic problems of disadvantage, discrimination and inequality. The development of Fair Employment Legislation and initiatives such as Targeting Social Need (TSN) and Policy Appraisal and Fair Treatment (PAFT) Guidelines for government departments, while not without their critics (Osborne, 1996) signalled an acknowledgement on the part of government that something should be done to address these socio-economic disadvantages most acutely felt by the Catholic community. Juxtaposed with this, community relations became a policy priority at the beginning of the 1990s. Concerned primarily with promoting greater cross-community contact, the approach adopted at the time was criticised by those who believed that government was promoting an assimilist/integrationalist agenda that offered little more than a 'sticking plaster' solution to the conflict (Cairns and Hewstone, 2001; Hughes, forthcoming).

### Background

Concurrent with policy interventions, a long and often tortuous multi-party talks process aimed to find a constitutional settlement that would appease both unionists and nationalists. The process gained momentum following Irish Republican Army (IRA) ceasefires and a major development was the signing of the Good Friday Agreement in April 1998. Supported by 71 per cent of the electorate in Northern Ireland, the Agreement emphasises a pluralist agenda and is underpinned by the commitment of all signatories to the principles of inclusiveness and equality. An important structural outcome has been the devolution of power from Westminster to a 108 member local assembly with responsibility for policy on devolved matters such as economic development, education, agriculture, environment, financial allocations, health, housing and social services. Under the terms of the Agreement, some decisions can only be taken on a cross-community, consensual basis.

## Community Relations in Northern Ireland

In the wake of political developments in the late 1990s, there are some signs that the community relations agenda has shifted from being 'symptom driven' to addressing root causes of conflict. Current practice is less concerned with promoting cross-community contact *per se* than with promoting cultural, religious and political pluralism, and the equality agenda has begun to define the nature of some community relations activity (Hughes, forthcoming). Measured by outcomes such as greater understanding of cultural diversity, increased willingness to engage in shared working, and, in some cases, an ability to influence wider political processes (Deloitte and Touche, 2001a; 2001b), a growing body of evidence suggests that community relations initiatives are having some positive impact at grass roots level (Knox, Hughes, Birrell and McCready, 1994; Capita, 1997; Deloitte and Touche, 2001a; 2001b). Despite this, and against the support for local level power sharing and the principles of equality and equity (as evidenced by the 71 per cent who voted in favour of the Agreement in the referendum) some research indicates that Northern Ireland has become a more divided society.

In housing, for example, time-series research has shown progressively higher levels of residential segregation with a majority of people choosing to live in polarised districts (Poole and Doherty, 1996; Doherty and Poole, 1997). Compounding the problem over the last few years, segregation has been accompanied by an increase in 'chill factors', referring to demarcation of sectarian boundaries with graffiti, flags, kerb painting and other manifestations of cultural/political identity and paramilitary association (Northern Ireland Housing Executive (NIHE), 1999). An increase in polarisation is also evident in voting behaviour where, in the period immediately following the signing of the Good Friday Agreement, voting preference reflected increasing support for the political extremes, with religion continuing to be the key determining factor (Carmichael and Knox, 1999). More recently, the Democratic Unionist Party (DUP) and Sinn Féin made substantial gains in the 2001 parliamentary and local council elections. The swing in the unionist vote from the pro-Agreement Ulster Unionist Party (UUP) and the Alliance Party towards the anti-Agreement DUP party has been interpreted as reflecting a growing Protestant disillusionment with political reforms (which will be discussed later in this chapter).

In addition to these developments, and undoubtedly linked to them, the ongoing parades dispute between the Orange Order and residents of Catholic/nationalist areas has continued to sour community relations. The latter have demanded re-routing of traditional Orange Order marches through nationalist districts, regarding them as triumphalist and inciting. An increase in Orange parades,[1] however, and the refusal of the Orange Order to take alternative routes has resulted in some of the worst periods of civil unrest and disruption seen in over 30 years of conflict (Hughes, 1998).

It could be argued that increased polarisation is a logical outcome of a pluralist agenda which promotes and embraces diversity and difference. This does not, however, explain ongoing intercommunity tension, hostility and intimidation. A range of explanations is offered in support of this apparent paradox. Wilson (2000), for example, argues that the Good Friday Agreement, although affirming the 'consent principle' – that is, that there can be no change in the constitutional position of Northern Ireland, except by the consent of the majority – has left in place 'the polarised political battlefield' because the constitutional position of Northern Ireland as part of the United Kingdom remains unchanged. On the one hand, unionists continue to defend their 'Britishness', upheld by the Agreement. On the other, nationalists contend that under the terms of the Agreement their 'Irishness' must be given due expression. Sectarian tension, manifest in the 'profusion of flags on the street' is attributed to the conflict of interests inherent in these positions. 'Unionists perceive [the] Nationalist stance as reflecting a reluctance to genuinely accept the consent principle. Nationalists, in turn, perceive the Unionist stance as reflecting a reluctance genuinely to accept the new relationship of equality the agreement envisages' (Wilson, 2000).

Focusing less on the Agreement *per se*, some academics have argued that increasing polarisation and sectarian tension, particularly with regards to the parades issue, can be attributed to a growing sense of alienation within the Protestant community (Knox, 1995; Hughes, 1998; O'Neill, 2000). O'Neill argues that unionists feel particularly insecure about their position within the UK because they perceive that nationalists will ultimately accept nothing less than 'political and cultural domination throughout Ireland'. This insecurity is intensified by British government engagement with the Irish government since the signing of the Anglo-Irish Agreement of 1985 (O'Neill, 2000, pp. 27–8). Concessions made to republicans during the implementation of the Good Friday Agreement have also exacerbated the problem. In particular, the British government's continued willingness to accommodate the demands of republicans,[2] against the repeated failure of republican paramilitaries to deliver decommissioning within stipulated timeframes, has caused ructions at both political and grass roots levels within the Protestant community that threaten to destabilise the peace process (Aughey, 2001). The theme of increasing Protestant marginalisation, implicit in this analysis, is reflected in the social attitudes data discussed below.

## Social Attitudes – Survey Evidence

The following analysis is based on data derived from the Community Relations modules included in the 1989 and 1996 NISA surveys and the 1999 Northern Ireland Life and Times survey. Five questions asked in the 1989 and 1996 surveys can be compared with identical or virtually identical equivalents from the 1999 survey. In addition, we have provided an analysis of new questions in the 1999 survey that relate to the equality agenda. All the findings presented in the chapter relate to Protestant and Catholic respondents, and to the two groups combined.

### Relations Between Protestants and Catholics

Respondents were asked whether relations between Protestants and Catholics were better, worse or the same as they were five years ago (Table 3.1). In the period 1989 to 1996 there was an increase of 25 percentage points in the proportion of Catholics and Protestants who believed that relations had improved. This is in contrast with the picture that emerges after 1996 where there was only a slight overall increase of four percentage points. Of particular significance however is the growing disparity in attitudes between Protestants and Catholics after 1996. In the period 1989 to 1996 those who thought that relations had improved increased from 20 per cent to 44 per cent, and 23 per cent to 47 per cent, for Protestants and Catholics respectively. From 1996 to 1999 the positive trend continued for Catholics with the figure rising to 60 per cent. Conversely the Protestant response to the same question fell to 42 per cent.

Table 3.1 Are relations between Protestants and Catholics better than they were five years ago? (%)

|  | 1989 | | | 1996 | | | 1999 | | |
|  | Total | Cath. | Prot. | Total | Cath. | Prot. | Total | Cath. | Prot. |
|---|---|---|---|---|---|---|---|---|---|
| Better | 21 | 23 | 20 | 46 | 47 | 44 | 50 | 60 | 42 |
| Worse | 28 | 31 | 26 | 11 | 10 | 11 | 7 | 4 | 10 |
| Same | 47 | 44 | 50 | 42 | 41 | 43 | 41 | 33 | 46 |
| Other | 2 | 2 | 2 | – | – | – | 1 | 1 | <1 |
| Don't know | 2 | 2 | 2 | 2 | 1 | 2 | 1 | 1 | 2 |
| No answer | <1 | <1 | 1 | <1 | <1 | <1 | – | – | – |

Similarly, when asked whether relations between Protestants and Catholics would be better, worse or the same in five years time (Table 3.2) the percentage who believed that they would be better increased from 25 per cent to 56 per cent in the period 1989 to 1999. Again, however, Catholics were more favourable than Protestants in their assessments. Compared to 1996, the 1999 data show a rise of 19 percentage points among Catholics and only a rise of 7 percentage points among Protestants who believed that relations would improve.

Table 3.2 Will relations between Protestants and Catholics be better in five years time? (%)

|  | 1989 | | | 1996 | | | 1999 | | |
|  | Total | Cath. | Prot. | Total | Cath. | Prot. | Total | Cath. | Prot. |
|---|---|---|---|---|---|---|---|---|---|
| Better | 25 | 30 | 22 | 43 | 48 | 39 | 56 | 67 | 46 |
| Worse | 16 | 16 | 16 | 8 | 4 | 10 | 4 | 2 | 7 |
| Same | 54 | 51 | 56 | 42 | 43 | 41 | 32 | 25 | 39 |
| Other | <1 | <1 | 1 | 2 | 1 | 3 | <1 | <1 | 1 |
| Don't know | 5 | 4 | 5 | 6 | 4 | 7 | 7 | 6 | 8 |
| No answer | 1 | <1 | 1 | – | – | – | – | – | – |

The growing disparity between the Protestant and Catholic responses is perhaps an endorsement of a Catholic community growing in confidence and a Protestant community feeling increasingly marginalised by wider political developments. It has been argued that in the most recent elections the key deciding factors for those who changed their vote from UUP to DUP were the failure of the Good Friday Agreement to deliver decommissioning and the reform of the Royal Ulster Constabulary (RUC) (*Belfast Telegraph*, 2001a). UUP party member John Taylor, when interviewed on Radio Ulster, reported that at some polling stations RUC warrants were flashed at UUP candidates who were told that the holder would be voting for the DUP (Friday, 8 June 2001). Attempts to generate a political culture based on equality and fair treatment have been interpreted by the Protestant community as undermining their interests (*Belfast Telegraph*, 2001b). This is likely to influence attitudes to, and relations with, the Catholic community.

*Continuing Segregation in Housing, Employment and Education?*

Although questions about relations between Protestants and Catholics may be relatively superficial because they are impressionistic, a series of questions that aim to gauge behaviour was also included. These refer to residential, workplace and educational segregation and the willingness of respondents to engage with the other community.

The total proportion of respondents wishing to live in neighbourhoods with people of only their own religion increased from 14 per cent in 1996 to 23 per cent in 1999, while the total preferring to live in mixed religion neighbourhoods decreased from 82 per cent to 73 per cent in the same period. In 1999 more Protestants (26 per cent) than Catholics (18 per cent) prefer to live in neighbourhoods with only their own religion and there is a greater decline from 1996 to 1999 in the proportion of Protestants (80 per cent to 68 per cent) relative to Catholics (85 per cent to 79 per cent) who prefer to live in a mixed religion neighbourhood (Table 3.3).

Table 3.3 Would you prefer to live in a neighbourhood with people of only your own religion? (%)

|  | 1989 | | | 1996 | | | 1999 | | |
|  | Total | Cath. | Prot. | Total | Cath. | Prot. | Total | Cath. | Prot. |
|---|---|---|---|---|---|---|---|---|---|
| Only own | 23 | 18 | 27 | 14 | 11 | 17 | 23 | 18 | 26 |
| Mixed | 70 | 75 | 67 | 82 | 85 | 80 | 73 | 79 | 68 |
| Don't know | 5 | 6 | 5 | 4 | 5 | 3 | 5 | 4 | 5 |
| No answer | 1 | 1 | 2 | – | – | – | – | – | – |

When asked 'if you were working and had to change your job, would you prefer a workplace with people of only your own religion, or a mixed religion workplace?', the total proportion of respondents expressing a desire to work with only those from their own religion increased from 3 per cent in 1996 to 9 per cent in 1999 (Table 3.4). There was a greater tendency in 1999 than in 1996 for both Catholics and Protestants to express a desire to work in religiously segregated workplaces, although this trend was more pronounced for Protestants. In 1999, fewer respondents overall suggested that they would prefer to work in mixed religion workplaces when compared with 1996 data (86 per cent and 96 per cent respectively).

Table 3.4 Would you prefer a workplace with people of only your own religion? (%)

|  | 1989 | | | 1996 | | | 1999 | | |
|  | Total | Cath. | Prot. | Total | Cath. | Prot. | Total | Cath. | Prot. |
| --- | --- | --- | --- | --- | --- | --- | --- | --- | --- |
| Only own | 11 | 7 | 14 | 3 | 2 | 4 | 9 | 6 | 12 |
| Mixed | 83 | 86 | 81 | 96 | 97 | 95 | 86 | 91 | 82 |
| Don't know | 5 | 6 | 3 | 2 | 2 | 1 | 5 | 4 | 6 |
| No answer | 1 | 1 | 2 | – | – | – | – | – | – |

The proportions of both Protestants and Catholics preferring to live and work with only their own religious group fell between 1989 and 1996, but by 1999 had more or less returned to the 1989 figures. In 1996 the marked increase in preference for living and working in mixed religion environments could be explained by the more congenial and sanguine atmosphere inspired by the 1994 ceasefires and the low level of violence in the inter-ceasefire period. However, an increase in other forms of sectarianism since the ceasefires, such as intimidation and harassment, may underpin current preferences for residential and workplace segregation.

Aside from residential segregation, community support for separate schools for Catholics and Protestants has traditionally been regarded as a barometer of the depth and breadth of social and cultural division in Northern Ireland. Any movement towards greater educational integration is closely monitored and often interpreted as a sign of better relationships between the two communities. When respondents were asked about their preference of school (Table 3.5) the total proportion stating a preference to send their child to a mixed religion school increased slightly from 62 per cent in 1996 to 64 per cent in 1999. This is complemented by a decrease in the total preferring to send their child to a school with only those from their own religion from 34 per cent in 1996 to 25 per cent in 1999.

Table 3.5 Would you prefer to send your children to a school with children of only your own religion? (%)

|  | 1989 | | | 1996 | | | 1999 | | |
|  | Total | Cath. | Prot. | Total | Cath. | Prot. | Total | Cath. | Prot. |
| --- | --- | --- | --- | --- | --- | --- | --- | --- | --- |
| Only own | 39 | 37 | 41 | 34 | 38 | 31 | 25 | 21 | 29 |
| Mixed | 53 | 54 | 52 | 62 | 57 | 65 | 64 | 72 | 57 |
| Don't know | 8 | 9 | 6 | 5 | 6 | 4 | 11 | 8 | 14 |
| No answer | 1 | – | 1 | – | – | – | – | – | – |

However, there are discernible differences between Catholic and Protestant views on mixed religion schooling. In the period 1989 to

1996, the proportion of Protestants preferring their own schools decreased by 10 percentage points while the proportion of Catholics preferring their own schools remained fairly static. Between 1996 and 1999 the proportion of Catholics who would prefer to send their child to a Catholic-only school fell by 17 percentage points, while the numbers of Protestants who would prefer to send their child to a Protestant-only school fell by only 2 percentage points in 1999. Moreover, the proportion of Catholics (72 per cent) who would prefer a mixed religion school has increased by 15 percentage points since 1996, while the proportion of Protestants who would prefer a mixed religion school has decreased from 65 per cent to 57 per cent and is now only 5 percentage points higher than the figure recorded in 1989. The gap between the proportions of respondents expressing a desire for integrated education in Northern Ireland and the numbers actually attending these schools has been well documented (Hughes and Carmichael, 1998). The survey was, however, concerned about *attitudes* towards integration and it is significant that there has been a decline in the numbers of Protestants who would prefer to send their child to a mixed religion school.

This waning enthusiasm may be further evidence of increasing disenchantment with changes at the macro level. More specifically though, the reduced support for integration between 1996 and 1999 may be related to a perceived shift in government policy in the mid-1990s to prioritise the transformation of schools to integrated status rather than to support the development of new schools. Existing schools could transform to Controlled Integrated status if a ballot indicated that there were sufficient levels of parental support and if the school could make a case that it would attract reasonable numbers of Catholics and Protestants. The way in which this policy of transformation has been interpreted has introduced differentials into the school system.

The trend towards transformation in the state-controlled sector, which has an overwhelming majority of Protestant pupils, has encouraged some to lament the loss of 'their' schools and has led to the development of a more defensive attitude towards 'Protestant education' (McGrath, 2000; Stephen, 2000). There is a tangible fear within the Protestant community that integrated schools are having a negative impact upon the viability of the state-controlled school system. This is compounded by declining enrolments in state-controlled schools. The long-term effects are difficult to predict but as Smith suggests, the transformation of Protestant schools while Catholic schools remain largely intact may have a 'negative impact on relations between these two communities' (1999, p. 9).

*Perceptions of Equality*

As noted earlier, since the Good Friday Agreement, the equality agenda has begun to define the nature of some community relations activity. In view of this, it was deemed important to include a set of questions within the 1999 Life and Times survey to explore perceptions of equality and equity within Northern Ireland. Table 3.6 reveals the importance attached to the equality agenda in Northern Ireland by respondents, and also provides some grounds for cautious optimism.

Table 3.6 It should be a top priority for government to make sure that Protestants and Catholics are treated equally (%)

|  | Total | Catholic | Protestant |
|---|---|---|---|
| Strongly agree | 51 | 63 | 42 |
| Agree | 40 | 33 | 45 |
| Neither agree nor disagree | 6 | 2 | 8 |
| Disagree | 1 | <1 | 2 |
| Strongly disagree | <1 | <1 | 1 |
| Can't choose | 2 | 1 | 2 |

However, while Table 3.6 shows general agreement (91 per cent) that equality *should* be a top priority for government, just over half (52 per cent) of respondents actually believe that Protestants and Catholics are treated equally (Table 3.7). Almost two thirds (64 per cent) of Protestants think that Protestants and Catholics are treated equally while 21 per cent believe they are not. It is notable, however, that 38 per cent of Catholics believe that there is equality. Had this question been asked ten years ago this figure is likely to have been substantially less.

Table 3.7 Are Protestants and Catholics in Northern Ireland treated equally? (%)

|  | Total | Catholic | Protestant |
|---|---|---|---|
| Yes | 52 | 38 | 64 |
| No | 29 | 40 | 21 |
| It depends | 15 | 18 | 12 |
| Other | 1 | 1 | <1 |
| Don't know | 3 | 3 | 3 |

Respondents who think that Catholics and Protestants in Northern Ireland are not always treated equally were asked who is usually treated better. Almost half (48 per cent) of these respondents believe that it is Protestants (Table 3.8). Almost three quarters of Catholics (73 per

cent) believe that Protestants are treated better. However, it is significant, given the legacy of discrimination against the Catholic
community, that over half (52 per cent) of the Protestant respondents
believe that it is Catholics who receive better treatment. It is also particularly interesting that, as noted earlier, one in five (21 per cent)
Protestants believe that inequality exists in Northern Ireland. This
could be interpreted in one of two ways. Either, that Protestants
believe that Catholics continue to be unfairly disadvantaged in
Northern Ireland, or, that the tables have turned and Protestants now
believe themselves to be treated more unfairly than Catholics. Taking
into account the data presented in the next section concerning rights
and cultural traditions, it is more likely that the latter is the case.

Table 3.8 Who is usually treated better – Protestants or Catholics? (%)

|            | Total | Catholic | Protestant |
| --- | --- | --- | --- |
| Protestants | 48 | 73 | 11 |
| Catholics | 22 | 1 | 52 |
| It depends | 26 | 24 | 29 |
| Other | 1 | <1 | 2 |
| Don't know | 4 | 2 | 6 |

*Perceived Rights and Cultural Traditions*

As noted earlier, much of the policy change since the mid-1990s has
been concerned with the development of a context wherein the rights
and cultural interests of all communities are accepted and protected.
However, the survey evidence shows that Protestants are more likely
than Catholics to see the environment as 'de-emphasising' their rights
and are also more likely to believe that the rights of the 'other
community' are talked about more than their own.

Respondents were asked whether they agree or disagree that 'there
is always talk about the rights of Catholics but never about the rights
of Protestants' (Table 3.9). Ten per cent of Catholics and 53 per cent
of Protestants agree or strongly agree with the statement. Conversely,
when respondents are asked whether 'there is always talk about the
rights of Protestants but never about the rights of Catholics', one
quarter of Catholics (25 per cent) and 5 per cent of Protestants agree
or strongly agree with this statement (Table 3.10).

More than twice as many Protestants than Catholics agree or
strongly agree that the rights of the other community are talked about
more than their own. Although the numbers are small, it is also significant that twice as many Catholics than Protestants agree or strongly
agree that there is more emphasis on their own rights than those of

the other community. Ostensibly these data may reveal nothing more than a tacit acceptance of macro-political processes that are addressing the differential socio-economic experience of Catholics. However, the data below show that this is unlikely to be the case.

Table 3.9 There is always talk about the rights of Catholics but never about the rights of Protestants (%)

|                            | Total | Catholic | Protestant |
|----------------------------|-------|----------|------------|
| Strongly agree             | 12    | 2        | 19         |
| Agree                      | 23    | 8        | 34         |
| Neither agree nor disagree | 22    | 18       | 25         |
| Disagree                   | 28    | 47       | 14         |
| Strongly disagree          | 9     | 19       | 3          |
| Can't choose               | 5     | 5        | 5          |

Table 3.10 There is always talk about the rights of Protestants but never about the rights of Catholics (%)

|                            | Total | Catholic | Protestant |
|----------------------------|-------|----------|------------|
| Strongly agree             | 3     | 5        | 1          |
| Agree                      | 11    | 20       | 4          |
| Neither agree nor disagree | 26    | 22       | 28         |
| Disagree                   | 44    | 37       | 49         |
| Strongly disagree          | 12    | 9        | 13         |
| Can't choose               | 5     | 6        | 5          |

When asked to respond to the statement 'thinking about the real differences in viewpoints between the different cultural traditions my fear is that my own view will be lost among louder voices', 43 per cent of the total believe that their view will be lost among louder voices (Table 3.11). It is significant, however, that more Protestants than Catholics agree or strongly agree with the statement (48 per cent and 38 per cent respectively). Almost half (47 per cent) of the Catholic respondents disagree or strongly disagree that their view will be lost compared with only 28 per cent of Protestants.

Protestants are no more optimistic when it comes to future prospects for the universal acceptance of all cultural traditions. Only 38 per cent of Protestants compared to 60 per cent of Catholics agree or strongly agree with the statement that 'at some time in the future the viewpoints of all cultural traditions will be accepted by everyone in Northern Ireland' (Table 3.12). Just under a quarter (24 per cent) of Catholics and over a third (38 per cent) of Protestants disagree or strongly disagree that the viewpoints of all cultural traditions will be accepted in the future.

Table 3.11 Thinking about the real differences in viewpoints between the different cultural traditions my fear is that my own view will be lost among louder voices (%)

|                            | Total | Catholic | Protestant |
| -------------------------- | ----- | -------- | ---------- |
| Strongly agree             | 9     | 6        | 11         |
| Agree                      | 35    | 32       | 37         |
| Neither agree nor disagree | 17    | 13       | 20         |
| Disagree                   | 33    | 42       | 26         |
| Strongly disagree          | 3     | 5        | 2          |
| Don't know                 | 4     | 3        | 5          |

Table 3.12 At some time in the future the viewpoints of all cultural traditions will be accepted by everyone in Northern Ireland[3] (%)

|                            | Total | Catholic | Protestant |
| -------------------------- | ----- | -------- | ---------- |
| Strongly agree             | 8     | 9        | 7          |
| Agree                      | 40    | 51       | 31         |
| Neither agree nor disagree | 14    | 10       | 17         |
| Disagree                   | 27    | 23       | 30         |
| Strongly disagree          | 5     | 1        | 8          |
| Don't know                 | 7     | 6        | 8          |

In general, it seems that Protestants are more likely than Catholics to express a lack of confidence that their rights and cultural traditions will be protected. This lack of confidence is further reflected in the responses to a question concerning accommodation and compromise (Table 3.13). Almost half (48 per cent) of the total respondents disagree with the statement that 'compromise and accommodation simply means that everyone loses out', and a further 15 per cent strongly disagree. More Protestants (22 per cent) than Catholics (15 per cent) agree or strongly agree that compromise and accommodation means that everyone loses out; however, substantially more Catholics (75 per cent) than Protestants (53 per cent) do not believe that compromise or accommodation means that everyone will lose out.

Table 3.13 Compromise and accommodation simply means that everyone loses out (%)

|                            | Total | Catholic | Protestant |
| -------------------------- | ----- | -------- | ---------- |
| Strongly agree             | 3     | 2        | 4          |
| Agree                      | 16    | 13       | 18         |
| Neither agree nor disagree | 13    | 7        | 19         |
| Disagree                   | 48    | 54       | 43         |
| Strongly disagree          | 15    | 21       | 10         |
| Don't know                 | 5     | 4        | 6          |

Overall, the evidence on rights, cultural traditions and compromise seems to indicate something of the success of recent measures to inspire confidence and reduce marginalisation among Catholics. However, a different picture is emerging for Protestants, where responses suggest that they see the environment as less sensitive to their rights and cultural traditions than those of the Catholic community. This perceived lack of sympathy seems to have influenced the negative reaction of Protestants to questions concerning compromise and accommodation.

## Conclusion

Although the 1999 survey evidence indicates a general improvement in attitudes towards community relations over the ten-year period, the data show that, since 1996, the Catholic and Protestant communities have developed notably different attitudes on a range of issues. In general, Catholics seem more amenable to efforts to promote cross-community contact as demonstrated by their greater willingness to integrate. This complements responses to other questions which suggest that Catholics are more confident that their rights and cultural traditions will be protected. The general optimism inherent in Catholic responses is, however, tempered by a growing sense of distrust and unease within the Protestant community. Protestants expressed less enthusiasm for interreligious mixing, a pattern that becomes more pronounced after 1996. Taken together with evidence from the 1999 survey, where Protestant respondents are less confident than Catholics that their rights and cultural traditions will be protected, it is reasonable to assume that Protestants are experiencing greater difficulty than Catholics with the changes at the macro-political and the meso-institutional levels. Hence, although the intention of the Good Friday Agreement is to create an inclusive society, the survey findings provide little evidence to suggest that this is the type of environment which is currently perceived by most Protestants.

The disparity in attitudes between Catholics and Protestants could be explained in two ways. Firstly, it is not yet clear whether the responses recorded by the survey are a product of the transitional period, in which Northern Ireland currently finds itself. As such, it is difficult to make any conclusive comments about Protestant disillusionment. However, in the light of growing frustration within the Protestant community, endorsed by the gains of anti-Agreement unionists in the recent Westminster and local government elections, it may be that Aughey's argument (2001), which highlights the fallacy of creating an agreement that is perceived to be based on concessions to republicans, could prove prophetic.

Secondly, the more positive attitudes of Catholics may be rooted in their belief that the status quo in Northern Ireland has improved. Evans and O'Leary (2000), for example, in their study of political attitudes in Northern Ireland after the Good Friday Agreement, have suggested that Protestants are more likely to believe that the Agreement does not benefit them as much as it does Catholics, because of their resistance to anything which is perceived to threaten the Union and, therefore, the status quo.

The survey evidence, taken in conjunction with greater electoral polarisation, underlines the inherent tensions and dilemmas of a pluralist model of government. At present the Protestant community's dissatisfaction appears to be related to its interpretation of the pluralist arrangements for government. Protestants seem to observe a *neo-pluralist* rather than a *pluralist* agenda at work, in the sense that the state is negotiating and according greater legitimacy and recognition to the Catholic community than the Protestant community (Marsh, 2000). In any pluralist society the loss of social cohesion and the alienation of particular sections of interests becomes inevitable unless particular efforts are made to engender confidence that the state will protect the interests of *all* groups (Marsh, 2000). Many Protestants, it would seem, do not believe that their rights and culture have been accorded the same degree of legitimacy as the Catholic community. This argument was put rather starkly by the newly elected DUP MP for East Londonderry, Gregory Campbell: 'The Unionist community have given concession after concession to nationalists and Republicans ... now we're in the queue now we're going to the Prime Minister to say that we want equality and we want legitimacy for our cause' (*Belfast Telegraph*, 2001b). The emphasis that has been placed on the pluralist model of developing community relations arguably represents a more realistic interpretation of the community relations problem. However, its success inevitably depends on the confidence of particip-ating groups that the macro- and meso-environment will protect their interests.

Although at present the confidence of the Catholic community appears to be increasing, that confidence is still quite precarious as it remains that 62 per cent believe that there is not equality in Northern Ireland, and 73 per cent of these respondents believe that Protestants are treated better than Catholics. So while there is a clear need to develop a sense of trust and confidence within the Protestant community, it is important that the tentative optimism currently being expressed by the Catholic community is not diluted. At present the increased desire to live and work in isolation from the other community (particularly pronounced in Protestant responses) cannot be viewed as an unproblematic expression of a pluralist society but must be seen as a reflection of cultural defensiveness fuelled by Protestant perceptions of an unequal society.

## Notes

1. Statistics collected by the Royal Ulster Constabulary between 1985 and 1995 show that loyalist parades have increased in number by 684 over the ten-year period <http://cain.ulst.ac.uk/issues/parade/jarman.htm>.
2. Aughey (2001) lists the concessions the British government made to republicans in an effort to ensure the latter would engage in 'exclusively democratic' processes. These included the continued early release of prisoners, the reduction of troop levels (despite continued paramilitary involvement in punishment beatings and intimidation), an agreement to meet a long-standing republican demand for an inquiry into the events of Bloody Sunday, the acceptance of the central recommendations of the Patten Report on police reforms (which were lambasted by unionists), permission, against the advice of the Speaker, that Sinn Féin MPs should be allowed access to the facilities of the House of Commons, without having taken an oath of allegiance, and, crucially, the persuasion of David Trimble that he should recommend his party share power with Sinn Féin. This was based on an understanding that the Irish Republican Army (IRA) would cooperate with an Independent International Commission on Decommissioning and that there would be some gesture on arms to satisfy unionist sceptics. Neither happened, but devolved government went 'live' in November 1999 (Aughey, 2001, p. 217).
3. Although the question attempted to ascertain the extent to which *all* cultural traditions will be accepted it has been assumed that, when answering, respondents were referring to their own culture.

## References

Aughey, A. (2001) 'British policy in Northern Ireland' in S.P. Savage and R. Atkinson (eds), *Public Policy Under Blair* (Hampshire: Palgrave) pp. 205–20.

*Belfast Telegraph* (2001a) 'Leader column', 9 June.

*Belfast Telegraph* (2001b) 'Campbell says result reflects mood of people', 9 June.

Cairns, E. and Hewstone, M. (2001) *The Impact of Peacemaking in Northern Ireland on Intergroup Behaviour*, draft paper (Coleraine: Department of Psychology, University of Ulster).

Capita (1997) *Evaluation of the Community Relations Council, Final Report* (Belfast: Capita Management Consultants).

Carmichael, P. and Knox, C. (1999) 'Towards a new era? Some developments in the governance of Northern Ireland', *International Review of Administrative Sciences*, Vol. 65, pp. 103–16.

Deloitte and Touche (2001a) *Evaluation of the Adult and Community Education Initiatives, Final Report* (Belfast: Deloitte and Touche).

Deloitte and Touche (2001b) *Evaluation of the Community Relations Council, Final Report* (Belfast: Deloitte and Touche).

Doherty, P. and Poole, M. (1997) 'Ethnic residential segregation in Belfast, Northern Ireland, 1971–1991', *The Geographical Review*, Vol. 87, No. 4, pp. 520–36.

Evans, G. and O' Leary, B. (2000) 'Northern Irish voters and the British – Irish Agreement: foundations of a stable consociational settlement', *The Political Quarterly*, Vol. 71, No.1, pp. 78–101.

Hughes, J. (1998) 'Approaches to community relations in Northern Ireland: lessons from Drumcree', *Journal of Ethnic and Migration Studies*, Vol. 24, No. 3, pp. 433–50.

Hughes, J. (forthcoming) 'Constitutional reform in Northern Ireland: implications for community relations policy and practice', *International Journal of Conflict Management*.

Hughes, J. and Carmichael P. (1998) 'Community relations in Northern Ireland: attitudes to contact and integration' in G. Robinson, D. Heenan, A.M. Gray and K. Thompson (eds), *Social Attitudes in Northern Ireland: The Seventh Report* (Aldershot: Ashgate) pp. 1–19.

Knox, C. (1995) 'Alienation: an emerging Protestant phenomenon in Northern Ireland', *Ulster Papers in Public Policy and Management*, No. 53 (Jordanstown: School of Public Policy, Economics and Law, University of Ulster).

Knox, C., Hughes, J., Birrell, D. and McCready, S. (1994) *Community Relations and Local Government* (Coleraine: Centre for the Study of Conflict, University of Ulster).

McGrath, M. (2000) *The Catholic Church and Catholic Schools in Northern Ireland: The Price of Faith* (Dublin: Irish Academic Press).

Marsh, I. (2000) *Sociology Making Sense of Society* (London: Pearson Education).

Northern Ireland Housing Executive (NIHE) (1999) 'Community relations and community safety', internal report (Belfast: NIHE).

O'Neill, S. (2000) 'Liberty, equality and the rights of cultures: the marching controversy at Drumcree', *British Journal of Politics and International Relations*, Vol. 2, No. 1, pp. 26–45.

Osborne, R. (1996) 'Policy dilemmas in Belfast', *Journal of Social Policy*, Vol. 25, No. 2, pp. 181–99.

Poole, M. and Doherty, P. (1996) *Ethnic Residential Segregation in Northern Ireland* (Coleraine: Centre for the Study of Conflict, University of Ulster).

Smith, A. (1999) 'Education and the peace process in Northern Ireland', paper presented at the American Educational Research Conference, Montreal, April.

Stephen, F. (2000) 'Integrated education in Northern Ireland' in M. Cox, A. Guelke and F. Stephen, *A Farewell to Arms? From Long War to Long Peace in Northern Ireland* (Manchester: Manchester University Press).

Wilson, Robin (2000) *Flagging Concern: The Controversy Over Flags and Emblems* (Belfast: Democratic Dialogue)
<http://www.democraticdialogue.org/working/flags.htm>

# 4  Science in our Lives

*Bernie Hannigan*

The 1998 Northern Ireland Life and Times survey included a series of questions designed to probe the public's understanding of science. The survey's interpretation of 'science' was broad, ranging from healthcare, through nature study, to nuclear power stations. The influence of pseudoscientific topics such as astrology was also investigated, as were attitudes to the scientists themselves.

Since the time of the survey, science and scientists have become part of the public's daily diet of news and concerns on an unprecedented scale, and in many cases the issues in question cannot be presented as absolutes. The real uncertainties of scientific knowledge are often presented in the media along with the accompanying moral and ethical considerations. Major issues include the control of foot and mouth disease, stem cell research, human cloning and, following the September 2001 terrorist attacks on the United States, the threat of biological weapons, such as modified anthrax. Each of these issues has been debated in the media and in society in Northern Ireland. Locally based experts provided opinions, and legislation passed by United Kingdom and European Union governments was implemented.

The aim of this chapter is to examine the impact of the various issues on the Northern Irish population. Does the snapshot of attitudes and understanding revealed by the Life and Times survey provide any evidence of a population able to understand, appreciate and incorporate into their own lives the knowledge and wisdom to be gained through exposure to contemporary discourse in science?

A new European Union-wide survey, under the Eurobarometer survey programme, and entitled Europeans, Science and Society was undertaken in May and June 2001 (Eurobarometer, 2001). Among the 16,029 people questioned, 300 were from Northern Ireland so, in exploring the findings of the Life and Times survey, frequent reference is made to these Eurobarometer data. It is recognised, however, that direct comparisons between the two surveys must be viewed with caution, as the rapid scientific progress and revelations of the three intervening years may have had a profound impact on peoples' attitudes.

## *Interest in Science*

Are we interested in science? Alongside perceived majority interests such as sport and politics, how well can science compete for our attention? The answer is that it competes really very well indeed. A total of 59 per cent of respondents are interested (very or moderately) in sport, 62 per cent in new films and 66 per cent in politics. However, 73 per cent indicate similar levels of interest in new scientific discoveries, 74 per cent in new inventions and technologies, and a huge 84 per cent are interested in new medical discoveries. Table 4.1 illustrates that, within these global figures, distinct, and not wholly unexpected, gender differences are apparent. Sport and politics interest women relatively less than they do men and those aspects of science which are of greatest interest to women tend to relate to medical discoveries. It is widely recognised that most inventors are men, so this finding would not be unexpected in any developed country. Men do not appear to draw a distinction between medical sciences and advances or inventions in more technological areas. The Eurobarometer report echoed these overall positive trends, although 45 per cent of Europeans feel that they are neither interested nor informed about science and technology.

Table 4.1 Level of interest in a range of topics (% very or moderately interested)

|  | Male | Female | All |
|---|---|---|---|
| Medical discoveries | 79 | 87 | 84 |
| Inventions/technologies | 84 | 65 | 74 |
| Scientific discoveries | 80 | 67 | 73 |
| Politics | 76 | 58 | 66 |
| New films | 63 | 62 | 62 |
| Sport | 83 | 40 | 59 |

Age has very little bearing on people's interests, apart from in the area of new scientific discoveries. Within the 18 to 24 years age group, 75 per cent are interested in scientific discoveries. This figure declines across the age groups such that only 57 per cent of those aged 65 years and over are interested. In this oldest age group, 40 per cent indicate that they have no interest in scientific discoveries. It should be noted that a relative lack of interest in all suggested topics is apparent among these older people (Table 4.2). It is only in the area of new medical discoveries that respondents in the youngest age group (18 to 24 years) display slightly less interest than do those in the oldest group (26 per cent and 23 per cent respectively).

Table 4.2 Level of disinterest among the 65 years and over age group (% not at all interested)

| | |
|---|---|
| New films | 75 |
| Sport | 45 |
| Scientific discoveries | 40 |
| Politics | 39 |
| Inventions/technologies | 37 |
| Medical discoveries | 23 |

The expressed interest in science does not appear to influence leisure activities. Only 41 per cent of people would make a special point of watching television programmes about advances in medicine while programmes on stars and planets or new inventions and technology attract only 12 per cent and 25 per cent of watchers, respectively. Women and people aged 65 years and over are the least likely to watch programmes on the latter topics. In contrast, programmes on advances in medicine are popular across all age groups, with only 16 per cent of women and 22 per cent of men tending not to watch.

Visits to zoos, aquaria, safari or wildlife parks are particularly unpopular as 72 per cent of people generally, and 87 per cent of those aged 65 years and over, had not made a single visit in the previous 12 months. Respondents in the 25 to 34 years age group are the most frequent visitors to such attractions, presumably because this is the group most likely to include parents of small children. Science, technology or natural history museums or science centres are even less popular. Only 20 per cent of people had visited such a place in the previous 12 months, 89 per cent had not attended a festival, lecture or evening class on a scientific subject and 87 per cent had not gone to a technological, computer or electronic show or fair. Not surprisingly, around 95 per cent of those aged 65 years and over had not attended these events. The data do not show whether the lack of involvement in science is due to reluctance, to a lack of specific organised events or lack of awareness of events, or to other factors such as cost or accessibility.

Table 4.3 indicates a fall in the level of participation in science and technology events, particularly among those aged 65 years and over. Evidence of a culture of lifelong learning in science is very weak indeed. In the future it will be interesting to see whether this same age-related distancing from science and technology occurs, or whether those who become involved at an early age will maintain or develop their interest as they grow older. The data presented here would bear out the poor attendance rates at many science-related millennium projects throughout the UK and Europe. The Eurobarometer report stated that just 11 per cent of respondents across Europe attended science centres and that the figure for the Republic of Ireland was a very low 4 per cent. The long-term sustainability of Belfast's W5 (WhoWhat WhereWhenWhy) centre, or of the now annual Festival of Science and Innovation in Derry/Londonderry will depend on the enthusiasm and motivation of the population to visit and revisit. Northern Ireland has very few centres or events focusing on science and technology, and this is unlikely to change. It is difficult for planners to estimate whether an increased number of attractions would heighten people's interest, or add to the number of centres trying to attract a very small section of the population.

Table 4.3 Level of participation in science-related events in last 12 months by age group (%)

|  | 18–24 | 25–34 | 35–44 | 45–54 | 55–64 | 65+ | All |
|---|---|---|---|---|---|---|---|
| At least one visit to a zoo, aquarium, safari park or wildlife park | 29 | 45 | 32 | 24 | 22 | 11 | 28 |
| At least one visit to a science, technology or natural history museum or science centre | 27 | 23 | 25 | 17 | 19 | 5 | 20 |
| At least one visit to a technology/computer/electronic show or fair | 20 | 13 | 14 | 17 | 12 | 1 | 13 |
| At least one attendance at a festival, lecture or class | 21 | 11 | 15 | 7 | 9 | 4 | 11 |

Despite the overwhelming non-participation in science, 75 per cent of people agree (strongly or slightly) that science and technology are making our lives healthier, easier and more comfortable. Only 8 per cent disagree (strongly or slightly) with this statement. Not unexpectedly, given the preceding information on an age-related decline in interest and participation in science, only 66 per cent of those aged 65 years and over agree with the statement compared to 84 per cent of 18 to 24 year olds and 76 per cent of those in the middle range age group (35 to 44 years).

An interesting viewpoint emerges from attitudes to a similar statement: 'the benefits of science are greater than any harmful effects'. Table 4.4 shows the age-related profile of responses. The most striking point is that 21 per cent of people aged 65 years and over cannot evaluate whether science is beneficial or harmful. This is consistent with their evident lack of involvement with the subject. However, overall, this table suggests that only about half of all people perceive the benefits to outweigh the potential for harm. Could this be the reason for the very low level of active involvement with science?

Table 4.4 Level of agreement that the benefits of science outweigh the harmful effects by age (%)

|  | 18–24 | 25–34 | 35–44 | 45–54 | 55–64 | 65+ | All |
|---|---|---|---|---|---|---|---|
| Agree (strongly or slightly) | 46 | 48 | 58 | 62 | 53 | 46 | 53 |
| Neither | 28 | 19 | 15 | 13 | 16 | 15 | 17 |
| Disagree (strongly or slightly) | 20 | 28 | 19 | 19 | 23 | 18 | 21 |
| Don't know | 6 | 4 | 9 | 7 | 8 | 21 | 9 |

The survey probed the extent to which science is seen as a factor that can influence our daily lives. Asked whether 'science makes our way of life change too fast', 52 per cent of respondents agree (strongly or slightly). Only 21 per cent of the oldest age group do not believe this is the case compared with 41 per cent of 18 to 24 year olds. Reflecting earlier age-related findings, only 31 per cent of respondents aged 65 years and over feel that it is important to know about science in their daily lives, while 54 per cent of the 18 to 34 years age group do so. This need to know about science is expressed most strongly by those likely to be mid-career: 58 per cent, 62 per cent and 58 per cent respectively for the 25 to 34 years, 35 to 44 years and 45 to 54 years age groups. Women are less likely than men are to see a role for knowledge of science in their daily lives: 47 per cent compared to 59 per cent.

### *Understanding Basic Scientific Principles*

So far, the findings from the science section of the survey have drawn out something of a disequilibrium. The very high level of interest and the belief that science is beneficial are not matched by any real involvement in science-related activities or learning. How much of this picture is underpinned by an understanding of basic scientific principles? In order to explore this idea, respondents were presented with a science 'quiz', in which they were asked to state whether they thought a series of statements were true or false. These statements varied in their complexity. As an aide to the reader, the correct answers to the questions are presented in Table 4.5.

Table 4.5 Correct answers for science 'quiz'

| | |
|---|---|
| The centre of the earth is very hot | True |
| Lasers work by focusing sound waves | False |
| It is the father's gene that decides if the baby is a boy or a girl | True |
| Antibiotics kill viruses as well as bacteria | False |
| The earth goes round the sun? | True |
| The term DNA is to do with the study of... | Living things |

When asked whether it is true or false that 'the centre of the earth is very hot', 84 per cent of people know the right answer, including 89 per cent of males and 81 per cent of females. One fifth (21 per cent) of respondents aged 65 years and over say they don't know the answer. Respondents were then asked if it is true or false that 'lasers work by focusing sound waves'. Correct answers are now less frequent: 41 per cent get it right, and it is significant that 32 per cent don't know the answer. Males are much more likely than females to get the right answer (56 per cent and 30 per cent respectively). The age-related responses are also striking (Table 4.6). A significant decrease in correct answers is evident across the age groups. This might be interpreted as stemming from the relative newness of the term 'laser'. We have already seen that learning in science is confined largely to the younger age groups. It may be that few respondents aged 65 years and over would have been exposed to an explanation of this term whether in a formal educational sense or through the use of laser-based electronic devices, such as CD players.

Table 4.6 Responses to laser question by age group (%)

|            | 18–24 | 25–34 | 35–44 | 45–54 | 55–64 | 65+ | All |
|------------|-------|-------|-------|-------|-------|-----|-----|
| Correct    | 54    | 46    | 49    | 45    | 33    | 18  | 41  |
| Incorrect  | 24    | 26    | 23    | 30    | 32    | 30  | 27  |
| Don't know | 22    | 28    | 28    | 25    | 35    | 53  | 32  |

As shown previously, an interest in medical advances predominates among respondents. Many recent medical stories highlighted in the media involve the potential applications of new knowledge in the field of genetics, and a range of questions probed the level of penetration of that knowledge. Asked to respond true or false to the statement 'it is the father's gene that decides whether the baby is a boy or girl', 61 per cent of answers are correct. Females (66 per cent) are much more likely than males (54 per cent) to know the correct answer. Interestingly, there does not appear to be a direct association with age, although the proportion of correct answers ranges from 51 per cent (65 years and over) to 70 per cent (35 to 44 years).

The most obvious and apparent interface between medical advances and people is the availability of drugs to combat common infections. Bacterial and viral infections affect people of all ages, and visits to healthcare providers are often expected to yield a prescription for a medicine that will limit the duration and effects of the ailment. Antibiotics rank highly among the most frequently prescribed medicines. But how many of us know what types of infectious organisms can be combated by antibiotics? Survey participants were asked whether it is true or false that 'antibiotics kill viruses as well as bacteria'. Only 44 per cent of people get this one right, including 39 per cent of males and 48 per cent of females. Once again, the 35 to 44 years age group is the best informed (54 per cent correct) and 26 per cent of the oldest age group do not know the answer.

Our most common infection, the common cold, is caused by the rhinovirus. Influenza, which affects many of the more vulnerable members of our society each winter (especially older people and young children), is also a viral illness. Unfortunately we have very few antiviral drugs that can cure it with anything like the efficiency with which antibiotics can combat microbial infections. A strong tendency has been for clinicians to use antibiotics prophylactically, that is, to deal with the possibility of microbial infections associated with colds and 'flu. Prophylactic antibiotic use has also been endemic in livestock farming and the entry of these drugs into human food sources is highly likely. The problem that has now emerged is that bacteria, which evolved originally many millions of years before humans, are now evolving antibiotic resistance. The greater our exposure to antibiotics, the greater is the chance of us developing antibiotic-resistant bacterial illnesses. Therefore, clinicians are urged to be cautious in prescribing antibiotics, and the public must know why it is inappropriate for them to ask continually for such a prescription. However, this apparently simple, but vitally important, public health message must be backed up by information to the public so that they know why the overuse of antibiotics is dangerous. The results from the Life and Times survey would suggest that a very simple fact, of the kinds of illnesses that can be treated by antibiotics, has not been absorbed by a wide section of the population.

If understanding of a twentieth-century phenomenon such as antibiotics is scant, can we see a different picture for knowledge of a topic that first came to public prominence in the 1600s? Asked whether the earth goes around the sun, or the sun around the earth, an amazing 37 per cent of women and 25 per cent of men cannot supply the correct answer. Twenty-eight per cent of people aged 65 years and over give the wrong answer and 17 per cent of this age group say they don't know the correct answer. On the subject of evolution, an element of opinion, as opposed to knowledge, is to be expected. Two thirds of respondents (66 per cent) believe it is true (either definitely or probably) that humans descended from earlier species of animals. The sex of respondents does not influence opinions but age most certainly does: 39 per cent of those aged 65 years and over say that this is untrue (either definitely or probably) compared with 20 per cent of 25 to 34 year olds. It may be that attitudes towards evolution are likely to be influenced by religious belief, something that will be explored further in the section on Science, Religion and Pseudoscience.

### *Genes, Families and Probabilities*

As stories of genes and genetics hit the mainstream media, the acronym DNA has been repeated more and more frequently. How many people know what it relates to? Reassuringly, 86 per cent of respondents know that it is related to the study of living things, although 30 per cent of those aged 65 years and over say they don't know whether it has to do with stars, rocks, living things or computers.

Genetic inheritance is linked inextricably to probabilities. It is this element of chance that provides one of the principal driving forces behind the diversification of living traits that underlies natural selection. In modern human societies we remain subject to the laws of probability as we produce children. Concerns about the quality of life of our children fuel a demand for genetic counselling services. Genetic counselling involves, in part, explanations to parents about their chances of producing a child bearing certain characteristics. To date, these services may be regarded as very crude, in that our knowledge of genetic determination is robust only for those genes that encode specific serious inherited diseases. Survey participants were asked about the impact of a genetically inherited disease upon children. Table 4.7 outlines their understanding of the possible implications of a couple being told by doctors that they have a one in four chance of having a child with such a disease.

Table 4.7 Understanding of the implications of an inherited illness (% of correct answers)

|  | Male | Female | All |
| --- | --- | --- | --- |
| If the first child has the illness will the next three be healthy? | 85 | 78 | 81 |
| Will each of the couple's children have the same risk of having the illness? | 80 | 75 | 77 |
| If the first three children are healthy, will the fourth have the illness? | 82 | 74 | 78 |

The peak for right answers to this set of three questions occurs, unsurprisingly, in the middle age ranges, with those aged 65 years and over giving the least frequently correct answers. Further, a significant proportion of those aged 65 years and over are unsure: approximately three in ten respondents within this age group say that they don't know the answer to each question. The answers required not only some thought, but also a level of numeracy. This is a very good example of the application of science to real life situations that may confront people of childbearing age. Therefore, the preponderance of correct answers among the intermediate age groups may reflect an understanding born of an immediate interest in, and possible experience of, the topic.

The genetic information recoverable by modern analytical techniques can potentially be used to map an individual's chance of succumbing to a range of diseases. For a fuller discussion on genetics, refer to the chapter by Barr and Thompson in this volume. Other characteristics can, perhaps, also be divined through genetic profiling and these would include characteristics that could cause a person to be more or less effective in a particular job. How likely do people think it is that, within the next 25 years, genetic information will be used to judge a person's suitability for getting a job they have applied for? This question seems to cause real difficulty because 23 per cent of respondents (44 per cent of those aged 65 years and over) cannot decide whether it is likely or not. Forty-one per cent consider it likely (very or quite) and 36 per cent view it as being unlikely (not very likely or not at all likely). When asked if it is likely that genetic information will be used to judge a person's suitability for getting credit at the bank within the next 25 years, almost exactly the same results are found as for the previous question. So, even among those who venture an answer to these questions, the 'likelies' are pretty well balanced by the 'unlikelies'. Thus, there is no overall consensus, and the oldest members of our society appear to feel that they do not have sufficient knowledge or understanding to express an opinion.

In order to uncover attitudes towards scientists, respondents were asked who, from a list of six, they would have most confidence in if they made a statement about mad cow disease (BSE infection). A real mistrust of information published in newspapers is evident: scientists writing in newspapers are the most trusted by only 2 per cent of respondents, and journalists fared even worse – only 1 per cent trust them the most. The most trusted of all is a university-based scientist (43 per cent). Working in the meat industry or a government department definitely erodes the trust placed in scientists, with their ratings falling to only 18 per cent and 7 per cent respectively. A surprising finding is that scientists working in a consumer organisation are trusted by exactly the same proportion of people as those in the meat industry. These responses would suggest a belief in the influence of scientists' working environments, or other vested interests, on their data interpretation and media comments. A recent national survey (OST, 2000) carried out by the Wellcome Trust <http://www.wellcome.ac.uk> and the Office of Science and Technology <http://www.dti.gov.uk/ost/> also indicated a widespread distrust of industrial and government scientists, with academic scientists faring only a little better. Overall, that survey found that a substantial minority of the UK population does not have confidence in the government's ability to ensure that science is conducted in a responsible and ethical manner. In the Eurobarometer survey, the majority of respondents (80 per cent) supported the view that 'the authorities should formally oblige scientists to obey ethical rules'.

The concepts of risk, and relative risk, have come to the fore latterly because of the emergence of new food-borne potential pathogens. It is disconcerting for many people that scientists apparently do not, or cannot, provide a single clear answer on the safety of eating particular foods, for example, beef. Survey participants were asked to select, from a range of possible reasons, why scientists disagree on whether the presence of mad cow disease makes it dangerous to eat British beef. Table 4.8 shows the spectrum of responses.

Table 4.8 Reasons why scientists disagree on whether BSE makes eating British beef dangerous (%)

| | |
|---|---|
| No one has all the facts | 54 |
| Scientists interpret the facts using different theories | 28 |
| Scientists have different political beliefs | 6 |
| Scientists have different personal and career interests | 6 |
| Don't know | 6 |

This table shows that people believe that the availability and interpretation of facts are the most significant factors, rather than the scientists' personal, political or career influences. The recent exposé of scientists who apparently couldn't figure out whether they were working on sheep or cattle brains has added to the level of scepticism about scientific 'facts'. Currently the organisation of research to underpin the agriculture and agri-foods sectors is under review throughout the UK. This review is timely and must ensure that the public money that is spent on research on our food chain funds the best possible research.

The often very local issues of food have replaced, in large part, preoccupations with more global phenomena, such as nuclear power. Scientists still do not give a clear answer on whether or not it is safe to live around nuclear power stations. Table 4.9 identifies what respondents feel are the underlying reasons for this disagreement.

Table 4.9 Reasons why scientists disagree on whether living around nuclear power stations is safe (%)

| | |
|---|---|
| No one has all the facts | 49 |
| Scientists interpret the facts using different theories | 26 |
| Scientists have different personal and career interests | 9 |
| Scientists have different political beliefs | 8 |
| Don't know | 8 |

Again, most people appear not to attribute any personal bias on the part of scientists in their expressed views. Almost a quarter (24 per cent) of respondents aged 65 years and over say that they don't know. Data from both these questions contrast with the evidence detailed above on how scientists working in different environments could be trusted to a greater or lesser degree. However, the apparent recognition of the difficulty of bringing all relevant facts together is somewhat reassuring.

### Science, Religion and Pseudoscience

In order to investigate whether there is a link between religion and attitudes to science, the survey data have been analysed according to the religion of participants, that is, Catholic, Protestant or no religion. In addition, the interaction between attitudes to science and other beliefs is investigated.

Alongside the low numbers engaging regularly in a science-related activity, 31 per cent of people say that they read a horoscope or personal astrology report either often or fairly often (44 per cent of women and 15 per cent of men). However, 88 per cent of those who read a horoscope do not take very seriously what it 'reveals'. In this case, the age-related trend is for older age groups to be less likely to read a horoscope or astrology report than younger age groups: 66 per cent of respondents aged 65 years and over compared to 40 per cent of those aged 18 to 24 years.

A large proportion of respondents (45 per cent) feels that we depend too much on science and not enough on faith. Men and women are equally convinced on this point, and the tendency to agree increases with age, ranging from 39 per cent of 18 to 24 year olds to 54 per cent of those aged 65 years and over. So, on the whole, science and faith would still appear to be opposing influences on our lives.

Do holders of Catholic or Protestant faiths view science differently either to each other, or to those not belonging to any religion? The answer is that, for most questions in the survey, there is no real difference between representatives of the three groupings. We might be prompted to view some similarities between Christian faith and scientific thinking. Both seek to answer fundamental questions. So doubt, questioning, striving for 'truth' and belief in the uncovered truths are key to both pursuits.

The survey topic on which Catholic and Protestant views diverged somewhat came as no real surprise: it was evolution. Of people with no religion, 83 per cent consider that it is true (definitely or probably) that human beings, as we know them today, developed from earlier species of animals. Among Catholics, the proportion is 76 per cent, while only 57 per cent of Protestants express this view. This difference in religion does not appear to greatly influence the level of under-standing of DNA or the impact upon our lives of genetic profiles, whether in conferring risk of inherited disease, or in judging employment potential or credit risk among the different groups. Is this question on evolution probing a matter that is considered to be a given aspect of faith for some Protestants, rather than a matter of science on which individuals can make a decision?

## *Conclusion*

The opinions expressed in the Public Understanding of Science module may be viewed in two ways: attitudes towards science, and attitudes towards scientists. In addition, we must bear in mind the extent to which all opinions are coloured by a knowledge of, or at least familiarity with, relevant scientific concepts.

The data suggest that a lifestyle change would be necessary for many people to take the time to really engage with science. While data on age differences are interesting, it is not possible to say whether the enhanced knowledge of science evident in the younger age groups will continue to be a feature of the current generation as people grow older. Is science a metaphor for what is interesting and wonderful in our world, or does it symbolise, for older people, an unknown of which to be fearful and shrink from?

Nationally, the need to improve the public's understanding of science has been addressed through a range of schemes, some government-backed and others promoted by public or charitable bodies or universities. In recent years, the term 'public understanding of science' has been replaced somewhat by increased emphasis on the need for scientists to communicate their ideas effectively to the public. Schemes include the Copus (Committee on Public Understanding of Science) initiative, which is supported by the Royal Society <http://www.royalsociety.org>. Copus describes itself as the remodelled partnership for people who communicate science. Its aim is to provide a strategic focus for science communication in all its forms, to improve connections between science and public audiences <http://www.royalsociety.org/copus/intro.htm>. Several UK univer-sities have established Chairs in the Public Understanding of Science and, not surprisingly, the holders of such positions are among the best known of all UK academic scientists, for example, Professor Richard Dawkins and Professor Louis Wolpert. Perhaps such an appointment should now be promoted in a Northern Ireland university.

In its report, the House of Lords' Select Committee on Science and Technology (2000) expressed:

- the need to create a new culture of dialogue between scientists and the public;
- the need to heed public values and attitudes;
- a perceived crisis of public trust in scientific advice to government;
- the need for all advisory and decision-making bodies in areas involving science to adopt an open and transparent approach to their work; and
- the need for scientists and the media to work constructively with each other.

A fundamental component of our modern society's view of science is that the public should be consulted before major decisions are made. The Royal Society wish to make sure that the voice of the public is heard when discussing and shaping science policy, to embrace a culture of openness in decision-making and to ensure that what the public thinks and feels about key scientific issues is taken into account. It is extremely important that all members of society have sufficient scientific knowledge and information to allow them to participate in such a key component of a democracy. As society desires to know more about scientific research, medical advances and technological developments, scientists and their various organisations and professional bodies must ensure that society's needs are met. The Wellcome Trust /OST report (OST, 2000) suggested that science communication activities tend to be skewed towards activities that provide facts about science, rather than activities that highlight the ethical and policy issues raised by science. The majority of those surveyed for that report were 'amazed' by the achievements of science. Largely this is because they can see the benefits for themselves – two thirds agreed that science and technology are making our lives healthier, easier and more comfortable. In that report, eight out of ten people agreed that Britain needs to develop science and technology in order to enhance its international competitiveness.

The data provided by the Life and Times survey indicate that attitudes towards science in Northern Ireland are similar to those identifiable nationally. The different levels of understanding and interest have implications for the way in which people might most effectively be engaged in scientific issues. Currently there is no single framework within which people can access information about science, allowing them to assess and judge information and its implications. Perhaps coordination of activities of disparate groups or organisations could be a starting point.

The Wellcome Trust also commissioned a large-scale survey of more than 1,600 UK scientists funded by a range of academic, charity and industry sources in order to determine the scientists' involvement in, and satisfaction with, public communication of their science. While more than half of the scientists had participated in some form of communication of research to non-specialist audiences in the previous year, fewer than one in five had training to deal with the media and/or to communicate with the public. Discussing the social and ethical implications of their research seemed to create the greatest difficulties. Public lack of education about, and interest in, science will also be barriers to effective communication and interaction between scientists and the public. A final point about the Eurobarometer survey is worthwhile. That survey enquired about what might cause an age-related trend towards a lesser interest in science. Causes cited included science classes at school are not sufficiently appealing (60 per cent), scientific subjects are too difficult (55 per cent) and career prospects are not sufficiently appealing (42 per cent). Would similar answers have been given if this question had been asked within the Life and Times survey? Given the concordance noted above between responses to other questions within the two surveys, we must consider it highly likely.

High quality scientific education, and lifelong education at that, is essential for any country or region that expects to develop and maintain an economy that can be competitive in the twenty-first century. It is pertinent to ask if scientific education is accorded the very high priority on the agendas of our local and national governments that it merits. If it is not, we risk producing a population that does not feel that science is a real part of their lives. Down that path lie the twin dangers of economic non-viability and social exclusion. Northern Ireland cannot take that risk.

## References

Eurobarometer (2001) *Europeans, Science and Society*, Eurobarometer 55.2.
<http://europa.eu.int/comm/public_opinion/archives/eb/ebs_154_en.pdf>.
House of Lords Select Committee on Science and Technology (2000) *Science and Society*, 3rd Report, Session 1999–2000, HL 38 <http://www.publications.parliament.uk/pa/ld199900/ldselect/ldscte ch/38/3801.htm>.
Office of Science and Techology (OST) (2000) *Science and the Public. A Review of Science Communication and Public Attitudes to Science in Britain* (London: OST)
<http://www.wellcome.ac.uk/en/1/mismiscnepubpat.html>.

# 5 Trusting People with Genetic Information

*Owen Barr and Kate Thompson*

During the twentieth century, rapid developments have occurred in relation to genetic knowledge and understanding, the pace of which has often been underestimated (Bell, 1998). Indeed, it has been proposed that a new paradigm centred on genetics as the key explanation of health, illness, normality and abnormality could replace the 'lifestyles' paradigm that previously existed (Chapple, May and Campion, 1995). As a consequence of media coverage regarding genetically modified crops, cloning of animals (for example, Dolly the sheep), the Human Genome Project, and more recently, the cloning of the first human embryo, the terms genetics and genetic engineering are now familiar to the majority of adults in the United Kingdom.

The uptake of genetic screening and the use of genetic information as a basis to support decisions about pregnancy, abortion, genetic selection, employment and life insurance raises complex personal and ethical dilemmas for many people. These highly individual decisions are heavily influenced by wider social factors, including one's values and beliefs about life, family loyalties, perceived proneness to genetic illness and personal judgements on the severity of different genetically inherited conditions (Richards, 1993). This is consistent with the views of Durant, Hansen and Bauer who postulated that

> public understandings of the new genetics are not passive reflections of professional, scientific understandings, but rather, they are active constructs, the products of multiply-mediated historical and cultural (including mass media) influences, which may be expected to diverge significantly from those professional understandings of science with which they co-exist. (1996, p. 236)

While Northern Ireland is part of the UK, it has a very distinct identity and strong cultural traditions that have been repeatedly shown to influence social attitudes across a wide range of topics. Earlier analysis of the Northern Ireland Social Attitudes (NISA) series has shown that attitudes are particularly influenced by religion, for example, Robinson, Heenan, Gray and Thompson (1998). Moreover, attitudes towards topics such as pregnancy and abortion can differ considerably from the rest of the UK. It is therefore likely that social attitudes within Northern Ireland regarding the developments in, and the understanding of, genetic inheritance together with the related impact on prenatal and postnatal genetic screening, genetic selection, employment and life insurance will differ from other areas within the UK. Other international and multinational studies have also noted significant variation in attitudes between countries towards these issues (Berg, Pettersson, Rils and Traney, 1995; Drake, Reid and Marteau, 1996; Cohen, Wertz, Nippert and Wolff, 1997).

As such attitudes are likely to be a major factor in the uptake of genetic tests and the utilisation of any related information in future life decisions, it is important to have access to detailed and up-to-date information on social attitudes towards this topic. The need for insight into the understanding and attitudes held by members of the general public towards genetic research is further supported by the limited amount of such information which is presently available.

This chapter reports some key findings from the Attitudes to Genetics Research module included in the 1999 Northern Ireland Life and Times survey. The main topics covered were levels of trust in various sources of genetic information, attitudes towards the use of genetic tests by insurance companies and employers, and in making decisions about abortion. The survey also collected information about lay beliefs in inherited characteristics and attitudes towards altering genes to change an individual's personal characteristics. While recent media attention has increased concern about the future direction of genetic engineering, the more immediate concerns for members of the general public relate to the availability of accurate information on genetic developments and the use of genetic tests and their results.

## The Need for Public Understanding and Trust

It has been argued that recent news reports on genetic developments tend to highlight the contribution genetic inheritance can make to health and how new developments can be used to improve health, without presenting the limitations of such developments (Peterson, 1998). Media reports are heavily influenced by 'experts', who are largely researchers or scientists in the genetics field, and little opportunity is taken to present the views of people affected by, or advocating for groups potentially affected by, the developments (Conrad, 1999). Due to this imbalance, media reports may not be representative of the range of opinions held by the wider public. It has been reported that the public understanding of, and attitudes towards, genetics may differ considerably from that of professionals. In fact, it is increasingly recognised that the views of members of the public need to be incorporated into the growing understanding of genetics (Richards, 1996; Kerr, Cunningham-Burley and Amos, 1998). The engagement of lay people in discussions about genetic developments and how these may impact on them is important if their level of understanding and trust in the developments is to be enhanced. Public distrust of information presented in the media may result in a reluctance to consider the possible benefits of genetic investigation.

### Who Do We Trust?

Respondents were asked to indicate how much they would trust six specified sources to provide them with information on the dangers of research into human genes. As Table 5.1 shows, scientists working in more independent settings are trusted more than those working for private companies or the government. The majority of respondents have very little or no trust in journalists working in national newspapers (64 per cent), government health ministers (61 per cent) and government scientists (53 per cent).

Table 5.1 Level of trust in sources of information on dangers of research into human genes (%)

|  | A lot | Some | Very little | None | Don't know |
|---|---|---|---|---|---|
| Scientists in health research charities | 30 | 55 | 8 | 4 | 3 |
| University scientists | 19 | 55 | 15 | 7 | 4 |
| Scientists in pharmaceutical companies | 10 | 42 | 26 | 18 | 4 |
| Government scientists | 6 | 38 | 31 | 22 | 4 |
| Government health ministers | 2 | 35 | 36 | 25 | 2 |
| Journalists on national newspapers | 2 | 32 | 36 | 28 | 2 |

Gender, age, religion and the presence of a genetic condition in the family all have a significant influence on the degree of trust held in the information sources. Women tend to be more trusting than men of government health ministers (41 per cent and 31 per cent), government scientists (48 per cent and 38 per cent), scientists working in pharmaceutical companies (57 per cent and 46 per cent) and journalists working on national newspapers (37 per cent and 30 per cent), as shown in Table 5.2.

Table 5.2 Trust in sources of information on dangers of research into human genes by gender (% saying a lot or some trust)

|  | Males | Females |
|---|---|---|
| Scientists in health research charities | 84 | 85 |
| University scientists★ | 75 | 74 |
| Scientists in pharmaceutical companies★ | 46 | 57 |
| Government scientists★ | 38 | 48 |
| Government health ministers★ | 31 | 41 |
| Journalists on national newspapers★ | 30 | 37 |

★ denotes that the association between gender and level of trust (a lot/some; little/none; don't know) is significant at p<0.05

Younger people (aged 18 to 24) are more trusting than older people (aged 65+) of genetic information provided from various sources, as shown in Table 5.3. The younger population have more trust than older people in scientists working in charities (89 per cent and 77 per cent), scientists in universities (84 per cent and 59 per cent), government scientists (50 per cent and 36 per cent), government health ministers (46 per cent and 33 per cent) and journalists working on national newspapers (37 per cent and 27 per cent).

Table 5.3 Trust in sources of information on dangers of research into human genes by age group (% saying a lot or some trust)

|  | 18–24 | 25–64 | 65+ |
|---|---|---|---|
| Scientists in health research charities★ | 89 | 86 | 77 |
| University scientists★ | 84 | 77 | 59 |
| Scientists in pharmaceutical companies★ | 51 | 53 | 51 |
| Government scientists★ | 50 | 44 | 36 |
| Government health ministers★ | 46 | 36 | 33 |
| Journalists on national newspapers★ | 37 | 35 | 27 |

★ denotes that the association between age and level of trust (a lot/some; little/none; don't know) is significant at p<0.05

It can be seen from Table 5.4 that the level of trust in people to provide the truth about the dangers of genetic research is not associated with religion in every case. However, those who described themselves as having no religious affiliation have more trust in government health ministers (42 per cent) than Catholic (40 per cent) or Protestant respondents (33 per cent). These differences are statistically significant.

Table 5.4 Trust in sources of information on dangers of research into human genes (% saying a lot or some trust)

|  | Genetic condition in family | | Religious group | | |
|  | Yes | No | Catholic | Protestant | No religion |
| --- | --- | --- | --- | --- | --- |
| Scientists in health research charities | 87 | 85 | 83 | 86 | 87 |
| University scientists | 71 | 76 | 74 | 76 | 77 |
| Scientists in pharmaceutical companies | 56 | 51 | 51 | 52 | 56 |
| Government scientists | 40 | 44 | 45 | 41 | 45 |
| Government health ministers* | 30 | 37 | 40 | 33 | 42 |
| Journalists on national newspapers** | 28 | 34 | 37 | 31 | 33 |

* denotes that the association between religion and level of trust (a lot/some; little/none; don't know) is significant at p<0.05
** denotes that the association between the presence of a genetic condition in the family and level of trust (a lot/some; little/none; don't know) is significant at p<0.05

Almost one in ten respondents (9 per cent) say that someone in their family has a serious genetic condition. Statistically significant differences are observed between these and other respondents with regard to the level of trust in journalists from national newspapers. Respondents with a genetic condition in their family have less trust in journalists. These respondents are also more likely to remain undecided about their level of trust in all information sources compared to other respondents.

Respondents to the Life and Times survey are less trusting of government health ministers and government scientists than are respondents to the 1998 British Social Attitudes (BSA) survey (Jowell, Curtice, Park and Thomson, 1999). The reason for this is unclear. A possible explanation is that government credibility has declined since the BSA survey was carried out, in part due to revelations about misleading the public over concerns in relation to BSE. This is dealt with in more detail in the chapter by Hannigan in this volume. Another possible factor for the apparent level of distrust is the nature of the political climate within Northern Ireland, which may contribute to a reduced trust in the British government.

In response to the level of distrust identified in this survey, it is important to develop strategies to engage members of the public in Northern Ireland in discussions about genetic developments. Some previous attempts to do so in the UK and the United States have included a people's parliament (King, 1997), citizen juries (Dunkerley and Glasner, 1998), community meetings (Garland, 1999), lay memberships on advisory committees, involving a wide range of people in the development of guidelines (Wertz and Gregg, 2000) and consultation exercises such as those by the Human Genetics Commission <http//:www.hgc.gov.uk>. Such events, facilitated by a range of people including those 'least trusted', could provide the opportunity to share information about genetic developments and engage members of the public in open discussion. This process should lead to an increased understanding of genetics and contribute to an enhanced level of trust in information provided about genetic developments.

## Public Attitudes Towards the Use of Genetic Tests

Developments in genetic understanding have the potential to impact on several key areas of one's life. In particular, three main areas have received the majority of attention to date. Firstly, the use of genetic information to identify the possible risk of an inherited condition being present, either prenatally or with adults who are presymptomatic, for instance with Huntington's Disease or some forms of familial cancer. Secondly, the use of genetic tests and their results by insurance companies and employers, and thirdly, the use of such tests and new technologies in genetic engineering that could alter an individual's genetic makeup.

Support for the use of genetic tests can be influenced by a number of different factors, including personal values, age, gender, religious beliefs, cultural traditions and having a person with a genetic condition in the family. The effectiveness of screening programmes in reducing the incidence of any particular condition will be dependent, in part, on personal decisions made by people who are expected to use the screening programmes. For instance, some parents choose not to use genetic counselling services, because of the association with the termination of pregnancies, whereas others may undergo screening tests prior to making a decision about the future of a pregnancy.

Age and gender have been shown to influence support for genetic tests, although conflicting findings have been reported. In Finland, men and younger people were generally more supportive of prenatal genetic testing and the use of tests in the context of making plans for marriage and family planning (Aro, Hakonen, Hietala, Lonnquist, Niemela, Peltonen and Aula, 1997). However, results from the BSA survey revealed that younger people in Britain were less supportive of the use of genetic tests than older people and gender was not found to influence attitudes (Stratford, Marteau and Bobrow, 1999).

Religion has been identified as having a major influence, resulting in tensions that may arise for some people between their beliefs about fate, freedom and the status of the foetus (Cole-Turner, 1999). The 1998 BSA survey found that Catholic respondents who attended a religious ceremony once a month or more were more opposed to prenatal genetic testing than respondents from other religious groups who attended a religious ceremony once a month or more, although 75 per cent of Catholics did support some use of prenatal testing (Stratford, Marteau and Bobrow, 1999). In addition, people who state that they have religious beliefs that influence any decisions that they make have been reported as more likely to view human genetic research as unethical. They are also more opposed to the use of genetic tests to establish family relationships (Human Genetics Commission (HGC), 2001).

Much discussion has taken place since the early 1990s across a number of countries in relation to the use of genetic tests and their results by employers, insurance companies and government agencies. Age and religious beliefs have been found to be influencing factors: older people in the UK have been reported as being more supportive of the use of genetic information by insurance companies and employers than younger people. People with religious beliefs which influenced their decisions were also more in support of the disclosure of existing genetic test results to insurance companies (HGC, 2001). There has been some acknowledgement of the potential usefulness of such test results to employers, but at the same time concern has been expressed about the potential risk of discrimination against people with specific genetic profiles by insurance companies, employers and health providers. This possibility raises particular concerns for people with disabilities and some ethnic groups (Singer, Corning and Lamias, 1998; Appleyard, 1999; Shakespeare, 2001) and restrictions on the use of such test results have been sought and in some instances put in place (Low, King and Wilkie, 1998; Frankel, 1999).

It is likely that attitudes towards genetic testing will continue to change and be influenced by a number of factors. Therefore it is useful to undertake research into public attitudes towards key aspects of developments in genetics at international, national and regional levels. This will provide information of use to policy-makers, service planners and people delivering services. In addition, the collection of information at regular intervals will provide an indication of changes in public attitudes over time (Stratford, Marteau and Bobrow, 1999). Within the Life and Times survey, respondents were asked their views about the use of genetic tests and their results in three scenarios, namely, use by insurance companies, employers and during pregnancy.

*Should Genetic Tests Be Used by Insurance Companies?*

Respondents were asked two questions relating to genetic tests that tell people whether they are likely to develop a serious genetic condition in the future. Firstly, 'should such tests be used by insurance companies to accept or refuse people for life insurance?', and secondly, 'should such tests be used by insurance companies in deciding how much to charge people for their life insurance policies?' The results show that the majority of respondents feel that such tests should not (probably or definitely) be used in accepting people for, or pricing, life insurance policies (77 per cent and 78 per cent respectively). However, it is clear from Table 5.5 that a level of support does exist for the use of such tests by insurance companies (approximately 16 per cent).

Table 5.5 Support for the use of genetic tests by insurance companies (%)

|  | Use tests to accept people for life insurance | Use tests to price life insurance |
|---|---|---|
| Definitely should | 3 | 2 |
| Probably should | 13 | 13 |
| Probably should not | 22 | 21 |
| Definitely should not | 55 | 57 |
| Don't know | 6 | 6 |

Men are significantly more in favour of using genetic tests to accept people for life insurance (19 per cent) than women (14 per cent). More women (8 per cent) than men (4 per cent) are undecided about using genetic testing for this reason. Similar trends are observed when considering the use of genetic tests in pricing life insurance policies, with more men (19 per cent) than women (13 per cent) in favour of this. More women (7 per cent) compared to men (5 per cent) are undecided about this, as shown in Table 5.6.

The level of indecision about the use of genetic tests in accepting people for life insurance is much higher among people aged 65 years and over (15 per cent) than in the two younger age groups (7 per cent for 18 to 24 year olds and 4 per cent for 25 to 64 year olds). Similar observations can be made in relation to the pricing of life insurance policies. The level of indecision among people aged 65 years and over is four times greater than the level within the 25 to 64 years age group, and twice that in the 18 to 24 years age group.

These findings reinforce those from similar surveys in the US and Britain, which found that between 70 and 80 per cent of respondents were opposed to the use of genetic tests by insurance companies (Singer, Corning and Lamias, 1998; Stratford, Marteau and Bobrow, 1999; HGC, 2001). Interestingly, though, research in Britain has also reported variation in support depending on the type of insurance being sought. Although approximately four in five people were opposed to the use of genetic information to set overall insurance premiums, approximately one third thought it was appropriate for existing genetic test results to be used in pricing health insurance (35 per cent), long-term care insurance (33 per cent) and life insurance (30 per cent). There was lower support for the use of genetic information for pricing motor and travel insurance, and pensions.

Table 5.6 Support for the use of genetic tests by insurance companies, by gender and age group (%)

|  | Use test to accept people for life insurance | | | Use test to price life insurance | | |
|---|---|---|---|---|---|---|
|  | Definitely/ probably should | Definitely/ probably should not | Don't know | Definitely/ probably should | Definitely/ probably should not | Don't know |
| *Gender** |  |  |  |  |  |  |
| Male | 19 | 77 | 4 | 19 | 77 | 5 |
| Female | 14 | 78 | 8 | 13 | 80 | 7 |
| *Age** |  |  |  |  |  |  |
| 18–24 years | 18 | 75 | 7 | 17 | 77 | 6 |
| 25–64 years | 15 | 81 | 4 | 15 | 81 | 4 |
| 65+ years | 20 | 65 | 15 | 15 | 68 | 17 |

* denotes that the association between these variables and attitude to the use of genetic tests is significant at p<0.05

## Should Genetic Tests Be Used By Employers?

Within the Life and Times survey, the attitudes of respondents were sought in respect of three applications of genetic tests. Firstly, 'should an employer have the right to see previous test results of someone applying for a job?' Secondly, 'should an employer have the right to make an applicant have a test?' Finally, 'should an employer who is aware of a previous test result have the right to take this information into consideration when the chance for promotion of the employee comes up?'

For all three scenarios, the majority of respondents definitely oppose the use of genetic tests or a consideration of the results. The suggestion that an employer should have the right to make an applicant have a test was opposed most. For all three situations, 6 per cent of respondents remain undecided (Table 5.7).

As Table 5.8 shows, gender is not a significant factor in attitudes towards genetic tests by employers, but age and the presence of a genetic condition within the family appear to influence some of the attitudes expressed. For example, respondents under the age of 65 are more likely to oppose employers' use of genetic testing in these three scenarios, than are older respondents. More of the older respondents are undecided in their views regarding the use of genetic testing by employers than their younger counterparts. Interestingly, the presence of a serious genetic condition in the family is not a significant variable in relation to employers seeing previous test results. However, respondents who have a serious genetic condition in their family are more likely to be undecided about making employees have a test (10 per cent) or the use of genetic test results in promotion cases (11 per cent) than other respondents.

Table 5.7 Support for the use of genetic tests by employers (%)

|  | See results of previous test | Require applicant to have a test | Consider known results in promotion |
|---|---|---|---|
| Definitely should | 2 | 1 | 2 |
| Probably should | 14 | 9 | 12 |
| Probably should not | 21 | 19 | 23 |
| Definitely should not | 57 | 65 | 57 |
| Don't know | 6 | 6 | 6 |

Table 5.8 Support for the use of genetic tests by employers by characteristics of respondents (%)

|  | See results of previous test (1) | | | Require applicant to have a test (2) | | | Consider known results in promotion (3) | | |
|---|---|---|---|---|---|---|---|---|---|
|  | Should | Should not | Don't know | Should | Should not | Don't know | Should | Should not | Don't know |
| *Gender* | | | | | | | | | |
| Males | 18 | 76 | 6 | 11 | 83 | 6 | 12 | 82 | 6 |
| Females | 15 | 79 | 6 | 10 | 85 | 6 | 14 | 80 | 6 |
| *Age*★ | | | | | | | | | |
| 18–24 years | 17 | 77 | 7 | 11 | 81 | 8 | 13 | 81 | 6 |
| 25–64 years | 16 | 80 | 4 | 9 | 88 | 3 | 12 | 84 | 4 |
| 65+ years | 17 | 68 | 15 | 15 | 70 | 16 | 17 | 68 | 15 |
| *Genetic Condition*★★ | | | | | | | | | |
| Yes | 19 | 74 | 7 | 8 | 82 | 10 | 12 | 77 | 11 |
| No | 16 | 79 | 5 | 10 | 86 | 4 | 13 | 82 | 5 |
| *All* | 16 | 78 | 6 | 10 | 84 | 6 | 13 | 81 | 6 |

★ denotes that the association between this variable and attitude to the use of genetic tests in all three situations is significant at p<0.05
★★ denotes that the association between this variable and attitude to the use of genetic tests in situations (2) and (3) is significant at p<0.05

Respondents appear to have drawn a distinction between the use of existing test results and the requirement that a potential employee should have to undergo a genetic test. Only 10 per cent of all respondents say an employee should have a genetic test, while 84 per cent would reject the imposition of such a test. Similar findings have been reported in Britain, with 83 per cent of respondents rejecting the requirement of such tests (Stratford, Marteau and Bobrow, 1999) and figures of between 86 and 91 per cent have been reported in a series of polls in the US (Singer, Corning and Lamias, 1998). Similarly, both the Life and Times and BSA surveys report that people with a serious genetic condition in their families are most opposed to the use of genetic test results in decisions about job promotions. This could be influenced by the belief that they would be most likely to be affected, but there may also be an underlying assumption that the consideration of such tests would disadvantage them.

Concern about possible discrimination is not unanimous and, in particular, varies with age. People aged 65 years and over are less opposed to the use of genetic tests in employment settings than those aged 64 years and under and similar findings have been reported in other surveys in the UK (Stratford, Marteau and Bobrow, 1999; HGC, 2001). One possible explanation is the converse of the above, which is that people aged 65 years and over perceive the use of such tests as not having a direct impact on them.

These findings are an indication of the need for clear guidelines about the use of genetic tests by insurance companies and employers. The presence of such formal guidelines or legislation that are widely publicised could help to reduce public concern about the misuse of genetic tests in these situations. It may also have the knock on effect of increasing public confidence that developments in genetic research will be used for the advantage of all people and not to assist in discrimination against a minority. Without confidence in the uses such test results may be put to, it is possible that people who could benefit from the information gained from a genetic test may not take up such tests due to concerns about possible discrimination at a later date.

## Should Genetic Tests Be Used During Pregnancy?

Respondents were informed that genetic tests could be undertaken when a baby is still in the womb to indicate the likelihood of the baby being born with a serious medical condition, and that such tests carry some risks. Following this they were asked if these tests should be available to all pregnant women, only to those with a special reason to suspect a problem, or not available at all. Opinions are divided, with 46 per cent of respondents supporting the view that tests should be available to all pregnant women and 41 per cent of the view that tests should only be available to those women with a special reason to suspect a problem. Only 8 per cent feel that tests should not be available at all and the remaining 5 per cent are undecided.

Age is a significant variable in influencing attitudes, with respondents aged 65 years and over more likely to oppose or to be undecided about the use of genetic testing during pregnancy compared to younger respondents (Table 5.9). Slightly more Catholics are opposed to the use of tests in pregnancy compared to Protestants (10 per cent and 8 per cent respectively) or those who report having no religious affiliation (4 per cent). However, the majority of Catholics (86 per cent) support the use of these tests in some or all pregnancies, and overall, religion does not have a significant impact on attitudes.

Table 5.9 Attitudes towards the availability of genetic tests during pregnancy by age and religion (%)

|  | All pregnant women should be offered tests | Should be available only if a reason to suspect a problem | Should not be allowed at all | Don't know |
|---|---|---|---|---|
| *Age** |  |  |  |  |
| 18–24 years | 47 | 44 | 6 | 3 |
| 25–64 years | 48 | 41 | 8 | 3 |
| 65+ years | 37 | 39 | 12 | 13 |
| *Religion* |  |  |  |  |
| Catholic | 42 | 44 | 10 | 5 |
| Protestant | 47 | 40 | 8 | 5 |
| None | 55 | 39 | 4 | 3 |
| *All* | 46 | 41 | 8 | 5 |

* denotes that the association between age and the availability of genetic tests during pregnancy is significant at $p<0.05$

## Conclusion

The findings from the Life and Times survey confirm that members of the public have strong opinions about genetic developments and demonstrate that, overall, attitudes to genetics in Northern Ireland are similar to those reported by surveys carried out in Britain and the US.

The findings of this survey illustrate the increased credibility attached to information provided from what could be viewed as more 'independent' sources, such as charities and universities, but less trust in scientists within the pharmaceutical industry. Conversely, the majority of the people surveyed have little or no trust in government sources and journalists on national newspapers. This situation is further compounded by differences that arise between men and women, people of different ages and religious affiliations.

It is evident from these findings that further efforts are needed to build credibility of some sources and gain the trust of members of the public about genetic developments. An important aspect of this should be the provision of accurate information on the dangers and limitations of research in this area. Without such balanced information, members of the general public are likely to continue to speculate on such dangers and arrive at erroneous conclusions on the basis of limited accurate information. There needs to be recognition of the importance of presenting information from credible sources and targeting information to account for differing levels of trust among various sections of the public (Frewer, Howard, Hedderley and Shepard, 1999).

Public distrust of key information sources can also have real implications for funding and other forms of support for research and clinical developments in genetics. A greater involvement of the public in decision-making may sit uneasily with some researchers and scientists, but could increase public accountability, transparency and trust (Garland, 1999). Members of the public have views in this area and there is much to be gained by recognising the potential of this to generate trust and acceptance of new initiatives through acknowledging what Kerr, Cunningham-Burley and Amos (1998) called 'lay expertise'. Appleyard (1999) felt that pursuing a model of decision-making in which scientists, researchers and doctors have exclusive control over future direction could be vulnerable to abuse.

The findings of this survey show that the level of support for the use of genetic tests varies depending on the situation in which their use is proposed. The majority of respondents support the use of genetic tests during pregnancy to indicate the likelihood of the baby being born with a serious medical condition. However, respondents are less supportive of the use of genetic tests by insurance companies and employers, which the majority of respondents oppose. Respondents seem to make a distinction between the use of existing test results and the imposition of a test by insurance companies or employers, as they show more support for the disclosure of previous test results. This could be interpreted as a degree of support for the use of genetic tests, or alternatively, may reflect the honesty of respondents towards disclosing known information.

The results of this module also show a high level of indecision in the use of genetic tests and their results. It is important to be sure that reduced support for a particular aspect of genetic developments does not necessarily mean an increased opposition to it, as it could also mean an increased level of uncertainty among a particular group of people. Therefore, it is imperative that survey findings should clearly identify people who are uncertain in their opinions, so that a more complete picture can be gained about the level and nature of uncertainty among the public.

## Future Developments

In the space of 50 years, the state of genetic knowledge has moved from a situation in which 'mutation as a direct cause of disease' was viewed as 'extremely rare and of little practical significance' (Journal of the American Medical Association (JAMA), 1947, cited in Pace and Sullivan-Fowler, 1997, p. 1,288) to a belief that the contribution of genetics and the Human Genome Project to medicine can 'hardly be overstated' (Collins, 1997, p. 1,286). However, since 2000, some reports on the potential of genetics to achieve major developments in health and medicine over the next decade have been reframed within longer timescales. The need to have rational and well-informed debate that places genetics into perspective has also been highlighted. Some authors have directly challenged the promises of the Human Genome Project as 'an illusion' (Lewontin, 2000) and others have urged a cautious approach to interpreting information available (Zimmern, Emery and Richards, 2001).

It is accepted that genetic developments to date, and knowledge and understanding derived from further research, have the potential to contribute to the development of public health. However, this potential may be underachieved due to the level of mistrust of key information sources, opposition to the imposition of genetic tests and varying degrees of uncertainty in relation to specific aspects of genetic developments. Further initiatives that seek to inform the public about genetic research, therefore, need to address the specific issues of enhancing trust (particularly of government sources) and provide reassurance that genetic tests will not be imposed nor the test results used for discriminatory reasons.

As indicated by the findings of the Life and Times survey and other surveys, members of the public do have views in relation to the development of genetic research and the future application of genetic knowledge. These opinions are products of a wide range of personal and social characteristics and their complexity needs to be understood. The fact that such opinions may be different from those of some professionals, and less supportive in relation to some aspects of genetic research, makes them different but not less important or necessarily incorrect (Michie, Drake, Bobrow and Marteau, 1995). If the potential of genetic developments to improve public health is to be achieved then health professionals, government agencies and members of the public must work effectively in partnership to provide direction and support to research, as well as to generate greater confidence and a wider acceptance of the clinical application of new knowledge.

The developments in genetic understanding that will arise from the findings of the Human Genome Project and other genetic research means that the situation is very fluid at present. Only time will truly tell if the potential advances promised will materialise or if it will turn out to be 'a false dawn' (Zimmern, 1999).

## References

Appleyard, B. (1999) *Brave New Worlds: Genetics and the Human Experience* (London: HarperCollins).

Aro, A.R., Hakonen, A., Hietala, M., Lonnquist, J., Niemela, P., Peltonen, L. and Aula, P. (1997) 'Acceptance of genetic testing in a general population: age, education and gender differences', *Patient Education and Counselling*, Vol. 32, No. 1–2, pp. 44–9.

Bell, J. (1998) 'The new genetics in clinical practice', *British Medical Journal*, Vol. 316, pp. 618–20.

Berg, K., Pettersson, U., Rils, P. and Traney, K. (1995) 'Genetics in democratic societies – the Nordic perspective', *Clinical Genetics*, Vol. 48, pp. 199–208.

Chapple, A., May, C. and Campion, P. (1995) 'Lay understanding of genetic disease: a British study of families attending a Genetic Counselling Service', *Journal of Genetic Counselling*, Vol. 4, No. 4, pp. 281–300.

Cohen, P.E., Wertz D.C., Nippert, I. and Wolff, G. (1997) 'Genetic counselling practices in Germany: a comparison between East and West German geneticists', *Journal of Genetic Counselling*, Vol. 6, No. 1, pp. 61–80.

Cole-Turner, R. (1999) 'Faith meets the Human Genome Project: religious factors in the public response to genetics', *Public Understanding of Science*, Vol. 8, pp. 207–14.

Collins, F.S. (1997) 'Preparing health professionals for the genetic revolution', *Journal of the American Medical Association*, Vol. 278, No. 15, pp. 1285–6.

Conrad, P. (1999) 'Uses of expertise: sources, quotes, and voice in the reporting of genetics in the news', *Public Understanding of Science*, Vol. 8, pp. 285–302.

Drake, H., Reid, M. and Marteau, T.M. (1996) 'Attitudes towards termination for fetal abnormality: comparisons in three European countries', *Clinical Genetics*, Vol. 49, pp. 134–40.

Dunkerley, D. and Glasner, P. (1998) 'Empowering the public? Citizen juries and the new genetic technologies', *Critical Public Health*, Vol. 8, No. 3, pp. 181–92.

Durant, J., Hansen, A. and Bauer, M. (1996) 'Public understanding of new genetics' in T. Marteau and M. Richards (eds), *The Troubled Helix: Social and Psychological Implications of the New Human Genetics* (Cambridge: Cambridge University Press) pp. 235–48.

Frankel, M.S. (1999) 'Genetic privacy, discrimination and the U.S. Congress', *Public Understanding of Science*, Vol. 8, pp. 215–22.

Frewer, L.J., Howard, C., Hedderley, D. and Shepard, R. (1999) 'Reactions to information about genetic engineering: impact of source characteristics, perceived personal relevance and persuasiveness', *Public Understanding of Science*, Vol. 8, pp. 35–50.

Garland, M.J. (1999) 'Experts and the public: a needed partnership for genetic policy', *Public Understanding of Science*, Vol. 8, pp. 241–54.

Human Genetics Commission (HGC) (2001) *Public Attitudes to Human Genetic Information* (London: Human Genetics Commission).

Jowell, Roger, Curtice, John, Park, Alison and Thomson, Katarina (eds) (1999) *British Social Attitudes: the 16th Report – Who Shares New Labour Values?* (Aldershot: Ashgate)

Kerr, A., Cunningham-Burley, S. and Amos, A. (1998) 'The new genetics and health: mobilising lay expertise', *Public Understanding of Science*, Vol. 7, pp. 41–60.

King, S. (1997) *The People Decide: Report on an Event 19th March 1997* (London: Wellcome Trust).

Lewontin, R. (2000) *It Ain't Necessarily So: The Dream of the Human Genome Project and Other Illusions* (London: Granta).

Low, L., King, S. and Wilkie, T. (1998) 'Genetic discrimination in life insurance: empirical evidence from a cross sectional survey of genetic support groups in the United Kingdom', *British Medical Journal*, Vol. 317, pp. 1632–5.

Michie S., Drake, H., Bobrow, M. and Marteau, T.M. (1995) 'A comparison of public and professionals attitudes towards genetic developments', *Public Understanding of Science*, Vol. 4, pp. 243–53.

Pace, M.A. and Sullivan-Fowler, M. (1997) 'JAMA 50 years ago: mutation as a cause of disease', *Journal of the American Medical Association*, Vol. 278, No. 15, p. 1288.

Peterson, A. (1998) 'The new genetics and politics of public health', *Critical Public Health*, Vol. 8, No. 1, pp. 59–71.

Richards, M.P.M. (1993) 'The new genetics: some issues for social scientists', *Sociology of Health and Illness*, Vol. 15, No. 5, pp. 565–86.

Richards, M.P.M. (1996) 'Lay and professional knowledge of genetics and inheritance', *Public Understanding of Science*, Vol. 5, pp. 217–30.

Robinson, G., Heenan, D., Gray, A.M. and Thompson, K. (eds) (1998) *Social Attitudes in Northern Ireland: The Seventh Report* (Aldershot: Ashgate)

Shakespeare, T. (2001) 'Foreword' in L. Ward. (ed.) *Considered Choices? The New Genetics, Prenatal Testing and People with Learning Disabilities* (Kidderminster: British Institute of Learning Disabilities) pp. 3–5.

Singer, E., Corning, A. and Lamias, M. (1998) 'The polls- trends: genetic testing, engineering and therapy', *Public Opinion Quarterly*, Vol. 62, pp. 633–44.

Stratford, N., Marteau, T. and Bobrow, M. (1999) 'Tailoring genes' in Roger Jowell, John Curtice, Alison Park and Katarina Thomson (eds), *British Social Attitudes: The 16th Report – Who Shares New Labour Values?* (Aldershot: Ashgate) pp. 157–78.

Wertz, D.C. and Gregg, R. (2000) 'Genetics services in a social, ethical and policy context: a collaboration between consumers and providers', *Journal of Medical Ethics*, Vol. 26, pp. 261–5.

Zimmern, R.L. (1999) 'The human genome project: a false dawn?', *British Medical Journal*, Vol. 319, p. 1282.

Zimmern, R.L., Emery, J. and Richards, T. (2001) 'Putting genetics in perspective', *British Medical Journal*, Vol. 332, pp. 1005–6.

# 6 On the Move: Attitudes to Transport in Northern Ireland

*Liz Fawcett*

There are a number of features of transport policy and behaviour in Northern Ireland which set it apart from the rest of the United Kingdom. Among the most significant is the fact that most public transport in Northern Ireland is still in the public sector, unlike Britain where private companies run most bus and rail services.[1] Yet, ironically, privately-run public transport services in Britain received much higher levels of public funding through various subsidies than did bus and rail services in Northern Ireland during the 1990s. Two unpublished studies commissioned by Northern Ireland's public sector bus and rail operator, Translink, show that, between 1991/92 and 1998/99, public sector revenue funding for railways in Northern Ireland amounted to just 17 per cent of that in Britain on a per capita basis (Steer Davies Gleave, 2000; 2001).[2] Public sector revenue support for buses in Northern Ireland equated to less than half that provided in Britain between 1993/94 and 1998/99 on a per capita basis (Steer Davies Gleave, 2000; 2001).[3] Moreover, the largest share of the public funding available for transport in Northern Ireland has tended to go on roads in the past few years. While 77 per cent of transport expenditure was allocated to roads in 1997–2001, just 20 per cent was allocated to public transport (Department for Regional Development (DRD), 2001).

At the same time, there has been much less integration of sustainable transport and land use planning policies in Northern Ireland (McEldowney, 2000). This is another important factor in determining the extent of car use. Finally, widespread violence during the worst years of the Troubles contributed to segregated residential patterns which may well have made it difficult to operate an efficient and cost-effective public transport system in certain areas (Smyth, 2000).

It is, therefore, not surprising that Northern Ireland has become a very car-dependent society. For example, while 70 per cent of those in employment travelled to work by car in Britain in 2000, the figure for Northern Ireland is 81 per cent (Northern Ireland Statistics and

87

Research Agency (NISRA), 2000; Department of the Environment, Transport and the Regions (DETR), 2001). By 1998, traffic volumes in Northern Ireland were increasing at almost twice the rate seen in Britain and the relative rate of growth in traffic in this region was increasing (Department of the Environment (DoE) and DRD, 1991–1998; DETR, 2000a).

At the same time, these figures disguise the extent to which a large proportion of the population in Northern Ireland relies on public transport, walking and cycling. Recent figures show that 30 per cent of households in Northern Ireland do not have a car, a figure which has remained unchanged since 1996–97 (NISRA, 2000). Data from the 1991 Census of Population provide more detailed information on car ownership and travel patterns (Department of Health and Social Services (DHSS), 1992a). This is unlikely to have changed greatly, as the overall proportion of those without cars has declined only slightly since 1991. The Census found that 36 per cent of households in Northern Ireland did not have a car. The proportion was even greater in the Belfast City Council area. In 1991, 54 per cent of households in the city did not have a car and that proportion rose to as high as 89 per cent in some of the poorer areas of the city (DHSS, 1992b). However, this lack of car ownership is not confined to Northern Ireland's largest cities. Thirty per cent of households in local government districts outside the Belfast conurbation area and Derry did not have a car in 1991 (DHSS, 1992a). Where such households do not have access to good quality, affordable public transport, they suffer from what has become known as 'transport poverty'.

However, the problem of transport poverty is still largely unrecognised in Northern Ireland, and was neglected in Britain until relatively recently (DETR, 2000b; General Consumer Council for Northern Ireland (GCCNI), 2001). The extent of under-investment in public transport in Northern Ireland only became a matter of widespread public and political debate in 2000, when the UK government (during a period of suspension of the Northern Ireland Executive), and subsequently the Northern Ireland Executive, considered closing most of the rail network. The Executive set up a Railways Task Force which examined closure and other options (Railways Task Force, 2000). It was informed by a report commissioned by Translink which revealed that much of its rail rolling stock and track needed to be replaced (Little, 2000). A 'Save Our Railways' campaign evolved and attracted widespread support. There is no doubt that this campaign turned public transport into a far bigger issue in the public mind than it had been hitherto. The relative lack of any such media coverage and public debate for many years prior to this campaign must therefore be borne in mind in assessing the data on attitudes towards transport from the 1999 Northern Ireland Life and Times survey.

Within the Life and Times survey, half the total sample were asked the questions on transport. A number of the same questions were also included in the 1998 and 1999 British Social Attitudes (BSA) surveys, thus allowing for comparison (National Centre for Social Research, 1998; 1999).

## Car Ownership and Driving Patterns

Just over three quarters (76 per cent) of respondents to the Life and Times survey say they or someone in their household has the use of a car or van. The proportion of households in Britain with use of a car is similar (81 per cent). A slightly lower proportion of respondents in Northern Ireland (65 per cent) than in Britain (68 per cent) say they drive a car. In contrast, while 73 per cent of car drivers in Northern Ireland say they travel by car every day or nearly every day, the figure for Britain is lower at 64 per cent.

### The Impact of Demographic Factors

In Northern Ireland, the single most important factor influencing a respondent's mode of transport is undoubtedly social class. Not surprisingly, a much higher proportion of people in higher social class categories drive cars than those in the lower categories (Table 6.1). Those in higher social class categories are also more likely to live in households where at least one member has regular use of the car, and they are more likely to be frequent car drivers.

Table 6.1 Car use by social class (%)

|  | Someone in household has use of car | Car drivers | Frequent car drivers (drive car every day or nearly every day*) |
|---|---|---|---|
| Professional/managerial | 86 | 83 | 65 |
| Skilled non-manual | 82 | 72 | 48 |
| Skilled/partly-skilled manual | 73 | 62 | 47 |
| Unskilled | 58 | 39 | 29 |

* This question was asked only of those who said they drive a car. However, the figure stated has been calculated as a percentage of all respondents within the relevant social class category.

There are also marked gender and age differences in patterns of car use. Forty-four per cent of women say they do not drive a car, compared to just 23 per cent of men. The oldest and youngest age groups are the least likely to drive a car (Table 6.2). Men are much more likely than women to drive a car frequently; 62 per cent of men say they drive a car every day or nearly every day while just 36 per cent of women say they do likewise. The oldest and youngest age groups are also much less likely than other age groups to drive a car frequently; 25 per cent of those aged 65 years and over drive a car every day or almost every day, compared to 62 per cent of 35 to 44 years olds, for example.

Table 6.2 Proportion of respondents who drive a car by age (%)

|     | 18–24 | 25–34 | 35–44 | 45–54 | 55–64 | 65+ |
| --- | --- | --- | --- | --- | --- | --- |
| Yes | 57 | 75 | 76 | 70 | 60 | 43 |
| No | 43 | 25 | 24 | 30 | 40 | 57 |

Respondents who are not in work (including the unemployed, retired, students and those who are looking after the home) are less likely to live in a household where someone has regular use of a car and are much less likely to drive a car themselves than those who are in work. Half of those (50 per cent) who say they are not working do not drive a car, compared to just 20 per cent of those who have jobs.

There is also a difference between respondents who live in urban and rural areas in terms of car use. ('Urban' respondents are those who say that they live in a big city, the suburbs or outskirts of a big city or a small city or town. 'Rural' respondents are those who say that they live in a country village or a farm or home in the country.) However, the difference is not as great as one might have expected. While 27 per cent of respondents in urban areas live in a household where no one has regular use of a car, this applies to 12 per cent of those in rural areas. Significantly, 24 per cent of respondents in rural areas say they do not drive a car, compared to 37 per cent of those in urban areas. Fifty-nine per cent of respondents in rural areas say they drive a car every day or nearly every day, compared to 46 per cent of those in urban areas. Thus, it is clear that a significant proportion of rural residents have to rely on public or community transport, walking, cycling, and/or lifts from friends or family in order to get around.

### Which Transport Issues Concern People?

Transport appears to come very low down the agenda for the Northern Ireland public. When respondents were presented with a list of day-to-day policy issues and asked to choose which one they felt would be the most important for the Assembly to deal with, a mere 1 per cent put 'improving transport' as the top issue. This compares with 42 per cent who select 'improving the health service' and 28 per cent who choose 'improving the economy of Northern Ireland'. A further 1 per cent put 'improving the environment' as the most important issue.

However, this approach gives little indication of where transport lies in the priority list of most respondents. It is very likely that, had a different set of questions been asked, the survey data would have indicated a strong concern about transport in relation to other issues. A more recent survey conducted in Northern Ireland for the DRD also examined the significance of transport as an issue for respondents (Atkins, 2001). Respondents were asked to say what they felt were the most pressing problems facing Northern Ireland and the areas in which they lived. They were not prompted with a list of issues. Fourteen per cent of respondents mentioned transport as one of the most significant problems for the region, while 11 per cent felt it was an important issue at local level. Transport was seen as a particularly important local issue in rural areas with 19 per cent of rural respondents saying it was a pressing concern compared to just 5 per cent in the greater Belfast area.[4]

The Life and Times survey did ask a number of questions designed to ascertain which transport issues were of particular concern to respondents. It should be noted that these focused on two particular areas – traffic on roads and the standard of bus services. The responses to these questions certainly suggest that transport is a matter of considerable significance to many respondents.

*Traffic-related Problems*

Two issues of great concern are traffic congestion and pollution from traffic. Forty-three per cent of respondents feel that it is definitely or probably true that 'the amount of traffic on the roads is one of the most serious problems in Northern Ireland'. A higher proportion of respondents feel that these problems are more serious in urban areas than in rural areas. Two thirds (67 per cent) of respondents feel that traffic congestion in towns and cities is a serious or very serious problem, while 50 per cent feel that exhaust fumes from traffic in towns and cities is an issue of concern. However, there is also concern about traffic volumes and congestion outside the main urban centres and along motorways. Thirty-eight per cent of respondents believe that 'increased traffic volumes on country roads and lanes' is a serious or very serious problem, while a slightly lower proportion (33 per cent) believes that congestion on motorways is a serious or very serious problem. Most people feel that traffic congestion is going to become a very serious regional problem in the future: 65 per cent feel it is definitely or probably true that 'within the next twenty years or so, traffic congestion will be one of the most serious problems for Northern Ireland'.

### Bus Services

Respondents were asked 'are there bus services around here that link your neighbourhood with nearby shops and services?' The data suggest that Northern Ireland compares poorly with Britain in terms of the provision of accessible bus services. Just under one quarter of respondents (23 per cent) say such services are not available near where they live, while 29 per cent feel that the buses stop too far away from their home. The same questions were asked of respondents in the 1998 BSA survey. Just 10 per cent of respondents in Britain say that there are no bus services linking their neighbourhood with nearby facilities, while only 13 per cent say that the buses stop too far from their home.

The problem of lack of accessible bus services is more acute in rural than in urban areas in both Britain and Northern Ireland. The 1998 BSA survey found that 16 per cent of respondents in rural areas do not have bus services nearby to take them to local facilities and 14 per cent say that the nearest bus stop is too far from their home. Yet, in Northern Ireland, no less than 42 per cent of the rural respondents say that there are no bus services nearby to take them to local facilities while 38 per cent say that the nearest bus stop is too far from where they live.[5] This compares with 27 per cent of urban respondents in Northern Ireland who feel the nearest bus stop is too far away.

Apart from the serious lack of accessible bus services for many people, the most significant criticisms of bus services concern the cost and frequency of those services. Just over half (53 per cent) of respondents agree that their local buses generally cost too much while a similar proportion (51 per cent) feel that buses in their area generally do not run often enough. Not surprisingly, the respondent's social class makes some difference to their views on the cost of bus services: while 60 per cent of those from an unskilled background feel that buses are too expensive, this opinion is shared by only 47 per cent of those from a professional/managerial background. However, this difference is perhaps not as great as one might have expected. On the issue of whether their local buses run often enough, there is a difference between the views of those living in urban and in rural areas. Sixty-three per cent of respondents in rural areas feel that buses do not run frequently enough compared with 49 per cent of people in urban areas. The fact that bus services in rural areas are less accessible and frequent than those in urban areas, taken together with the finding that a significant proportion of rural residents do not have access to a car, points to a clear problem of inadequate public transport provision in rural areas.

On the plus side, the majority of people (59 per cent) feel that their local buses are generally clean and tidy and that these buses take people to where they mostly need to go (62 per cent). Forty-five per cent also agree or strongly agree that buses serving their neighbourhood are safe to travel in after dark, while 21 per cent disagree with this statement. This is interesting in view of the widely held belief that many people have been deterred from using public transport in Northern Ireland by conflict-related violence. However, there is an association with social class suggesting that those from less well-off households feel less safe using public transport than the better off. Thirty per cent of those from unskilled backgrounds say they do not believe that buses are safe after dark, while only 13 per cent of those from professional backgrounds share this view. Women are more likely than men to think that buses are not safe at night (23 per cent and 17 per cent respectively) but the gender difference is not as marked as one might have expected. No questions were asked in the survey about the quality of the rail service in Northern Ireland.

### Influencing Travel Behaviour

Fifty-seven per cent of respondents feel it is very or fairly important to reduce the number of cars on Northern Ireland's roads, while 39 per cent feel this is not very important or not at all important. Many people do not feel that building roads adds to the traffic problem, although views are divided on this issue. Exactly half of the respondents (50 per cent) reject the proposition that 'building roads just encourages more traffic' while 39 per cent support it. Three out of five (61 per cent) respondents agree that the government should build more motorways to reduce traffic congestion, while 30 per cent disagree with this view. Many people have clearly not thought through their views on this issue, however; almost half (46 per cent) of those who agree that building roads encourages more traffic also feel that the government should build more motorways to combat traffic congestion!

### Car Driver Behaviour

Respondents were asked a number of questions about what measures might encourage them to reduce their own use of the car. The results suggest that there are many measures that car drivers feel would encourage them to use their car less, especially those which would affect the relative cost of car use and of public transport (Table 6.3).

More than half of all car drivers (58 per cent) say they might use their car less if fares for local public transport were halved, and the same proportion say they might use their car less if the cost of petrol was gradually doubled over the next ten years. Fifty-six per cent say they might use their car less if congestion charging in the form of a £2 charge for driving through a city or town centre was introduced. The same proportion (56 per cent) say that they might use their car less if the reliability of local public transport was improved.

A somewhat lower but still fairly substantial proportion of respondents feel that improvements and fare cuts for long distance public transport services might persuade them to cut their car use. Respondents are less inclined to believe that tighter parking restrictions, higher parking charges or road tolls would make a difference; nevertheless, a significant minority do believe that these measures might alter their travel behaviour. The installation of special cycle lanes is the measure least likely to make a difference (24 per cent).

In general, frequent car users are slightly less likely to feel that such measures would persuade them to change their travel behaviour, but the differences are not as great as one might have expected. There is no difference with regard to increasing the cost of petrol; 58 per cent of frequent drivers feel that measure might reduce their car use.

Table 6.3 Support for measures to reduce the number of car journeys (% of car drivers who might use their car less)

| | All car drivers | Frequent car drivers (drive car every day or nearly every day) |
| --- | --- | --- |
| Cutting in half local public transport fares | 58 | 55 |
| Gradually doubling the cost of petrol over the next ten years | 58 | 58 |
| Greatly improving the reliability of local public transport | 56 | 53 |
| Charging £2 for town/city entry | 56 | 55 |
| Cutting in half long distance rail and coach fares | 47 | 45 |
| Greatly improving long distance rail and coach services | 46 | 43 |
| Making parking penalties and restrictions much more severe | 41 | 40 |
| Charging £1 for every 50 miles motorists travel on motorways | 39 | 38 |
| Special cycle lanes on roads round here | 24 | 23 |

The 1999 BSA survey also asked drivers about the potential effectiveness of most of the same measures. While the proportions that feel each specific measure might make a difference were remarkably similar, there are two notable differences. The first relates to halving long distance rail and coach fares. Fifty-six per cent of drivers in Britain feel this might persuade them to reduce their car use compared to 47 per cent in Northern Ireland. However, long distance rail and coach fares in Northern Ireland appear to be considerably lower than in Britain and this may well explain the difference. The second variation relates to improving the reliability of local public transport: 64 per cent of drivers in Britain feel this might persuade them to change their travel habits compared to 56 per cent of drivers in Northern Ireland.

However, the results from a survey carried out in England in 2000 for the Commission for Integrated Transport (CfIT) are somewhat at odds with the BSA survey findings. They suggest far less faith among English car drivers in the effectiveness of such measures. For example, only 22 per cent of drivers who took part in the CfIT survey feel that congestion charging might encourage them to use their car less, while just 23 per cent think that either maintaining or improving bus services, or providing more of them, would persuade them to reduce their car use. It is hard to explain the difference in the CfIT and BSA survey results. However, the findings from the Life and Times survey strongly support those of the BSA survey and suggest that it may be worth investigating possible reasons for the differences in the findings between these surveys and the CfIT.

Three out of five respondents (60 per cent) to the Life and Times survey feel it would be too inconvenient to give up using a car for the sake of the environment. However, 26 per cent disagree with this sentiment. Car users were asked how convenient or otherwise it would be if they were forced to give up a proportion of their regular car trips. No assumption was made with these questions that any carrots or sticks were being put in place. Most respondents say it would be a nuisance to cut their car use. However, 21 per cent say it would be either not at all inconvenient or not very inconvenient to reduce by a quarter the number of regular car journeys they make, and 14 per cent say it would be not at all or not very inconvenient to cut their regular car use by as much as half. These results suggest a greater readiness among Northern Irish car drivers to cut their car use than among drivers in Britain. Just 17 per cent of British drivers say it would not be inconvenient to cut their regular car trips by a quarter while only 9 per cent say it would not be inconvenient to reduce their regular car journeys by a half.

These results do suggest that a range of both carrot and stick measures have the potential to have at least some impact on the extent of car use in Northern Ireland. In particular, making public transport services at local level more attractive, increasing the cost of petrol and introducing congestion charging might be effective.

### Paying for Improved Transport

Not surprisingly, given respondents' views on the current state of bus services in Northern Ireland, there is strong support among all respondents for the need to improve public transport: 57 per cent of respondents feel this is very important while a further 32 per cent feel it is fairly important. All the questions in the Life and Times survey relating to paying for improved transport provision looked only at what people were prepared to do to fund public transport. They were not asked any similar questions with regard to roads expenditure.

Having said this, politicians may well be surprised by the degree of enthusiasm which exists for raising taxes to fund public transport. More than half (57 per cent) of all respondents feel the Northern Ireland Assembly should have tax varying powers and of these, 57 per cent say they would be prepared to pay a penny more in income tax to finance improvements in public transport. This proportion represents 32 per cent of all respondents.

However, much higher proportions of respondents are in favour of tax rises to fund improvements in health and education. For example, 90 per cent of those who feel the Northern Ireland Assembly should have tax varying powers say they would be prepared to pay a penny more in income tax to fund local health service improvements.

Most respondents (76 per cent) also support cross-border cooperation with the Irish Republic on transport, suggesting that they would be amenable to the use of Irish government and cross-border funds for transport measures. While a higher proportion of Catholics (90 per cent) support this measure, it is also endorsed by 68 per cent of Protestants, and only 7 per cent of Protestants actually oppose this idea. There is greater support for cross-border cooperation on transport than on health: 65 per cent of respondents support the latter measure and 14 per cent of Protestants oppose it.

Certainly, both of these measures find far more support than any of the other proposed means of funding public transport improvements included in the survey (Table 6.4). The most unpopular measure is gradually doubling the cost of petrol over the next ten years: this is opposed by no less than 80 per cent of respondents. There is least opposition to road tolls on motorways as a means of raising money for public transport: 59 per cent of respondents opposed this measure although it was supported by 19 per cent. Surprisingly, although many car drivers say that congestion charging might reduce their car use, respondents are not very enthusiastic about this measure. Two thirds (67 per cent) of respondents oppose it and only 16 per cent support it. As can be seen from Table 6.4, data from the 1999 BSA survey suggest that the level of support for, and opposition against, most of these measures is fairly similar in Britain. However, there is considerably more support for congestion charging in Britain. There is also much more support for cutting spending on new roads in order to fund public transport investment.

Table 6.4 Support for measures to fund public transport, Northern Ireland and Britain (%)

|  | Support or strongly support | | Oppose or strongly oppose | |
|---|---|---|---|---|
|  | N Ireland | Britain | N Ireland | Britain |
| Charging £1 for every 50 miles motorists travel on motorways | 19 | 24 | 59 | 55 |
| Charging around £2 for entering town/city | 16 | 25 | 67 | 58 |
| Halving spending on new roads | 13 | 21 | 61 | 54 |
| Increasing taxes like VAT | 8 | 9 | 75 | 71 |
| Halving spending on roads maintenance | 8 | 7 | 74 | 75 |
| Gradually doubling the cost of petrol | 6 | 8 | 80 | 75 |

The results of the more recent survey commissioned by the DRD, referred to earlier, suggest that support for congestion charging has not increased greatly across Northern Ireland but is more widely accepted in the greater Belfast area (Atkins, 2001). One in five respondents (19 per cent) to the DRD survey said they would support the introduction of a congestion charge for entering Belfast city centre if the revenue went towards transport improvements. Perhaps more notably, it was supported by 25 per cent of residents in the greater Belfast area who were also more likely to support workplace carpark charges (23 per cent) and road tolls (21 per cent) if the resulting income was spent on transport improvements. The measure that found most favour with respondents in all areas was a proposal that developers should be encouraged to fund transport alternatives such as bus services and cycle routes.

The DRD survey also found that 49 per cent of respondents thought that money for transport improvements should come from sources other than simply government and regional taxes. However, there was little support for most of the options for raising revenues by other means, particularly outside greater Belfast. The one exception was raising money from developers, but it is unlikely that this measure would raise a significant amount of additional revenue.[6] At the same time, it is also of interest that 37 per cent of respondents, while appearing to believe that additional funding was needed for transport, felt all the money should come from government and regional taxes. The results from both the DRD and Life and Times surveys do suggest that there might be support for a modest tax increase to boost transport funding in Northern Ireland.

## Conclusion

The clear policy implication for decision-makers which arises from responses to the Life and Times survey is that public transport provision has to be improved greatly. The Northern Ireland Executive has committed itself to tackling social exclusion and discrimination in every aspect of its policy. If it is to follow through this commitment as regards transport, it will have to make a significant investment in improving and extending public transport in Northern Ireland.

Investment in public transport will undoubtedly help to tackle the other major concern that emerges from this survey – traffic congestion. Given the extent to which respondents believe both carrot and stick measures might work, it would seem the Executive also needs to invest in promoting measures such as congestion charging, which might help deter people from using their cars unnecessarily. It is clear that support for these measures is fairly low at the moment in Northern Ireland. However, the perceived effectiveness of such steps and the growth in support for such measures in Britain suggest that the Northern Ireland public could be persuaded that some sticks as well as carrots are needed in order to get people out of their cars.

Findings from the survey also reveal a surprising degree of readiness to pay extra taxes to fund public transport. Undoubtedly, the Northern Ireland Executive would be wary of taking on or, indeed, using tax varying powers in order to raise more revenue. The Executive ran into trouble in 2000/2001 when its intention to increase the Northern Ireland regional rate became apparent. However, initially no attempt was made to sell this increase to the public, and revenue from it was not hypothecated towards improvements in specific policy areas. The results from the Life and Times survey and, to a lesser extent, the DRD survey, suggest that there might be support for, or at least tolerance of, a regional rise in income tax that was clearly hypothecated for improvements in health, education and transport. The Life and Times survey results certainly suggest that the Northern Ireland Assembly should be brought into line with the Scottish parliament by being given its own tax varying powers.

Northern Ireland decision-makers have suffered from a serious paucity of data on both regional travel behaviour and attitudes to transport in the past. The 1999 Life and Times survey is the first social attitudes survey in Northern Ireland to have included such a comprehensive set of questions on transport. It is imperative that this topic is included again at regular intervals and that as many of the questions as possible are repeated to enable a time-series picture to be built up, especially as there is no doubt that the transport needs of a significant proportion of the Northern Ireland public are not being met. Lack of information on the scale of the problem has obviously played a part in this. It is very encouraging that a concerted effort is now being made to improve the quantity and quality of available data.

### Notes

The author would like to gratefully acknowledge the patient and thorough work of Katrina Lloyd in producing a wide range of cross-tabulated data for this chapter. This chapter could not have been produced without her assistance. The author would also like to acknowledge the assistance of Translink, the Northern Ireland Statistics and Research Agency, and the Department for Regional Development in providing information.

1.  At the time of writing, in November 2001, the government had put the private rail infrastructure company, Railtrack, into administration which effectively meant it was being wound up. The government had announced its intention to replace Railtrack with a not-for-profit trust. The London Underground was a public sector operation but was due to become a Public Private Partnership.

2.  It should be noted that each of these reports presents different figures for per capita rail revenue funding in Northern Ireland and Britain in 1996/97. The figures in the more recent report were used to arrive at the percentage figure used in the text. In the latter report, the figure for Britain does not include London and what the report refers to as 'the Metropolitan areas'. It is not clear whether or not the earlier report does likewise.

3.  The 2000 report presented average figures for the years 1993/94–1996/97 which showed that per capita bus revenue support in Northern Ireland was less than half that in Britain during those years. The 2001 report presented figures which showed that the same was also true for the years 1995/96–1998/99. In both instances, the figures for Britain do not include London and the Metropolitan areas.

4.  The greater Belfast area in this instance is the Belfast City Council area and the urban areas of a number of neighbouring district councils. Rural areas were defined in the report as being those outside urban centres with a population of more than 5,000, and rural areas in the greater Belfast area.

5.  It must be borne in mind that Northern Ireland has a relatively low density of population compared to the UK average. Northern Ireland has 123 persons per square kilometre, compared to a UK average of 242 per square km. It also has a slightly lower population density than Wales which has 141 people per square km but a considerably higher density than the Scottish average which is 66

people per square km. However, none of these figures distinguish between urban and rural areas, and so they are of limited use in determining how sparse the density of population in rural parts of Northern Ireland is compared to rural areas elsewhere. The calculations are based on 1996 figures taken from the Office for National Statistics (1999).

6. For example, the DRD estimates that an annual sum of between £5.5m and £7m might be raised by this means, see DRD (2001), p. 19. This compares with current unofficial DRD estimates, which suggest that some £20m a year might be raised through a congestion charge in the Belfast area, although similar calculations for the greater Bristol area, which has a lower population than the greater Belfast area, have suggested that a congestion charge of between £1.20 and £1.90 might produce between £30m and £50m a year in revenue. (The DRD estimate was also included in correspondence from the DRD to the author. Councillor Helen Holland, Bristol City Council, cited the figures relating to greater Belfast in a talk entitled 'Road user charging: policy in Bristol' (1998)).

### References

Atkins W.S. (2001) 'Regional transport strategy: market research: final report' (unpublished).

Commission for Integrated Transport (CfIT) (2000) *The CfIT Report: Public Attitudes to Transport in England* (London: CfIT) <www.cfit.gov.uk/reports/mori/index.htm>.

Department of the Environment and Department for Regional Development Roads Service (1991–1998) *Vehicle Kilometres of Travel Survey of Northern Ireland: Annual Reports 1991–1998* (Belfast: DoE; DRD).

Department of the Environment, Transport and the Regions (DETR) (2000a) *Transport Statistics Great Britain: 2000 Edition* (London: DETR) Table 4.7.

Department of the Environment, Transport and the Regions (DETR) (2000b) *Social Exclusion and the Provision and Availability of Public Transport* (London: DETR) <http://www.mobility-unit.dtlr.gov.uk/socialex/inde6.htm>.

Department of the Environment, Transport and the Regions (DETR) (2001) *Personal Travel Factsheet 3 – March 2001* (London: DETR) <www.transtat.dtlr.gov.uk/facts/ntsfacts/travwork/travwork.htm>.

Department of Health and Social Services (DHSS) and Registrar General Northern Ireland (1992a) *The Northern Ireland Census 1991 Summary Report* (Belfast: HMSO) Table 13, pp. 121–4.

Department of Health and Social Services (DHSS) and Registrar General Northern Ireland (1992b) *The Northern Ireland Census 1991: Belfast Urban Area Report* (Belfast: HMSO) Table 13, pp. 450–67.

Department for Regional Development (DRD) (2001) *Developing a Regional Transportation Strategy for Northern Ireland: Conference Papers* (Belfast: DRD) p. 15.

General Consumer Council for Northern Ireland (GCCNI) (2001) *The Transport Trap: How Transport Disadvantages Poorer People* (Belfast: GCCNI) <www.gccni.org.uk/publications/pdf/transport_trap.pdf>.

Holland, Helen (1998) 'Road user charging: policy in Bristol' paper presented at 1st Local Authority UK Chairs of Transport Conference, London, September.

Little, Arthur D. (2000) *Strategic Safety Review of Northern Ireland Railways* (Cambridge: Arthur D. Little) <http://www.railwaystaskforceni.gov.uk/rtfni_little.htm>

McEldowney, M. (2000) 'Planning and transportation: the need for integration' in *Northern Ireland Environment Link Fact Sheet*, Vol. 1, No. 2, pp. 6–7.

National Centre for Social Research (1998) 'British Social Attitudes Survey'.

National Centre for Social Research (1999) 'British Social Attitudes Survey'.

Northern Ireland Statistics and Research Agency (NISRA) (2000) 'Northern Ireland Labour Force Survey'.

Office for National Statistics (1999) *Regional Trends 34* (London: HMSO).

Railways Task Force (2000) *Interim Report of the Railways Task Force* (Belfast: Department for Regional Development and Northern Ireland Transport Holding Company) <http://www.railwaystaskforceni.gov.uk/rtfni_intrmrpt.htm>.

Smyth, Austin (2000) *The Implications of Segregation for Transport within Northern Ireland* (Belfast: Community Relations Council).

Steer Davies Gleave (2000) 'Translink – update of key funding indices' (unpublished).

Steer Davies Gleave (2001) 'Translink – update of key funding indices: final report (unpublished).

# 7 Housing and Social Exclusion

*Deirdre Heenan and Katrina Lloyd*

Within the social sciences, concepts and theories move in and out of vogue. Rarely, though, have any been accepted as wholeheartedly as social exclusion. It has been hailed as the key to our understanding of poverty, inequality and disadvantage. As noted by Ratcliffe (1998), it has been adopted with seemingly equal fervour by a broad section of academics, media commentators and politicians. Much of the debate on social policy within the European Union is currently set in the context of social exclusion, and numerous books and reports have attempted to define, identify and measure it. What is clear from this literature is that the housing system and housing policies are central to any discussion or debate on inequalities and cycles of deprivation. Not only can it be argued that there is a relationship between an individual's housing situation and access to employment, education and health services, but, due to its capital value, it can also be seen to perpetuate the growth of inequalities and social exclusion. Existing research has focused largely on the links between deprivation and large social housing estates. As poorer people are concentrated in social housing, it has been suggested that social exclusion is largely tenure specific.

This chapter examines data from the 1998 Northern Ireland Life and Times survey and assesses the relationship between social exclusion and housing tenure. It concludes by considering how useful the concept of social exclusion is to understanding housing disadvantage, and outlines the implications of these findings for future housing and urban regeneration policies.

## Social Exclusion

Targeting social need and promoting social inclusion have become key policy areas in Britain and Northern Ireland. Government accepts that there is inequality in relation to housing, health and education, which has important social, economic and political consequences. The 1980s and 1990s have witnessed huge social and economic changes, resulting

102

ning divisions between those on the highest incomes and those
west. Pantazis (2000) notes that the divide between the rich
poor is probably the most significant social change to have
d under 18 years of Conservative government (1979–97).
inequality is now wider than at any time since the Second
War. These trends are not confined to the United Kingdom, but
rather can be seen as part of the profound changes taking place in many
European societies. The changes are usually explained in the context
of the deregulation of labour markets and globalisation. These concerns
have led to the emergence of the term social exclusion, where there is
a belief that certain sections of the community are being cut off from
the mainstream (Room, 1995). The significance of the discourse on
social exclusion has been commented on by Levitas, who noted that
'it represents the primary significant division in society as one in an
included majority and one in an excluded minority' (1998, p. 7).

Social exclusion has been described by the government as one of
the most serious social issues of our time. It refers to much more than
simply a lack of financial resources, but also to the identification of the
processes that cause poverty and deprivation. In 1997 the Labour
government established a Social Exclusion Unit (SEU) to coordinate
and publicise policies to combat inequalities. The SEU refers to social
exclusion as 'a shorthand term for what can happen when individuals
or areas suffer from a combination of linked problems such as unemployment, poor skills, low incomes, poor housing, high crime
environments, bad health and family breakdown' (SEU, 2001a, p. 10).

In the context of housing, inclusion concerns the access to good
quality, affordable housing, in a safe and healthy environment.
Basically, it is a matter of differential access to what Marshall (1950)
referred to as social citizenship rights. According to Lee and Murie
(1999), social exclusion is more than simply poverty: it includes
concerns about power, participation and integration. It recognises the
compound nature of disadvantage and the concentration of inequality
among some social groups. Government stresses that policies must
be formulated which not only repair the damage caused by exclusion
but which also address the roots of the problem. Many of the attempts
to address this increasing polarisation and inequality have been
explicitly focused on spatial patterns of deprivation (Lee, 1998).

Increasingly, the role that housing policy can play in strategies to
combat social exclusion is being emphasised. Despite the fact that
housing policies in the 1980s and 1990s have directly led to increased
inequality and polarisation, New Labour has not formulated a housing
policy based on specific housing objectives. Instead the focus has been
on the ways in which housing policy can play a role in combating social
exclusion and contribute to urban regeneration. New Labour has
described strengthening communities as a vital element of effective

policies for tackling social exclusion in areas with high levels of social and economic deprivation – the 'worst neighbourhoods' as New Labour has termed them. The third report from the SEU, 'Bringing Britain Together' (1998), states that the gap between the worst estates and the remainder of the country has grown substantially during the 1980s and 1990s. The report noted that while most areas have gained from rising standards of living, the poorest neighbourhoods have not enjoyed this prosperity. They have become more run down, more prone to crime, and more cut off from the labour market. The report states that there are 'pockets of intense deprivation' where there are serious problems with crime and unemployment intertwined with poor health, housing and education.

### The Policy Context

During the 1980s and 1990s the aims and objectives of housing policy have had a huge impact on the nature and status of social rented housing. At the turn of the twentieth century, private renting dominated the housing system, accounting for over 90 per cent of the total housing stock in 1914. Gradually, the sector went into decline, as it became increasingly apparent that it was ill equipped to cope with the demands of a growing population. Initially, when the government intervened in the housing system, it was to reduce overcrowding, clear slums and ensure that a minimum standard was achieved. There was an underlying assumption that the aim of housing policy was to reduce social divisions and encourage social cohesion (Lee and Murie, 1997). Council housing, which accounted for less than 1 per cent of the total stock in 1914, had expanded to a peak of 29 per cent by 1971 (Kemp, 1999). Significantly, council housing was originally designed for the more affluent working classes, not for the poor. Malpass and Murie (1987, p. 74) point out that access to good quality council housing built during this period reflected the political and economic power of organised skilled labour – the better-off working class, as distinct from the poor. Council housing represented an attractive option for many working-class families, as it was less expensive and of a higher standard than private rented housing.

However, the dynamics of this sector have changed radically since the 1960s, and when the Conservative government was returned to power in 1979, its housing policies underlined and stressed the socio-economic residualisation which was already underway. These tenure-focused policies aimed to turn Britain into a nation of homeowners. In 1980, the then Secretary of State for the Environment hailed homeownership as the tenure which ensures the wide spread of wealth through society, encourages a personal desire to improve and modernise one's home, enables people to accrue wealth for their children and stimulates the attitudes of independence and self-reliance that are a bedrock of a free society. (Monk and Kleinman, 1989, p. 122)

Significantly then, while social differences related to housing conditions were diminishing, the importance of housing tenure as an indicator of social position was increasing. The best housing has been sold off into owner occupation through the right to buy. Levels of new build have been kept at a minimum and have not kept pace with the numbers of houses being sold into owner occupation. The social rented sector is diminishing numerically and has been abandoned by the better-off members of the working class who have purchased their local authority dwellings or entered directly into low cost homeownership. Conservative attempts to revitalise the private rented sector have not been overturned by New Labour, which accepts that this sector has a significant role to play within the housing market. Indeed as Kemp (1999) notes, New Labour's approach to housing is underpinned by an unquestioning acceptance that the free market is the best way to provide shelter.

### The Northern Ireland Context

Housing policy has been a particularly contentious issue in Northern Ireland prior to and during the most recent period of troubles. The allocation of public housing was one of the key issues that led to the creation of the Civil Rights Movement in Northern Ireland in the late 1960s. Following the report of the Cameron Commission (Cameron, Biggart and Campbell, 1969), public housing management was removed from local government and placed in the hands of a new central authority – the Northern Ireland Housing Executive (NIHE). The NIHE was established in 1971 as a single purpose, efficient, and streamlined central housing authority to take over responsibility for the building, management and allocation of all public sector housing. The NIHE, still in place today, is an appointed board with responsibility for all functions relating to public sector housing including building, design, rent collection, and repairs and maintenance. It also has functions relating to the private sector; for example, it administers improvement grants for owner occupiers. Since the 1990s, the NIHE has adopted a more strategic role within the housing market while responsibility for providing and managing new build public sector housing has been placed with housing associations. These voluntary organisations have grown rapidly; however, they are only responsible for 13 per cent of the public rented stock in Northern Ireland (Department for Social Development (DSD), 2001).

The history of housing policy in Northern Ireland has largely mirrored developments in the rest of the UK but the unique political situation in Northern Ireland has had important implications for policy and practice. Conflict and civil unrest have necessitated that housing has been organised around sectarian and political boundaries, which in turn has resulted in reduced choice especially for social rented sector tenants. Keane (1990) described Belfast as one of the most highly segregated areas in Europe, if not in the world. Throughout the 30 years of the Troubles, much of the segregated space in Northern Ireland has been divided along religious lines. An examination of data from the 1991 Census of Population highlighted the extent of this segregation. Of the 117 wards that made up the Belfast Urban Area, 62 had a population that was more than 92 per cent of one religion (McPeake, 1998). Figures produced by the NIHE and reported by Hughes and Donnelly (2001) show that 71 per cent of public sector housing estates are segregated, based on a threshold of 10 per cent present for either religion. The findings from the 1998 Life and Times survey show that respondents who live in the social rented sector are more likely to be housed in segregated areas than homeowners or those who rent their homes from private landlords (Table 7.1).

Table 7.1 Tenure by religious mix of area (%)

|  | Totally Cath. | Mainly Cath. | Mixed Cath. and Prot. | Mainly Prot. | Totally Prot. | Don't know |
|---|---|---|---|---|---|---|
| Owner occupied | 8 | 17 | 35 | 34 | 3 | 2 |
| Social rented* | 17 | 11 | 22 | 28 | 19 | 3 |
| Private rented | 6 | 10 | 55 | 14 | 5 | 11 |

* NIHE and Housing Association

### Housing Finance

A key area where policy in Northern Ireland has differed radically from the rest of the UK is housing finance. A combination of a history of neglect by successive unionist governments in the interwar years and political pressures meant that the huge cuts in finance for public housing which took place in Britain would not have been expedient in Northern Ireland. Consequently, during the 1970s and 1980s, public housing in Northern Ireland was in a somewhat privileged position and, unlike other areas of the UK, standards here improved dramatically. The relatively high levels of public expenditure on housing were highlighted by Gaffikin and Morrissey in their assessment of the Thatcher years.

During the 1970s and early 80s public expenditure on housing in Northern Ireland grew about twice as fast as in Britain. In 1978–79 Northern Ireland's public sector housing expenditure was 4.1% of the UK total. By 1987–88 this figure had risen to 9.6%. In 1986–87 public expenditure on housing per head in Northern Ireland was nearly three times that of England and Wales and 20% higher than in Scotland. (1990, p. 158)

### Housing Tenure

In Northern Ireland, as in other parts of the UK, owner occupation is by far the preferred tenure and the sector is increasing every year. Two thirds of respondents who participated in the 1998 Life and Times survey live in owner occupied properties. This figure is similar to estimates reported by other surveys carried out in Northern Ireland (Table 7.2). According to the DSD (2001), 73 per cent of the total occupied stock in Northern Ireland is now owner occupied. The high levels of owner occupation across the UK can be partly attributed to a government housing policy that has vigorously promoted privatisation. When the right to buy legislation was introduced in 1980 in England and Wales a similar scheme was already operating in Northern Ireland. In May 1979, the NIHE introduced a Voluntary House Sales Scheme through which secure tenants could buy their own homes. This scheme operated until September 1983, when the Housing (NI) Order introduced the right to buy. The NIHE amended the Voluntary House Sales Scheme to take account of the additional rights contained within the Order. The Housing (NI) Order 1992 repealed the former right to buy legislation in Northern Ireland and replaced it with a Statutory Sales Scheme (NIHE, 2001a). By 2001, over 90,000 properties had been sold (NIHE, 2001b) and the NIHE now owns approximately 118,000 properties, which represents 19 per cent of the total occupied housing stock in Northern Ireland (DSD, 2001).

As in other parts of the UK, the type of public sector dwellings sold to tenants by the NIHE tended to be in the best locations, leaving an increasing proportion of less popular estates in the public sector. Those who took advantage of the right to buy their homes tended to be middle aged with a grown-up family, to work in skilled jobs and to be in the most favourable economic position. The remaining tenants were much more likely to be older, dependent on state benefits and on low incomes (Heenan, 1998). The volume of sales to sitting tenants reinforced the trend for public sector housing to become viewed as inferior housing stock suitable for the poorest in the population.

Table 7.2 Comparison of data on tenure from three Northern Ireland surveys (%)

|  | Owner occupied | NIHE | Other rented** | Other |
|---|---|---|---|---|
| 1998 Life and Times Survey* | 66 | 25 | 8 | 1 |
| 1998 Continuous Household Survey | 68 | 23 | 7 | 1 |
| 1996 Northern Ireland House Condition Survey*** | 67 | 25 | 8 | 1 |

*    Household characteristics are based on unweighted data from the Life and Times survey
**   Includes properties rented from a housing association and rented from a private landlord (source: 1998 Life and Times survey, <http://www.ark.ac.uk/nilt/1998/tech98.pdf>)
***  Occupied stock only (source: NIHE, 1998)

Two surveys carried out by the NIHE have provided unequivocal evidence of the impact of the house sales scheme on the socio-economic residualisation of its tenants. Analysis of data collected by the 1996 Northern Ireland House Condition Survey (NIHCS) has shown that the profile of ex-NIHE tenants who have bought their properties differs from that of current NIHE tenants. Those who have purchased are more likely than tenants to be employed (47 per cent compared to 20 per cent) and to have gross annual household incomes of £10,000 or more (43 per cent and 10 per cent respectively) (Murie and Leather, 2000). A more recent survey also found that heads of household living in ex-NIHE properties are much more likely than current NIHE tenants to be working (48 per cent and 16 per cent respectively). Furthermore, of those who provided information on their income, 46 per cent of households living in ex-NIHE properties, compared with 6 per cent of current NIHE tenants, had a gross annual household income of £10,401 or more (NIHE, 2000a).

*Housing Tenure and Income Poverty*

Figures produced by the NIHE in its 1998/99 Continuous Tenant Omnibus Survey (CTOS) report also highlighted the level of socio-economic disadvantage experienced by its tenants (NIHE, 1999a). The survey found that almost two thirds (64 per cent) of households had a gross annual income of £7,300 or less. Commenting on the results, the chairman of the NIHE, Sid McDowell, pointed out that

A worrying aspect of the Continuous Tenant Omnibus Survey was the high number of tenants on low income. Almost two-thirds of households had a gross income of £7,300 or less. This is a clear indication that housing is no longer just about 'bricks and mortar'. It supports our commitment to work with other agencies and local communities to tackle deprivation on our estates. (NIHE, 1999b)

The concentration of low income households in the social rented sector (NIHE and housing associations) is clearly evident from the 1998 Life and Times survey data. Table 7.3 shows that high earning households are concentrated in the owner occupied sector. Only 7 per cent of respondents living in social rented properties have an annual income of £10,000 or more. These findings are consistent with the results from other social surveys carried out in Northern Ireland and Britain. For example, the Continuous Household Survey (CHS) found that in Northern Ireland only 19 per cent of NIHE tenants compared with 40 per cent of owner occupiers had an annual income of £10,400 or more[1] (Northern Ireland Statistics and Research Agency (NISRA), 2001). The 1998 General Household Survey (GHS) also showed that in Britain those with the lowest incomes were in the social rented sector. Households buying with a mortgage had, on average, the highest gross annual income (£28,964). Those with the lowest gross annual income were households living in the social rented sector (council tenants £9,048, housing association tenants £9,568). Private rented tenants had, on average, a gross annual household income of £15,912 (Office for National Statistics (ONS), 1998).

Table 7.3 Tenure* by personal gross annual income (%)

| | £3,999 or less | £4,000–9,999 | £10,000–19,999 | £20,000+ | Don't know |
|---|---|---|---|---|---|
| Owner occupied | 17 | 20 | 25 | 16 | 22 |
| Social rented | 37 | 41 | 7 | 0 | 15 |
| Private rented | 38 | 32 | 14 | 3 | 14 |

* denotes that the difference between tenures is statistically significant at p<0.001

## Social Class and Economic Status

Since the move away from a considerable social mix in the social rented sector, the homeownership sector has become more diverse, although high earning households are almost exclusively concentrated in this sector. Better-off tenants left the social rented sector as the status of owner occupation increased and it became viewed as the superior tenure. As a result, tenure status has become closely associated with economic status and social class. Lee and Murie (1997) have described the link between poor households and social housing as a key element in patterns of urban social stratification.

Findings from the Life and Times survey support this view. As Table 7.4 shows, employment rates are highest among respondents who live in owner occupied properties. Only one quarter of respondents who live in the social rented sector have jobs. Figures from other surveys carried out in Northern Ireland support the findings from the Life and Times survey and show a link between employment rates and tenure status. The 1998/99 CTOS found that only 17 per cent of heads of household living in NIHE properties were working. Tenure differences in economic status were also found by the British Social Attitudes (BSA) survey: analysis by Kemp showed that almost twice as many owner occupiers as council tenants in Britain were in work (61 per cent and 32 per cent respectively) (Kemp, 2000).

Table 7.4 Tenure* by economic status (%)

|  | Working | Not working | Retired | Perm. sick/ disabled | Full-time educ. | Other |
|---|---|---|---|---|---|---|
| Owner occupied | 61 | 16 | 16 | 3 | 4 | 1 |
| Social rented | 25 | 42 | 19 | 9 | 3 | 1 |
| Private rented | 45 | 19 | 4 | 2 | 28 | 3 |

* denotes that the difference between tenures is statistically significant at p<0.001

Tenure status is also closely associated with social class, as measured by respondents' present or most recent job.[2] Table 7.5 shows that owner occupiers and private renters tend to be concentrated in the professional, managerial and technical occupations with social rented sector tenants much more likely to be employed in partly skilled or unskilled manual jobs.

Table 7.5 Tenure* by social class[3] (%)

|  | Professional, managerial and technical | Skilled non-manual | Skilled manual | Partly skilled/ unskilled manual |
|---|---|---|---|---|
| Owner occupied | 36 | 25 | 18 | 22 |
| Social rented | 11 | 16 | 27 | 46 |
| Private rented | 40 | 30 | 9 | 21 |

* denotes that the difference between tenures is statistically significant at p<0.001

## *Housing Tenure and Benefit Dependency*

Reflecting the significant relationship between tenure and socio-economic characteristics reported earlier, there is a continuing trend towards social housing tenants being disproportionately reliant on social security benefits. Claiming Income Support is associated with being a social rented tenant, with 29 per cent of those interviewed in receipt of Income Support compared to just 3 per cent of owner occupiers (Table 7.6). This association between tenure and dependency on Income Support has been borne out by other surveys carried out in Northern Ireland. For example, the 2000/01 CHS found that more than six times as many heads of household in the social rented sector as in the owner occupied sector were in receipt of Income Support (NISRA, 2001).

Table 7.6 Tenure* by receipt of Income Support (%)

|                | Yes | No |
|----------------|-----|-----|
| Owner occupied | 3   | 97  |
| Social rented  | 29  | 71  |
| Private rented | 11  | 89  |

* denotes that the difference between tenures is statistically significant at p<0.001

## *Housing Benefit*

Given the means tested nature of Housing Benefit, it is not surprising that very small numbers of owner occupiers are in receipt of this benefit (Table 7.7). Many more respondents who live in social rented accommodation (34 per cent) than homeowners (1 per cent) say that they receive Housing Benefit. However, the figure of 34 per cent is much lower than the 78 per cent of respondents in receipt of this benefit reported by the NIHE in its 1998/99 CTOS (NIHE, 1999a). One possible explanation for this disparity is the different methodologies employed by the two surveys. The CTOS asks whether the head of household or partner receives Housing Benefit while the Life and Times survey asks only whether the respondent is on Housing Benefit. Furthermore, many individuals are unaware that they are actually in receipt of this benefit as it can be paid directly to the landlord. Nevertheless, the figures reported by the NIHE and by the Life and Times survey indicate the higher dependence on Housing Benefit among tenants than homeowners.

Table 7.7 Tenure* by receipt of Housing Benefit (%)

|                | Yes | No |
|----------------|-----|----|
| Owner occupied | 1   | 99 |
| Social rented  | 34  | 66 |
| Private rented | 11  | 89 |

* denotes that the difference between tenures is statistically significant at p<0.001

### Excluded Neighbourhoods

Low demand housing areas are likely to be poorly serviced, and low income households are unlikely to have the resources to obtain better services elsewhere. As a result, people living in these areas are less able to secure opportunities which could improve their circumstances and allow them to move on. A number of previous studies have highlighted the fact that those with a choice elect to live elsewhere and new tenants are largely those without choice. This cyclical nature of disadvantage is exacerbated by the poor health and low levels of educational attainment which tend to be found among those who live in social rented sector estates (SEU, 1998).

Data from the Life and Times survey show that almost one third (30 per cent) of respondents who live in social rented properties have a long-standing health problem or disability, compared with 14 per cent of respondents from the owner occupied sector and only 8 per cent of those from the private rented sector (Table 7.8). This is compounded by the fact that few respondents with a long-term health problem have a job (18 per cent). The comparable figure for people who do not have such a health problem is 59 per cent. Worst off, however, are social rented sector tenants who have a long-term health problem: they are three times less likely than owner occupiers with a long-term health problem to have a job (8 per cent for the former and 24 per cent for the latter).

Table 7.8 Tenure* by long-standing health problem or disability (%)

|                | Yes | No | Don't know |
|----------------|-----|----|------------|
| Owner occupied | 14  | 86 | <1         |
| Social rented  | 30  | 70 | 1          |
| Private rented | 8   | 91 | 1          |

* denotes that the difference between tenures is statistically significant at p<0.001

So far it has been shown that low levels of employment and poor health are more prevalent among social rented sector tenants. This concentration of vulnerable people in poor neighbourhoods has been a contributory factor in the decline of many housing estates. According to government sources, too little attention has been paid to problems such as unemployment and poor health services in deprived areas (SEU, 2001b). The SEU report also acknowledges that poor skills and lack of educational qualifications compound the problems faced by those who live in deprived areas as they block their routes out of poverty.

In support of this view, it has already been shown that respondents living in the social rented sector are more than twice as likely as those living in the owner occupied sector to be employed in partly skilled or unskilled jobs. As Table 7.9 shows, data from the Life and Times survey also indicate that less than half as many respondents who live in the social rented sector as those who live in the owner occupied sector have some educational qualifications (32 per cent compared with 65 per cent). Thus, the chances of social rented sector tenants being able to secure employment, or acquire better jobs, and consequently escape the cycle of disadvantage are low. In recognition of the disadvantages experienced by people who do not have educational qualifications, the government introduced an Individual Learning Accounts (ILA) scheme (which has now been temporarily suspended in Northern Ireland, <http://www.my-ila.co.uk>) to encourage adults to enrol for courses that will give them the qualifications they need to secure employment. It would appear from the results of the 1998 Life and Times survey that efforts to encourage take-up of this scheme (or any replacement scheme if the ILA scheme is permanently withdrawn) should be concentrated on those who live in the social rented sector.

Table 7.9 Tenure* by educational qualifications (%)

|  | Any qualifications | No qualifications |
| --- | --- | --- |
| Owner occupied | 65 | 35 |
| Social rented | 32 | 68 |
| Private rented | 79 | 21 |

* denotes that the difference between tenures is statistically significant at p<0.001

## Family Breakdown

As discussed earlier, social exclusion occurs when there is an accumulation of linked problems, one of which is family breakdown (SEU, 2001a). As Table 7.10 shows, respondents who live in the social rented sector are up to five times more likely than are respondents from other sectors to be separated, divorced or widowed. These findings are consistent with those reported in the 1999/00 CTOS which showed that 22 per cent of heads of household living in NIHE properties were separated or divorced and 21 per cent were widowed (NIHE, 2000b). As Heenan and Gray (1997) noted, owner occupation could be described as the married person's tenure, with the social rented sector being increasingly seen as the tenure of widowed, divorced and single people, especially women.

Table 7.10 Tenure* by marital status (%)

|  | Single – never married | Married | Separated or divorced | Widowed |
|---|---|---|---|---|
| Owner occupied | 21 | 70 | 3 | 6 |
| Social rented | 29 | 43 | 15 | 14 |
| Private rented | 69 | 21 | 8 | 3 |

* denotes that the difference between tenures is statistically significant at p<0.001

## Housing Conditions

Housing deprivation in Northern Ireland has traditionally been understood in terms of the physical condition of properties, and since 1974, the NIHE has carried out House Condition Surveys to assess levels of unfitness and disrepair in the housing stock. The results of these surveys have been used to secure government funding for improving housing conditions. By the late 1970s, vast improvements had been made in the area of unfitness and the number of households who were living in poor housing conditions was in decline. The last survey, carried out in 1996, showed that overall, only 7 per cent of properties in Northern Ireland were classified as unfit compared with 20 per cent in 1974 (NIHE, 1974; 1998[4]). Furthermore, the 1996 NIHCS found that unfitness was lower in the social rented sector than in the owner occupied sector. This is in contrast to the pattern of unfitness by tenure reported by the 1996 English House Condition Survey (Department of Environment, Transport and the Regions (DETR), 1998) (Table 7.11). Data from both surveys revealed that the poorest housing conditions are found in the private rented sector.

Average disrepair costs in Northern Ireland's housing stock were also lower in the social rented sector (£303 for housing association stock and £696 for Housing Executive stock) than in the owner occupied (£1,848) or private rented (£2,905) sectors.

Table 7.11 Unfitness by tenure (% unfit 1996)

|                    | Owner occupied | LA*/NIHE | RSL**/HA*** | Private rented | All dwellings |
|--------------------|----------------|----------|-------------|----------------|---------------|
| Northern Ireland   | 6              | 2        | 2           | 16             | 7             |
| England            | 6              | 7        | 5           | 19             | 7             |

\* Local Authority
\*\* Registered Social Landlords
\*\*\* Housing Association
Source: NIHE, 1998 and DETR, 1998

These findings highlight the complex nature of the relationship between housing and deprivation and suggest that in Northern Ireland, the causes of social inequality are largely unrelated to physical housing conditions. They cast doubt on the assertion in the SEU's *Strategy for Neighbourhood Renewal* (1998) that poverty and poor housing go together. The strategy noted that, over the course of the 1990s, excluded groups are more likely to live in housing unfit for human habitation, in need of substantial repair or requiring essential modernisation. While the worst housing conditions in Northern Ireland are found in the private rented sector, people living in the social rented sector tend to be worst off in terms of poverty, inequality and disadvantage.

### Social Exclusion: A Limited Concept?

In terms of the relationship between housing and social exclusion, the findings from the 1998 Life and Times survey support what one might have expected. Those who live in social rented housing are more likely to be dependent on benefits, have lower incomes and experience higher levels of disadvantage than those in other tenure groups. In this sense, then, it can be said that social exclusion is tenure specific. Significantly though, due to higher levels of public spending on housing, the poorest sections of the population in Northern Ireland actually enjoy relatively good housing conditions, as unfitness rates are lowest in the social rented sector.

However, it is important to note that the expansion in owner occupation has led to increasing differentiation within this sector. The right to buy scheme has enabled the working class to enter home-ownership in large numbers and this has led to increasing diversity among those who live in this sector. This diversity has meant that significant numbers of owner occupiers may be in a perilous position at the margins of the tenure without any support or safety net. For example, Wilcox and Ford (1997) note that homeowners now represent more than two fifths of all households in the lowest income decile. In their analysis of the data from the 1996 NIHCS, Murie and Leather (2000) found that owner occupiers who had bought their homes from the NIHE were less affluent and less likely to have high earning jobs than owner occupiers who had never been NIHE tenants. Furthermore, the stock sold off by the NIHE through the right to buy scheme has tended to be relatively young and in good repair. It seems likely that those who took the opportunity to buy their homes will increasingly find maintenance and repair of their properties problematic.

People living in the private rented sector, however, experience the worst housing conditions. This is a serious problem as it is much more difficult to regulate and monitor standards in the private rented sector than in other rented housing sectors. Significantly then, it can be argued that many people living in the private rented sector and those at the bottom of the homeownership sector may also experience social exclusion in terms of poor standards and inadequate resources.

This suggests that policies to combat social exclusion which are focused on the social rented sector, and do not take account of needs within other tenures, are likely to be ineffective. Strategies aimed at regeneration and urban renewal need to focus on those who are at the margins of society, regardless of tenure. Also, concentrating solely on the association between social rented housing and social exclusion may further stigmatise tenants. In popular discourse, lone parents and unemployed young males have come to be associated with social housing tenants who in turn have been used as convenient scapegoats for explaining the difficulties experienced in some social housing estates. The relentless promotion of homeownership at the expense of other tenures has served to reinforce the association between social rented sector tenants and a morally deficient underclass (Card, 2001).

So is the concept of social exclusion useful when looking at housing policies and trends? On the one hand it could be suggested that the concept lacks theoretical precision and has become a 'catch all' notion used to describe a broad spectrum of disadvantage. The inevitable result is that the concept can actually obscure the nature and extent of inequalities. It could be described as an oppressive form of discourse, which labels social rented tenants as part of an excluded underclass. On the other hand, the concept can be useful if one is attempting to assess the role that the housing system plays in shaping and strengthening social exclusion. In this context, any analysis of housing processes should not be confined to tenure divisions but should also consider housing production, housing allocation, housing choices and housing finance. Social exclusion should be distinguished from tenure exclusion as the terms are not mutually exclusive and the compound nature of exclusion must be recognised.

What is clear is that policies and strategies for regeneration and renewal must be based on a sound understanding of the complex nature of disadvantage and inequalities. Social, political and economic factors have meant that, in many respects, housing in Northern Ireland has developed in a unique way within the UK. Initiatives in Northern Ireland must take account of the particular housing circumstances that exist here and not simply be poorly disguised imitations of strategies introduced in other areas of the UK.

## Notes

1. The CHS figures are for annual household income while the Life and Times survey figures are for personal income of respondent.
2. Respondents who were in work, looking for work or retired at the time of the 1998 Life and Times survey.
3. Due to the small numbers in some cells, the six social class categories were recoded into four.
4. Due to changes in definition, data for unfit dwellings are not directly comparable across the two surveys.

## References

Cameron, J., Biggart, J.H. and Campbell, J.J. (1969) *Disturbances in Northern Ireland: Report of the Commission Appointed by the Governor of Northern Ireland* (Belfast: HMSO) Cmd 532.

Card, P. (2001) 'Managing anti-social behaviour – inclusion or exclusion' in D. Cowan and A. Marsh (eds) *Two Steps Forward, Housing Policy Into the New Millennium* (Bristol: Policy Press) pp. 201–19.

Department of the Environment, Transport and the Regions (DETR) (1998) *English House Condition Survey 1996. Summary Report*, <http://www.housing.dtlr.gov.uk/research/ehcs96/summary/index.htm>.

Department for Social Development (DSD) (2001) *Northern Ireland Housing Statistics 2000–01* <http://www.dsdni.gov.uk/srb/pdf/0001section1.pdf>.

Gaffikin, F. and Morrissey, M. (1990) *Northern Ireland: The Thatcher Years* (London: Zed).

Heenan, D. (1998) 'The growth of home ownership: explanations and implications' in Gillian Robinson, Deirdre Heenan, Ann Marie Gray and Kate Thompson (eds) *Social Attitudes in Northern Ireland: The Seventh Report* (Aldershot: Ashgate) pp. 19–31.

Heenan, D. and Gray, A.M. (1997) 'Women, public housing and inequality: a Northern Ireland perspective', *Housing Studies*, Vol. 12, No. 2, pp. 157–71.

Hughes, J. and Donnelly, C. (2001) *Ten Years of Social Attitudes to Community Relations in Northern Ireland*, Northern Ireland Life and Times Survey Occasional Paper 1, <http://www.ark.ac.uk/nilt/occpaper1.pdf>.

Keane, M.C. (1990) 'Segregation processes in public sector housing' in P. Doherty (ed.) *Geographical Perspectives on the Belfast Region* (Belfast: Geographical Society of Ireland) pp. 88–107.

Kemp, P.A. (1999) 'Housing policy under New Labour' in M. Powell (ed.) *New Labour, New Welfare State?* (Bristol: Policy Press) pp. 123–47.

Kemp, P.A. (2000) 'Images of council housing' in Roger Jowell, John Curtice, Alison Park, Katarina Thompson, Lindsey Jarvis, Catherine Bromley and Nina Stratford (eds) *British Social Attitudes: The 17th Report Focusing on Diversity* (London: Sage and National Centre for Social Research) pp. 137–54.

Lee, P. (1998) 'Housing policy, citizenship and social exclusion' in A. Marsh and D. Mullins (eds) *Housing and Public Policy: Citizenship, Choice and Control* (Buckingham: Open University Press) pp. 57–78.

Lee, P. and Murie, A. (1997) *Poverty, Housing Tenure and Social Exclusion* (Bristol/York: The Policy Press/Joseph Rowntree Foundation).

Lee, P. and Murie, A. (1999) 'Spatial and social division within British cities', *Beyond Residualisation*, Vol. 14, No. 5, pp. 625–40.

Levitas, R. (1998) *The Inclusive Society? Social Exclusion and New Labour* (Basingstoke: Macmillan).

McPeake, J. (1998) 'Religion and residential search behaviour in the Belfast urban area', *Housing Studies*, Vol. 13, No. 4, pp. 527–48.

Malpass, P. and Murie, A. (1987) *Housing Policy and Practice* (London: Macmillan).

Marshall, T. (1950) *Citizenship and Social Class* (Cambridge: Cambridge University Press).

Monk, S. and Kleinman, M. (1989) 'Housing' in P. Brown and R. Sparks (eds) *Beyond Thatcherism: Social Policy, Politics and Society* (Milton Keynes: Open University Press) pp. 121–36.

Murie, A. and Leather, P. (2000) *A Profile of Housing Executive Sold Properties in Northern Ireland* (Birmingham: Centre for Urban and Regional Studies, University of Birmingham).

Northern Ireland Housing Executive (NIHE) (1974) *Northern Ireland House Condition Survey Final Report* (Belfast: NIHE).

Northern Ireland Housing Executive (NIHE) (1998) *Northern Ireland House Condition Survey 1996* (Belfast: Smith Ryan).

Northern Ireland Housing Executive (NIHE) (1999a) *Continuous Tenant Omnibus Survey 1998/99 Key Findings* (Belfast: NIHE) <http://www.nihe.gov.uk/publications/reports/CTOS_key_findings 98.pdf>.

Northern Ireland Housing Executive (NIHE) (1999b) <http://www.nihe.gov.uk/news>.

Northern Ireland Housing Executive (NIHE) (2000a) *Anti-Social Behaviour in Housing Executive Areas*, Research Report (Belfast: NIHE).

Northern Ireland Housing Executive (NIHE) (2000b) *Continuous Tenant Omnibus Survey, Annual Report 1999–2000* (Belfast: NIHE).

Northern Ireland Housing Executive (NIHE) (2001a) *The Housing Executive's House Sales Scheme: Proposals for Change. Consultation Document* (Belfast: NIHE) <http://www.nihe.gov.uk/publications/ consultation_documents/hsreviewfull.pdf>.

Northern Ireland Housing Executive (NIHE) (2001b) *30th Annual Report 2000/2001* (Belfast: NIHE) <http://www.nihe.gov.uk/publications/reports/ar2001.pdf>.

Northern Ireland Statistics and Research Agency (NISRA) (2001) 'Continuous Household Survey 2000–2001'.

Office for National Statistics (ONS) (1998) General Household Survey (London: Department of Health) <http://www.statistics.gov.uk>.

Pantazis, C. (2000) 'Introduction' in C. Pantazis and D. Gordon (eds) *Tackling Inequality: Where Are We Now and What Can be Done?* (Bristol: Policy Press) pp. 1–23.

Ratcliffe, P. (1998) '"Race" housing and social exclusion', *Housing Studies*, Vol. 13, No. 6, pp. 807–18.

Room, G. (1995) 'Poverty and social exclusion: the new European agenda for policy and research' in G. Room (ed.) *Beyond the Threshold. The Measurement and Analysis of Social Exclusion* (Bristol: Policy Press) pp. 1–9.

Social Exclusion Unit (SEU) (1998) *Bringing Britain Together: A National Strategy for Neighbourhood Renewal*, CM4045 (London: The Stationery Office).

Social Exclusion Unit (SEU) (2001a) *Preventing Social Exclusion* (London: The Stationaery Office).

Social Exclusion Unit (SEU) (2001b) *A New Commitment to Neighbourhood Renewal: National Strategy Action Plan*, <http://www.cabinet-office.gov.uk/seu/publications/reports/pdfs/ action_plan.pdf>.

Wilcox, S. and Ford, J. (1997) 'At your own risk' in S. Wilcox (ed.) *Housing Finance Review 1997/98* (York: Joseph Rowntree Foundation) pp. 23–9.

# 8 Attitudes to Academic Selection, Integrated Education and Diversity within the Curriculum

*Tony Gallagher and Alan Smith*

The education system has always played a key role in debates on public policy in Northern Ireland. Education has also featured in issues related to the conflict. In particular, three key themes have taken prominence within these debates: the selective system of secondary and grammar schools, de facto religious schools, and curriculum initiatives to promote tolerance and reconciliation. Reflecting the high level of public interest, as well as ongoing research and policy discussions, the Education module of the 1999 Northern Ireland Life and Times survey incorporated these three key themes. This chapter will first outline the policy context for each theme, and then discuss the attitudes of the public towards them.

The first issue is the selective system of grammar and secondary schools, and the transfer procedure used to select pupils. This issue has been hotly debated since the establishment of a selective system of post-primary education in 1947. Unlike most of the rest of the United Kingdom, Northern Ireland did not shift towards a comprehensive system of schools in the 1960s and 1970s. There was a move in this direction towards the end of the 1970s, but this was halted when the Conservative government was elected in 1979. Research in the 1980s highlighted some significant problems with the selective system (Sutherland and Gallagher, 1986; Wilson, 1986; Sutherland and Gallagher, 1987; Gallagher, 1988; Teare and Sutherland, 1988), but there was little interest in change at a policy level. This altered when the Labour government was elected in 1997 and the then minister with responsibility for education, Tony Worthington, commissioned two major research projects on the effects of the selective system of education (Alexander, Daly, Gallagher, Gray and Sutherland, 1998; Gallagher and Smith, 2000). Following the publication of the Gallagher and Smith (2000) report, the Minister for Education, Martin McGuinness, established the Post-Primary Review Body to consult on options for the future organisation of post-primary education. The findings of this body were published as the Burns Report (Post-Primary Review Body, 2001) and recommended the abolition of academic selection in the transfer from primary to post-primary school. It advocates the establishment of a new formative assessment system to run from the upper primary school and through post-primary school, and the establishment of collaborative collegiates of post-primary schools. At the time of writing, these recommendations are out for consultation and a final decision on future arrangements is expected sometime in 2002.

The second issue addressed in the survey is integrated education. In recent years a significant development in education in Northern Ireland has been the establishment of integrated schools, that is, schools which are attended in roughly equal numbers by Protestant and Catholic pupils. Although there is widespread evidence of popular support for more integrated education in Northern Ireland, the system continues to be characterised by a high level of segregation on the basis of religion. In large part this is linked to developments in the 1920s and 1930s when the basic framework of the education system was being developed (Akenson, 1973; Smith, 2001).

The first planned integrated school (Lagan College) was established in Belfast in 1981. An important feature that distinguishes the establishment of integrated schools is that the impetus has not come from state or church authorities. The main activists in the establishment of integrated schools have been parents, and the development process could therefore be characterised as 'voluntary integration' through parental consent rather than 'compulsory desegregation' by church or state authorities. A number of research studies (Agnew, McEwan, Salters and Salters, 1992; Morgan, Dunn, Cairns and Fraser, 1992) have highlighted some of the issues and concerns related to parental involvement and their implications for integrated schools. Other parent groups followed Lagan College's example and three more integrated schools opened in Belfast in 1985. Further schools opened throughout Northern Ireland, initially as independent schools with financial support from a great many charitable institutions, such as the Nuffield Foundation.

By the end of the 1980s the number of integrated schools had reached double figures and sufficient viability had been demonstrated for support for integrated education to be included in new legislation through the Education Reform (NI) Order 1989. The legislation introduced government funding for a central, representative body, underpinning the development role of the Northern Ireland Council for Integrated Education (NICIE) and also included provisions to permit existing schools to transform their status to become integrated. The 1990s has seen further growth and in September 2000 there were

45 integrated schools (28 primary and 17 post-primary) with approximately 14,000 pupils, representing 4 per cent of the school population.

The third issue relates to the contribution of the school curriculum to the improvement of relations between the two main communities in Northern Ireland. The 1989 Education Reform (NI) Order created a statutory curriculum with two education themes, Education for Mutual Understanding (EMU) and Cultural Heritage, which aimed to address community relations. As we will see later in this chapter, this initiative has had limited success. As we also note below, the review of the curriculum being undertaken by the Council for the Curriculum Examinations and Assessment (CCEA) includes proposals for the introduction of citizenship education as part of the statutory curriculum.

### The Eleven-Plus and Attitudes to Academic Selection

In this section we consider the questions that focused on the eleven-plus tests, and the selective system of secondary and grammar schools. In the context of responses to these questions, it should be noted that 27 per cent of respondents say that they had passed the eleven-plus, 35 per cent that they had not passed the eleven-plus and the remaining 38 per cent say that they had not taken the tests.

The first set of questions asked respondents whether they agree or disagree with a series of statements on various aspects of the eleven-plus and selection. Table 8.1 shows that there is no simple consensus on the current system. Thus, most respondents feel that the eleven-plus tests put too much pressure on young people, that children are too young at that age for selection tests and that the eleven-plus means that most children feel they are failures. However, most respondents also feel that selection has to happen at some time and that children who do not get to grammar school still get a first class education. On the remaining questions, opinions are more evenly divided.

Part of the explanation for the variation in the expressed opinions relates to respondents' experience of the system. In particular, the survey responses suggest that those who had passed the eleven-plus, or who went to grammar schools, are more positive about the current system.

The second set of questions explored respondents' views on the future of selection, beginning with a question that asked whether they felt the current system works well enough or whether it should be changed. Most tend to favour change, as only 37 per cent say that the system works well enough, while 55 per cent say it should be changed. We can see from Table 8.2 that opinion on this issue is only influenced to some degree by respondents' personal experience of the system.

Thus, the balance of opinion remains in favour of change, with personal experience only influencing the extent to which this view is held.

Table 8.1 Attitudes to the selection procedure (%)

|  | Strongly agree/agree | Strongly disagree/disagree |
|---|---|---|
| Selection has to happen at some time in a child's education | 82 | 10 |
| The eleven-plus puts too much pressure on 10 and 11 year olds | 78 | 14 |
| Children who don't get places at grammar schools still get a first class education | 75 | 13 |
| Children are far too young at 10 or 11 for selection tests | 70 | 19 |
| The eleven-plus system means that most children feel that they are failures | 61 | 24 |
| Grammar schools provide the best standard of education anywhere in the UK | 48 | 32 |
| A system of separate secondary and grammar schools is unfair | 40 | 43 |
| The eleven-plus is a good measure of ability | 30 | 53 |

Table 8.2 Attitudes to eleven-plus by transfer status (%)

|  | Works well enough | Should be changed |
|---|---|---|
| All respondents | 37 | 55 |
| Passed eleven-plus | 43 | 52 |
| Failed or did not take eleven-plus | 34 | 57 |

Respondents who feel that some aspects of the current system should be changed were asked whether they think that the eleven-plus tests, the system of secondary and grammar schools, or both should be changed. Table 8.3 shows that the most unpopular aspect of the current system is the eleven-plus tests. Almost all respondents say that the eleven-plus tests should be changed, while 58 per cent say that the system of secondary and grammar schools should be changed.

Table 8.3 Aspects of current system that should be changed (%)

| | |
|---|---|
| The eleven-plus test only | 42 |
| System of secondary and grammar schools only | 9 |
| Both eleven-plus and the system of secondary and grammar schools | 49 |

Respondents who feel that only the eleven-plus tests should be changed were given a list of options and asked to suggest whether they thought that these options were useful or not useful as possible alternatives to the current eleven-plus procedure. The options available were using primary teacher assessment for selection, delaying the eleven-plus tests until the end of the P7 year (age 10 to 11), using a different type of test, or delaying the point of selection to age 14 years or age 16 years.

Table 8.4 shows that those who would like to see the eleven-plus tests changed appear to prefer a delay in the point of selection to age 14 years, and are very much less supportive of a delay in selection until age 16 years. The second most favoured option is a different type of test, closely followed by a preference for the use of teacher assessment.

Table 8.4 Usefulness of alternative selection procedures (%)

|  | Useful | Not useful | Don't know |
| --- | --- | --- | --- |
| Selection later at age 14 years | 81 | 17 | 2 |
| Use a different type of test | 61 | 34 | 6 |
| Use teacher assessment instead of test | 58 | 40 | 3 |
| Selection later at age 16 years | 46 | 52 | 2 |
| Take eleven-plus test at the end of P7 | 42 | 55 | 3 |

Respondents who say that the system of secondary and grammar schools should be changed were given three alternatives to the current system and asked if each one would be useful or not useful. As Table 8.5 shows, all the stated options are seen as being useful by the majority of respondents. The most preferred scenario is for all pupils to go to the same school to age 14 years, followed by all pupils going to the same school to age 16 years.

Table 8.5 Usefulness of alternative school systems (%)

|  | Useful | Not useful | Don't know |
| --- | --- | --- | --- |
| All to same school to age 14 years | 73 | 23 | 5 |
| All to same school to age 16 years | 60 | 37 | 3 |
| Allow secondary schools to select a third of their intake | 57 | 35 | 8 |

Debates over the merits or otherwise of the selective system of schools in Northern Ireland and the procedures used to allocate pupils within the system have gone on for many years. This survey evidence highlights the complexity of opinions on these issues. Most people can readily identify problems with the current system, while believing that some form of selection is probably inevitable. However, while many advocate change in the system there is little consensus on the form that change should take.

## Integrated Education

As noted above, there have been debates on the merits of integrated schools since the outbreak of the violence in the late 1960s (Darby, 1973; Fraser, 1973; Darby and Dunn, 1987; Spencer, 1987; Moffatt, 1993; Gallagher, 1995). However, it was only in the last two decades of the last century that the planned integrated schools were opened. The 1999 Life and Times survey examines support for integrated schools, as well as a number of other aspects related to current levels of participation in these schools. When asked whether the government should encourage or discourage more integrated schools, or leave things as they are, almost three quarters (74 per cent) of respondents say that the government should encourage more integrated schools. However, this level of support is somewhat higher among Catholics (80 per cent) as compared with Protestants (67 per cent); as many as a quarter of Protestant respondents say that things should be left as they are, a view expressed by 15 per cent of Catholic respondents. The vast majority (86 per cent) of those respondents who are parents of school-age children say that none of their own children has attended an integrated school. However, the proportion who say their children have attended one of these schools is slightly higher among Protestants (16 per cent) as compared with Catholics (10 per cent).

To a large extent this pattern of results is unsurprising and, as previously noted, mirrors many past surveys of opinion on the general support for, but limited uptake of, integrated schooling. The Life and Times survey goes beyond this, and asks parents of school-age children who did not send their children to an integrated school to identify particular reasons which had influenced their decision. As shown in Table 8.6, the only reason attracting a significant degree of affirmation is that there was no integrated school nearby. The only other offered explanation which attracted more than one in ten affirmations is that parents had concerns that their children should learn about their own culture and religion. Interestingly, this is the only item on which there is any marked difference on the basis of religion, with 16 per cent of Catholic respondents identifying this reason in comparison with 10 per cent of Protestant respondents. Overall, however, this pattern of results implies a fairly widespread view that more parents would opt for integrated education for their children if more opportunities were available.

Table 8.6 Reason for not sending children to an integrated school (% indicating each reason)

| | |
|---|---|
| There was no integrated school nearby | 66 |
| Concerns that children should learn about their own culture and religion | 13 |
| Wanted child to go to a grammar school | 9 |
| Brother or sister was at another school | 8 |
| Because the facilities at other schools were better | 8 |
| Concerns that the integrated school would not be as good academically | 6 |
| Other reason | 6 |
| Don't know | 4 |

The third series of questions on this issue focused on respondents' views on how extra provision in integrated education might be provided. The initial wave of integrated schools came through the efforts of parents and some teachers who established new schools in the 1980s. Following the 1989 Education Reform (NI) Order the government indicated that while the possibility of entirely new schools would remain an option, its preference was for development through the transformation of existing schools: the Reform Order made provision for this by means of a parental ballot. The logic of this preference is understandable because of the existing high level of surplus places in the system already, a forthcoming reduction in the size of the cohort going through second-level schooling and the cost of new build arrangements. On the other hand, a transforming school not only has to develop a new character and ethos, which inevitably involves a significant degree of change from past practice, but also has to achieve targets for a balanced enrolment within a set time period. A further factor is that all the transformation schools to date have changed from being Controlled primary or secondary schools which had a majority Protestant enrolment; no ballot has yet taken place in any Catholic school.

All respondents were offered a series of options about the future of integrated education, and asked to choose between them. From Table 8.7 it can be seen that almost half (46 per cent) favour the transformation option, that is, schools changing their status in order to become integrated, with additional money to support this change. Interestingly, a higher proportion of Catholic respondents (49 per cent) as compared with Protestant respondents (41 per cent) choose this option, although it is by far the most popular option among the small number of respondents who said they had no religion (57 per cent). The second most favoured option, chosen by a little under a quarter (22 per cent) of respondents, is that schools should largely stay as they are, but provide a more diverse curriculum. This scenario, too, is more popular with

Catholics (27 per cent) than Protestants (20 per cent). The third most favoured option is to leave things as they are (16 per cent), chosen by many more Protestants (23 per cent) than Catholics (9 per cent). The option receiving the lowest level of support (13 per cent) is that money should be provided to create new integrated schools.

Table 8.7 Ways of increasing integrated education (%)

| | |
|---|---|
| Encourage existing schools to become integrated and give them additional money to do this | 46 |
| Keep schools as they are but make it compulsory to learn more about all cultures and traditions in Northern Ireland | 22 |
| Just keep things the way they are now | 16 |
| Spend money on setting up new integrated schools | 13 |
| Other | <1 |
| Don't know | 2 |

These data on integrated education highlight a number of conundrums. Firstly, the patterns of responses reflect the high degree of support that has been found consistently for integrated education in Northern Ireland. Furthermore, the evidence suggests that the reason why parents do not send their children to integrated schools is simply because there are insufficient schools or places at present. However, there is no evidence of widespread support for a programme to create new schools. Rather, the preferred option seems to be that more existing schools follow the transformation route and become integrated. It is noteworthy that this option receives a high level of support among Catholic parents, yet there have been no proposals to consider the transformation option in any Catholic school. In addition, there have been relatively few cases of transformed schools since 1989.

There would appear to be three possible explanations for this pattern of responses. Firstly, only a small number of schools currently have a minority enrolment that would allow them to be considered at all. Data from the Department of Education for Northern Ireland shows that this amounts to less than 4 per cent of all schools, or about 40 schools overall. Thus the criteria for starting the process may be set too high. Secondly, the procedure for starting a transformation process may be too complicated or cumbersome, or parents may not be aware of either the option or the mechanism for initiating a transformation process. Thirdly, the authorities of Catholic schools may actively discourage any proposals to consider transformation in their schools, although it should be noted that only 10 of the 40 schools with a significant minority enrolment are Catholic schools with a significant Protestant enrolment.

### Diversity within the Curriculum

We next turn to issues relating to the curriculum and, more particularly, views on the extent to which the compulsory curriculum in Northern Irish schools should reflect aspects of diversity in the wider society.

Respondents were asked if certain aspects of language and culture should be a compulsory part of the curriculum for all pupils in secondary-level schools, specifically, whether all pupils should learn about Irish language and culture, and about Ulster-Scots language and culture. The Northern Ireland Social Attitudes (NISA) survey series had only asked about the first of these, as the Ulster-Scots movement is of fairly recent origin. In the past, about 60 per cent of Catholic respondents have supported the teaching of Irish language and culture, while over 85 per cent of Protestant respondents have not supported this proposal (Gallagher, 1995). In essence this is exactly the pattern found in the 1999 Life and Times survey.

Table 8.8 shows that 61 per cent of Catholics but only 13 per cent of Protestants and 20 per cent of those with no religion say that all pupils at secondary-level schools should learn about Irish language and culture. Perhaps a little more surprising, however, is the pattern of responses when asked about the teaching of Ulster-Scots language and culture – a clear majority disagrees with the suggestion that pupils should learn about these. The level of support is highest among Catholics. Thus, while 28 per cent of Catholics say that all pupils should learn about Ulster-Scots language and culture, this is so for only 17 per cent of those with no religion and only 12 per cent of Protestants.

Table 8.8 Support for compulsory teaching of languages and cultures (%)

|  | Strongly agree/ agree | Neither | Strongly disagree/ disagree |
|---|---|---|---|
| *Irish language and culture* | | | |
| All respondents | 32 | 13 | 52 |
| Protestant | 13 | 14 | 71 |
| Catholic | 61 | 11 | 26 |
| No religion | 20 | 15 | 64 |
| *Ulster-Scots language and culture* | | | |
| All respondents | 18 | 17 | 59 |
| Protestant | 12 | 18 | 67 |
| Catholic | 28 | 16 | 48 |
| No religion | 17 | 17 | 63 |

The second aspect of a pluralist curriculum is the issue of the teaching of religion. Religious Education is a statutory part of the Northern Ireland Curriculum and as part of the Education Reform

(NI) Order 1989, a Core Syllabus for Religious Education was developed jointly by representatives from the three main Protestant churches (Church of Ireland, Presbyterian, Methodist) and the Roman Catholic church (Barnes, 1997). The NISA survey series asked about the teaching of Protestant and Catholic religious beliefs, as well as the teaching of religious beliefs in general, not specifically Catholic or Protestant (Gallagher, 1995). The emergent pattern was one where a majority of Catholics favoured the teaching of religion, whether as Catholic or Protestant religious beliefs, while a majority of Protestants did not. About one third of Protestants agreed with the teaching of Catholic religious beliefs, and about two in five agreed with the teaching of Protestant religious beliefs. The 1999 Life and Times survey also asked for respondents' views on the teaching of religious beliefs: Protestant, Catholic and religious beliefs in general.

The pattern of results shown in Table 8.9 is consistent with past evidence (Gallagher, 1995). Thus, Catholics support the teaching of Catholic and Protestant beliefs, while Protestant opinion is much more divided, with the modal opinion being to support the teaching of Protestant beliefs, but not the teaching of Catholic beliefs. Those who say they have no religion are firmly opposed to the teaching of either Protestant or Catholic religious beliefs. However, perhaps the more interesting finding relates to views on the teaching of religious beliefs in general, not specifically Protestant or Catholic. In response to this question, three quarters of respondents say they would favour the teaching of general religious beliefs, and clear majorities in support of this proposition are found among Protestants, Catholics and those who say they have no religion.

Table 8.9 Support for compulsory teaching of religion (%)

|  | Strongly agree/ agree | Neither | Strongly disagree/ disagree |
|---|---|---|---|
| *Protestant religious beliefs* | | | |
| All respondents | 46 | 18 | 35 |
| Protestant | 40 | 21 | 37 |
| Catholic | 55 | 14 | 29 |
| No religion | 30 | 15 | 54 |
| *Catholic religious beliefs* | | | |
| All respondents | 42 | 18 | 38 |
| Protestant | 30 | 23 | 47 |
| Catholic | 61 | 13 | 25 |
| No religion | 26 | 16 | 57 |
| *Religious beliefs in general* | | | |
| All respondents | 75 | 12 | 12 |
| Protestant | 72 | 14 | 13 |
| Catholic | 83 | 8 | 8 |
| No religion | 61 | 19 | 18 |

*Citizenship Education*

Since 1989, schools have operated under a statutory curriculum that provides a broadly common entitlement to all pupils throughout their period of compulsory education. One feature of the statutory curriculum is that it includes a series of educational themes that are meant to influence all areas. Two of these themes, EMU and Cultural Heritage, directly address issues related to community relations, and the promotion of tolerance and reconciliation through schools. However, despite the undoubted value of these themes in principle, and the high quality of the advice provided to schools on their implementation (Council for the Curriculum Examinations and Assessment (CCEA), 1997), there have been a number of critical assessments of the extent to which the original goals of these themes have been achieved (Smith and Robinson, 1992; 1996; Leitch and Kilpatrick, 1999).

The body responsible for the curriculum in Northern Ireland, CCEA <http://www.ccea.org.uk>, is undertaking a review of current provision with a view to establishing a new statutory framework from 2003 onwards. Partly in response to the critical appraisals of EMU and Cultural Heritage, this review includes a detailed consideration of introducing a version of citizenship education in schools. Development work towards achieving an effective and workable programme has already begun. Citizenship education in various forms has existed for many years in numerous countries throughout the world including many European countries and the United States (Kerr, 1999; Torney-Purta, Schwille and Amadeo, 1999). Recent developments in this area, however, have been largely based on concerns that the level of democratic participation and civic engagement by young people is dangerously low. Thus, there have been particular developments in England and Wales, and the Republic of Ireland, to try to address this issue. In Northern Ireland concerns about levels of political literacy are conjoined with a perceived need to address issues related to equality, justice, rights and responsibilities through any new curriculum programme, not least because this focuses on a range of issues that many teachers have tended to avoid through the EMU and Cultural Heritage programmes. However, most of the discussions on these proposals to date have taken place within the educational community rather than the wider society. Thus, the Life and Times survey provided the opportunity to seek popular views on some aspects of this new proposed initiative.

Firstly, respondents were asked about the role of schools in the teaching of politics and human rights. A number of themes are evident from the results shown in Table 8.10. A small majority of respondents feel that schools should tackle such difficult topics as the teaching of politics and human rights, although support for this among Protestants is less than among Catholics and those with no religion. Part of the reason for this reticence on the part of Protestants may be because many of them doubt whether teachers would present these topics fairly. It is perhaps also noteworthy that a majority of Protestant respondents agree with the suggestion that children should be able to get away from the political problems of Northern Ireland while at school. Despite the fact that most of those with no religion agreed that schools should address these issues, there is doubt that teachers would present these issues fairly. Respondents with no religion share a degree of support for the view that schools should represent havens from political conflict, although for these respondents these concerns may be mainly related to their views on the inappropriateness of segregated education.

Table 8.10 Attitudes to the teaching of politics and human rights in schools (%)

|  | Strongly agree/ agree | Neither | Strongly disagree/ disagree |
|---|---|---|---|
| *It isn't the job of schools to teach about politics and human rights* | | | |
| All respondents | 36 | 11 | 50 |
| Protestant | 43 | 11 | 41 |
| Catholic | 26 | 10 | 61 |
| No religion | 31 | 16 | 50 |
| *It's about time schools started to openly tackle such difficult issues* | | | |
| All respondents | 58 | 12 | 26 |
| Protestant | 49 | 13 | 34 |
| Catholic | 69 | 10 | 19 |
| No religion | 63 | 14 | 20 |
| *I doubt whether people teaching this kind of thing would do it fairly* | | | |
| All respondents | 42 | 20 | 34 |
| Protestant | 47 | 21 | 27 |
| Catholic | 32 | 19 | 44 |
| No religion | 51 | 15 | 29 |
| *Schools should be a place where children are able to get away from the political problems of Northern Ireland* | | | |
| All respondents | 48 | 16 | 32 |
| Protestant | 55 | 17 | 26 |
| Catholic | 39 | 15 | 43 |
| No religion | 49 | 15 | 32 |

Secondly, respondents' views were sought on the potentially positive aspects that might be gained from teaching politics and human rights in schools. The results in Table 8.11 show that around one half of respondents feel that teaching politics and human rights in schools will encourage young people to become more effective and active members of society and more active in their own communities. At the same time, the views of Protestant respondents on these items is somewhat more mixed. One issue on which a clear majority of respondents do agree is that teaching politics and human rights in school will lead to greater understanding of grievances held by communities in Northern Ireland. However, a cynical interpretation of this result may be that many people believe it will lead to a greater understanding of the grievances held by *their* community, rather than a greater understanding by them of the grievances held by *other* communities.

Table 8.11 Attitudes to the potentially positive effects on children of teaching politics and human rights in school (%)

|  | Strongly agree/ agree | Neither | Strongly disagree/ disagree |
|---|---|---|---|
| *Our children will never be effective members of society unless we allow them to learn about human rights and politics when they are young* |  |  |  |
| All respondents | 51 | 15 | 31 |
| Protestant | 44 | 17 | 35 |
| Catholic | 59 | 13 | 25 |
| No religion | 52 | 16 | 27 |
| *Teaching about human rights and politics at school will help young people become active members of their own communities* |  |  |  |
| All respondents | 50 | 18 | 28 |
| Protestant | 44 | 20 | 32 |
| Catholic | 58 | 15 | 25 |
| No religion | 55 | 19 | 23 |
| *Discussions about politics and human rights will help children understand why other traditions in Northern Ireland feel hard done by* |  |  |  |
| All respondents | 62 | 16 | 19 |
| Protestant | 56 | 19 | 20 |
| Catholic | 67 | 12 | 18 |
| No religion | 70 | 12 | 15 |

Thirdly, respondents were asked about some possible negative consequences of teaching politics and human rights in schools. Table 8.12 shows that just over half of respondents (52 per cent) reject the suggestion that teaching politics and human rights in school would lead to 'brainwashing', although among Protestant respondents this is not a majority view. Thereafter the responses indicate some concerns on the part of many about the difficulties that could arise in this area. Thus, for example, many respondents (34 per cent) feel that teaching about politics and human rights in school could run the risk of encouraging young people to adopt extreme political views, although this concern is not shared by Catholic respondents. In a related vein, about one half of respondents (49 per cent) feel that discussions on these topics in school would be difficult for young people who have suffered personally as a consequence of the violence, although again this view is held more strongly among Protestant respondents than others.

Table 8.12 Attitudes to the potentially negative effects on children of teaching politics and human rights in school (%)

|  | Strongly agree/ agree | Neither | Strongly disagree/ disagree |
|---|---|---|---|
| *Teaching children about politics and human rights at school is just trying to brainwash them* | | | |
| All respondents | 29 | 15 | 52 |
| Protestant | 36 | 16 | 45 |
| Catholic | 22 | 14 | 61 |
| No religion | 21 | 19 | 56 |
| *Teaching about human rights and politics at school runs the risk of encouraging children towards extreme political views* | | | |
| All respondents | 34 | 18 | 44 |
| Protestant | 39 | 18 | 38 |
| Catholic | 25 | 16 | 56 |
| No religion | 37 | 21 | 40 |
| *Discussions about politics and human rights at school will be too difficult for a lot of children who have suffered personally during the Troubles* | | | |
| All respondents | 49 | 20 | 27 |
| Protestant | 56 | 19 | 22 |
| Catholic | 40 | 20 | 35 |
| No religion | 42 | 24 | 30 |

These results suggest a reasonably favourable climate towards the possible introduction of some form of citizenship education in Northern Ireland schools, while also highlighting a number of possible concerns that many people hold on the possible consequences of this development. However, having gone through all these issues, when asked if, on balance, respondents felt that it was a good idea to teach about politics and human rights in schools, 60 per cent say definitely or probably 'yes'. This general view is shared across all groups, with the only difference lying in the extent to which the view is held. Thus, for example, whereas 69 per cent of Catholics and 65 per cent of those with no religion say definitely or probably 'yes' to the teaching of politics and human rights in schools, this was so for 53 per cent of Protestants.

## *Conclusion*

The two most distinctive aspects of the education system in Northern Ireland, as compared with schools in the rest of the UK, lie in the continued use of selection at age eleven years to divide pupils between grammar and secondary schools (Gallagher and Smith, 2000; Post-Primary Review Body, 2001), and the existence of de facto separate Protestant and Catholic schools, alongside a relatively small number of religiously integrated schools. In addition, while Northern Ireland has been influenced by the education policy in the UK generally, there has also been a commitment to working through the schools to promote improved community relations. In this chapter we have examined views on a number of issues that are related to all of these themes.

We have found a high degree of dissatisfaction with key aspects of the selective system of secondary education and, in particular, the tests used to select pupils at age eleven years. At the same time, there is a widespread view that some form of selection is probably inevitable and that grammar schools provide a high quality of education. Most respondents favour the end of the eleven-plus tests and many feel that pupils should attend the same school until age 14 or even 16 years. However, while there is general agreement that some change should occur, there is limited consensus on the exact nature of that change.

In the area of integrated education, there is a continuing high level of support for an expansion in integrated provision and a widespread perception that the limited number of places available in integrated schools at present is the main limiting factor in parental choice for this option. When asked how the number of places in integrated schools might be best expanded, the main view is that the government should encourage more schools to transform to integrated status. Only a small proportion of respondents favour the development of entirely new integrated schools.

One way in which the government has attempted to promote improved community relations is through the statutory curriculum in schools. Respondents were asked about certain aspects of diversity in the curriculum, in particular through the teaching of language and culture and the teaching of religious beliefs. There is limited evidence of strong support for a more diverse curriculum. In general Catholic respondents and, to a lesser extent, those with no religion, tend to favour a more diverse curriculum. By contrast, Protestant respondents display more reticence in this area and their views are much more evenly divided.

The final series of questions asked for views on the teaching of politics and human rights in schools, issues that could arise if current proposals to develop a citizenship education programme come to fruition in the revised statutory curriculum. In general, respondents give reasonable endorsement of these proposals and, in particular, feel that the teaching of these topics would probably increase understanding of aspects of the conflict in Northern Ireland. However, as with the views on diversity in the curriculum, Protestant respondents are somewhat more reticent than others on this issue. In addition, there are some issues on which respondents with no religion express a degree of concern, which is probably related to concerns about the way politics and human rights might be taught in the context of a religiously divided schools system. It is noteworthy also that many of the respondents do have some concerns about the potential impact of addressing these issues in schools when so many young people will have had direct personal suffering as a consequence of the violence.

## *References*

Agnew, U., McEwan, A., Salters, J. and Salters, M. (1992) *Integrated Education: The Views of Parents* (Belfast: Queen's University, School of Education).

Akenson, D.H. (1973) *Education and Enmity: The Control of Schooling in Northern Ireland, 1920–1950* (Newton Abbot: David and Charles).

Alexander, J., Daly, P., Gallagher, A.M., Gray, C. and Sutherland, A.E. (1998) *An Evaluation of the Craigavon Two-tier System* (Bangor: Department of Education for Northern Ireland).

Barnes, L.P. (1997) 'Reforming religious education in Northern Ireland: a critical review' *British Journal of Religious Education*, Vol. 19, No. 2, pp. 73–82.

Council for the Curriculum Examinations and Assessment (CCEA) (1997) *Education for Mutual Understanding and Cultural Heritage: Guidance for Schools* (Belfast: CCEA).

Darby, J. (1973) 'Divisiveness in education', *The Northern Teacher*, Vol. 11, No. 1, pp. 3–12.

Darby, J. and Dunn, S. (1987) 'Segregated schools: the research evidence' in R.D. Osborne, R.J. Cormack, R.L. Miller (eds)

*Education and Policy in Northern Ireland* (Belfast: Policy Research Institute) pp. 85–98.

Fraser, R.M. (1973) *Children in Conflict* (London: Secker and Wartburg).

Gallagher, A.M. (1988) *Transfer Pupils at 16* (Belfast: Northern Ireland Council for Educational Research).

Gallagher, A.M. (1995) 'Equity, contact and pluralism: attitudes to community relations' in R. Breen, P. Devine and G. Robinson (eds) *Social Attitudes in Northern Ireland: The Fourth Report, 1994–1995* (Belfast: Appletree Press) pp. 13–32.

Gallagher, T. and Smith, A. (2000) *The Effects of the Selective System of Secondary Education in Northern Ireland: Main Report* (Bangor: Department of Education for Northern Ireland).

Kerr, D. (1999) *Citizenship Education: An International Comparison*, International Review of Curriculum and Assessment Frameworks Paper 4 (London: QCA).

Leitch, R. and Kilpatrick, R. (1999) *Beyond the School Gates* (Belfast: Save the Children).

Moffat, C. (ed.) (1993) *Education Together for a Change* (Belfast: Fortnight Educational Trust).

Morgan, V., Dunn, S., Cairns, E. and Fraser, G. (1992) *Breaking the Mould. The Role of Parents and Teachers in the Integrated Schools in Northern Ireland* (Coleraine: Centre for the Study of Conflict, University of Ulster).

Post-Primary Review Body (2001) *Education for the 21st Century* (Belfast: Post-Primary Review Body) <http://www.deni.gov.uk/review/index.htm>.

Smith, A. (2001) 'Religious segregation and the emergence of integrated schools in Northern Ireland', *Oxford Review of Education*, Vol. 27, No. 4, pp. 559–75.

Smith, A. and Robinson, A. (1992) *Education for Mutual Understanding, Perceptions and Policy* (Coleraine: Centre for the Study of Conflict, University of Ulster).

Smith, A. and Robinson, A. (1996) *An Evaluation of Education for Mutual Understanding: The Initial, Statutory Years* (Coleraine: University of Ulster).

Spencer, A.E.C.W. (1987) 'Arguments for an integrated school system' in R.D. Osborne, R.J. Cormack, and R.L. Miller (eds) *Education and Policy in Northern Ireland* (Belfast: Policy Research Institute) pp. 99–114.

Sutherland, A.E. and Gallagher, A.M. (1986) *Transfer and the Upper Primary School* (Belfast: Northern Ireland Council for Educational Research).

Sutherland, A.E. and Gallagher A.M. (1987) *Pupils in the Border Band* (Belfast: Northern Ireland Council for Educational Research).

Teare, S. and Sutherland, A.E. (1988) *At Sixes and Sevens* (Belfast: Northern Ireland Council for Educational Research).

Torney-Purta, J., Schwille, J. and Amadeo, J.-A. (eds) (1999) *Civic Education Across Countries: Twenty-four Case Studies from the Civic Education Project* (Amsterdam: Eburon Publishers for the International Association for the Evaluation of Educational Achievement).

Wilson, J.A. (1986) *Transfer and the Structure of Secondary Education* (Belfast: Northern Ireland Council for Educational Research).

# 9 The Rights of the Child in Northern Ireland: Teenage Attitudes and Social Responsibilities

*Kerry O'Halloran*

As peace begins to bed down in Northern Ireland, this is an appropriate time to take stock of how the more vulnerable groups in our society are coping. The blanket effect of 30 years of violence has prevented a full appreciation of just how marginal and ignored some groups have become. A corollary to the legacy of violence, bitterness and lack of trust in this jurisdiction is the deficit in policy initiatives addressing the broader aspects of social inclusion. Whereas other modern Western societies have spent some decades wrestling with issues such as how best to respond to the problems suffered by those disadvantaged by a social perception of inadequacy due to disability, race, age, gender and so on, in this jurisdiction these issues have largely been on hold. Instead, as communities coped with the more immediate pressures of direct violence and the not unrelated phenomenon of the highest level of unemployment in these islands, social inclusion policies were quietly deferred. Now, with a return to normal politics, there is a growing awareness that those such as the disabled, the travelling community, the gay and lesbian community and other minorities belonging, for example, to non-white racial groups, are relatively more disadvantaged in this than in other United Kingdom jurisdictions. A priority for the Northern Ireland Assembly and for relevant government departments in the first years of representative democracy will have to be a social inclusion programme which addresses the neglected needs of the long overlooked minority groups in our society.

Children and young people are such a group. In no jurisdiction in these islands have the needs of children been so pushed to one side and so dominated by the violence of their elders. In the aftermath of the Westminster endorsement of the United Nations (UN) Convention on the Rights of the Child and the Declaration of Rights, it is appropriate to enquire as to how these provisions are now impacting upon the lives and perceptions of children and young people in Northern Ireland. In the years following the introduction of the Children (NI) Order 1995, which set the agenda for the most significant change to the law affecting children ever made in this jurisdiction, it is important to ask whether children are aware of its provisions. Has it made any difference to their rights and their capacity to exercise those rights? This chapter responds to that challenge by examining the rights of the child in Northern Ireland. It does so by considering the findings from the Rights of the Child module in the 1998 Northern Ireland Life and Times survey and Young Life and Times survey against the background of the current law.

In this jurisdiction, the rights of the child are legally determined within a context of rights and principles set by international, national and regional legislation as mediated through the appropriate courts. Increasingly, such rights, and the corresponding responsibilities of other parties in respect of a child, are now being considered against the backdrop of relatively recently introduced legislation applying governing principles. The chapter, therefore, begins by examining the new legal context for children's rights as established by the UN Convention on the Rights of the Child and the Declaration of Rights. It then moves to briefly consider the broad principles of equity, non-discrimination and rights established in recent years to protect the interests of all citizens in Northern Ireland. From that background, the chapter then focuses on some aspects of the current domestic law in relation to children's rights and how these play out in the courts. Having considered the broad rights context and identified the international and domestic law relating to the rights of the child the chapter then turns to examine the views of both young people and adults in Northern Ireland regarding their rights. The chapter concludes with some comments on the surveys and recommendations for improving general awareness of the rights of the child in Northern Ireland.

### International Conventions

There is now a raft of legislation emanating from Europe with a bearing on how the rights of children are to be given effect in our courts. Most of this is issue specific, for example relating to inter-country adoption. Two pieces of legislation are of more fundamental importance: the UN Convention on the Rights of the Child and the Convention for the Protection of Human Rights and Fundamental Freedoms.

The UN Convention on the Rights of the Child was ratified by the UK, but not incorporated into its legislation, on 16 December 1991. It requires the courts in Northern Ireland, in common with those elsewhere in the UK, to ensure that decisions broadly comply with the general and specific obligations set out in the Convention (Kilkelly, 1999). Of these obligations, the most important are set out in Articles 2 and 3. Article 2 declares that children shall not be discriminated against and shall have equal access to protection. Article 3 requires that in all actions concerning a child undertaken by courts of law, administrative authorities or legislative bodies, the best interests of that child shall be the primary consideration. The state must take all appropriate legislative and administrative measures to ensure such protection and care as is necessary for the child's wellbeing.[1] Articles 44 and 45 require the state to report on the measures it has adopted which give effect to the rights recognised in the Convention and on the progress made on enjoyment of those rights (HMSO, 1994; 1999). This is the most widely ratified of the UN Conventions and its effect on accelerating the modernising of the law relating to children in Northern Ireland cannot be overestimated.

The Human Rights Act 1998, giving effect to the Convention for the Protection of Human Rights and Fundamental Freedoms, came into force in October 2000. From that date the case law resulting from decisions of the European Commission on Human Rights (ECHR) has had a direct relevance for the courts in Northern Ireland. Article 2 of this act requires that parents be involved in any decision-making process to a degree sufficient to provide them with the requisite protection of their interests. If they are not so involved there will have been a failure to respect their family life. Article 8(1) guarantees the right to respect for private and family life and for home and correspondence. Article 8(2) declares that a public authority shall not interfere with the right to respect for family life.[2] Essentially, this article aims to provide protection for an individual against arbitrary action by public authorities, for example a Health and Social Services Trust. Article 14 provides that the rights enumerated in the Convention shall be assured without discrimination.

Both of these conventions are important because they provide a body of governing principles against which the law and practice of all signatory states can be benchmarked. This readily permits the identification of instances where a jurisdiction, such as Northern Ireland, is failing to meet international standards for protecting rights, such as those of children. Of the two, it is the Human Rights Act 1998 which will have the most far-reaching consequences for the rights of the child, and others. As the judgments given by the courts in this jurisdiction repeatedly illustrate,[3] decisions affecting the rights and welfare interests of a child must now be proofed against the requirements of the 1998 Act.

Arguably, however, there is more to embedding rights awareness than providing for their recognition and enforcement in legislation and related court proceedings. Rights require measures for their positive affirmation, not just measures which permit a victim to seek redress in the event of their breach. Rights are of primary importance to the minority group for which they were designed, but are also of importance to the rest of society. Their rights are our responsibility as they articulate and give effect to our collective values. It is not enough that a minority group is granted rights then left to defend them in court. There also has to be a preventative framework within which society as a whole can be alerted to the existence and significance of the new rights and the resulting practical implications for our customary way of treating that group. Positive initiatives are required to promote rights awareness, to prevent if possible their breach and to address the circumstances in which breaches have occurred. In relation to children, this approach points inescapably to the need for a new agency or post to be created and statutorily charged with such duties. The role and responsibilities of a body similar to the Equality Commission for Northern Ireland now needs to be applied to the rights context for children. Hopefully, this gap will shortly be filled by the office of Children's Commissioner (NI).[4]

### The Equality Legislation in Northern Ireland

The rights of the child must also be considered against the background of domestic legislation dealing with equality matters and administered by the Equality Commission for Northern Ireland. The main pieces of equality legislation are:

- Equal Pay Act (NI) 1970 (amended in 1994);
- Sex Discrimination (NI) Order 1976 (amended 1998);
- Disability Discrimination Act 1995;
- Race Relations (NI) Order 1997;
- Fair Employment and Treatment (NI) Order 1998;
- Northern Ireland Act 1998; and
- Equality (Disability, etc.) (NI) Order 2000.

For the purposes of children's rights, the statutory provisions providing for equality of opportunity and entitlement to non-discriminatory practices, as embodied in the 1976 Order, the 1995 Act and the 1997 Order, are the most important. This body of legislation dealing with equity, equality and non-discrimination provides a relatively new and important context for the rights of children in Northern Ireland. It sets out quite specific rights intended as much for their protection as for the protection of adults. It has also promoted the growth of a rights culture and established an expectation that the courts in this jurisdiction will be vigilant and vigorous in their recognition and protection of rights.

## The Rights of the Child within the Current Northern Ireland Legislative Context

The legal concept of a child as the bearer of rights rather than the subject of welfare concerns is a modern development (Freeman and Veerman, 1992; O'Halloran, 1999). It represents a very real paradigm shift in the way society views children (Eekelaar, 1986; Freeman, 1996; Fortin, 1998).

The history of the law relating to children is primarily a history of the changing grounds on which authority can or should be used to assign responsibility for their care, protection or control to a parent, other adult or body. Only in the last century or so has a recognition of their welfare interests emerged and it has taken until recent decades for this to evolve into the present quite sophisticated understanding of the relative importance of different elements of welfare depending on the age of the child (Goldstein, Freud and Solnit, 1973; 1986; Mnookin, 1985). Contemporary law provides for recognition of a child's welfare interests and determines their role and weighting in various decision-making processes and court proceedings. This seems appropriate. Children, by definition, are not as self-sufficient as adults and, depending on their age, must have their developmental and other needs recognised and protected by the law. Their wishes are to be sought and taken into account when decisions are made on matters affecting their interests.[5] Again, this is appropriate provided it is done in a manner and on issues which allow for age-related concerns. Contemporary law, however, now recognises that children also have rights to be asserted by them or on their behalf in competition with the rights of others. How to strike the most appropriate balance between welfare and rights, relative to the age and needs of a particular child and relative to the significance of the issue for the rights of others, is a dilemma of central importance to modern family law (Veerman, 1991).

Within the UK, the change from an emphasis on welfare to rights is one which arrived latest in Northern Ireland. Arguably, it has yet to be fully assimilated into our law and has a long way to go before we can say with confidence that it is reflected in the more generally prevailing attitudes of our society. There is a sense in which the law has embraced, or has had grafted on to it, new governing principles which have yet to be given effect through joined up legislative provisions in a coherent body of laws relating to children.[6] Practice and procedure have yet to catch up with principle.

In Northern Ireland, the legislative introduction of a new rights approach to issues affecting the upbringing of children in civil proceedings was signalled with the arrival of the Children (NI) Order 1995[7] and the setting up of the Family Proceedings courts.[8] The traditional welfare approach was not abandoned: indeed the provisions of the 1995 Order are largely concerned with identifying, safeguarding, promoting and ensuring paramountcy for the welfare interests of children across a range of proceedings. This approach is now balanced by provisions in the 1995 Order, which remove parental rights, substitute parental responsibilities and provide important rights for asserting and protecting the interests of children. In the latter context, perhaps the most important innovation has been the introduction of a *guardian ad litem* to provide independent representation for a child's welfare interests balanced by the availability of a solicitor to assert the rights of that child.[9] This statute and the ancillary body of rules and regulations have together established in Northern Ireland a wholly new legal platform for children's rights and constituted many new fora in which they may be exercised.[10]

## The Rights of the Child Module

Arguably, for any minority group to become genuinely empowered they must first know their rights and how they can be asserted (Flekkoy, 1991). Otherwise they will be left dependent upon the knowledge, skills, availability and agenda of others. So, what do our children know about their rights?

The data for this chapter are drawn from the Rights of the Child module, which examines the attitudes of young people and adults on a series of rights awareness issues. The data were collected in 1998 at a time when there was considerable media coverage of rights issues in the national and regional media. After all, this was the year when the Human Rights Act was passed in Westminster, the year after the Children's Law Centre was established in Belfast, and within the previous two years, legislation had been introduced to address the rights of children, disability discrimination and race relations in Northern Ireland. The issue of human rights was never more prevalent in Northern Ireland. It might be expected, therefore, that both children and adults would be alert to rights issues.

The issues included in the module are relevant and wide-ranging. However, in a quantitative survey of this nature, it is not appropriate to explore issues which might be regarded as more distinctively characteristic of the youth of Northern Ireland or the 'big' rights issues that are more generally prevalent among young people of all jurisdictions.

Fifteen questions from the Rights of the Child module were asked of both adults and young people aged between 12 and 17. This allows for comparative analysis between the responses of adults and young people.

*Young People and Their Treatment by Society*

Respondents were asked if they agreed or disagreed with the statement that 'these days schools encourage teenagers to express their views'. As Table 9.1 shows, there is overwhelming agreement among young people (80 per cent) and much the same response from the adults (81 per cent). Females are more likely to agree than males (83 per cent and 78 per cent respectively) and there is also some variation across religious groups, with more Catholic (83 per cent) and Protestant (80 per cent) respondents agreeing than those with no religion (75 per cent).

It is encouraging to see from these findings that most respondents believe that schools are positively supporting young people to find their voices and to be heard on matters concerning them.

Table 9.1 These days schools encourage teenagers to express their views (%)

|  | Strongly agree/agree | Neither agree nor disagree | Strongly disagree/disagree | Don't know |
|---|---|---|---|---|
| *Age* | | | | |
| 12–17 years | 80 | 8 | 9 | 4 |
| 18 years and over | 81 | 8 | 6 | 5 |
| *Gender* | | | | |
| Male | 78 | 9 | 7 | 6 |
| Female | 83 | 7 | 7 | 4 |
| *Religion* | | | | |
| Catholic | 83 | 7 | 6 | 5 |
| Protestant | 80 | 10 | 6 | 4 |
| No religion | 75 | 6 | 15 | 4 |

Approximately two out of five young people agree that 'most employers treat young people fairly', while a considerable proportion equivocate (14 per cent neither agree nor disagree and 13 per cent don't know) (Table 9.2). More adults than young people disagree and respondents with no religion are more likely to disagree (48 per cent) than Catholics (39 per cent) or Protestants (31 per cent).

There is a marked difference of opinion between young people and adults to the assertion that 'teenagers are always treated like second-class citizens in shops and cafes' (Table 9.3). Three out of five young people compared with only 37 per cent of adults agree. There is little variation across gender and religious groups except that Catholic respondents are more likely than Protestant respondents to agree (49 per cent and 41 per cent respectively).

Table 9.2 Most employers treat young people fairly (%)

|  | Strongly agree/agree | Neither agree nor disagree | Strongly disagree/disagree | Don't know |
|---|---|---|---|---|
| *Age* | | | | |
| 12–17 years | 43 | 14 | 30 | 13 |
| 18 years and over | 38 | 16 | 38 | 8 |
| *Gender* | | | | |
| Male | 42 | 14 | 36 | 9 |
| Female | 38 | 18 | 35 | 10 |
| *Religion* | | | | |
| Catholic | 40 | 13 | 39 | 9 |
| Protestant | 40 | 19 | 31 | 9 |
| No religion | 35 | 11 | 48 | 6 |

Table 9.3 Teenagers are always treated like second class citizens in shops and cafes (%)

|  | Strongly agree/agree | Neither agree nor disagree | Strongly disagree/disagree | Don't know |
|---|---|---|---|---|
| *Age* | | | | |
| 12–17 years | 60 | 12 | 24 | 5 |
| 18 years and over | 37 | 19 | 38 | 6 |
| *Gender* | | | | |
| Male | 43 | 17 | 35 | 6 |
| Female | 46 | 16 | 32 | 5 |
| *Religion* | | | | |
| Catholic | 49 | 15 | 30 | 6 |
| Protestant | 41 | 19 | 36 | 5 |
| No religion | 46 | 15 | 35 | 4 |

*Young People and Politics*

Given the political situation in Northern Ireland and the prominence of political issues in everyday life, it is not surprising that the Life and Times survey included a series of questions on attitudes to politics and politicians. Just under one third (32 per cent) of young people agree with the statement that 'none of our politicians are bothered about the problems facing young people in Northern Ireland today' (Table 9.4). Interestingly, adults are much more likely to agree with this statement than young people (44 per cent). Noticeably more men (39 per cent) than women disagree (34 per cent) while those with no religion are less likely to agree than Catholics or Protestants (32 per cent as opposed to 44 per cent of Catholics and 37 per cent of Protestants).

Table 9.4 Politicians are not bothered about the problems facing young people today (%)

|  | Strongly agree/agree | Neither agree nor disagree | Strongly disagree/disagree | Don't know |
|---|---|---|---|---|
| *Age* | | | | |
| 12–17 years | 32 | 12 | 41 | 15 |
| 18 years and over | 44 | 17 | 34 | 5 |
| *Gender* | | | | |
| Male | 38 | 15 | 39 | 8 |
| Female | 42 | 16 | 34 | 9 |
| *Religion* | | | | |
| Catholic | 44 | 12 | 35 | 9 |
| Protestant | 37 | 19 | 38 | 7 |
| No religion | 32 | 18 | 38 | 12 |

Table 9.5 shows that the suggestion that 'there should be a way to give young people a voice in politics in Northern Ireland' is strongly endorsed by young people (85 per cent agreeing), only a tiny minority disagreeing (4 per cent) and a few either not knowing or having no opinion (7 per cent and 4 per cent respectively). The majority of adults (81 per cent) also agree that there should be a way to give young people a voice in politics in Northern Ireland. The survey found little gender variation, but a clear difference across religious groups is evident: more Catholics than Protestants or those with no religion agree with the statement (87 per cent and 79 per cent respectively).

Table 9.5 There should be a way to give young people a voice in politics in Northern Ireland (%)

|  | Strongly agree/agree | Neither agree nor disagree | Strongly disagree/disagree | Don't know |
|---|---|---|---|---|
| *Age* | | | | |
| 12–17 years | 85 | 4 | 4 | 7 |
| 18 years and over | 81 | 10 | 6 | 3 |
| *Gender* | | | | |
| Male | 81 | 8 | 7 | 4 |
| Female | 83 | 8 | 4 | 4 |
| *Religion* | | | | |
| Catholic | 87 | 5 | 4 | 4 |
| Protestant | 79 | 11 | 6 | 3 |
| No religion | 79 | 10 | 6 | 5 |

There is a fairly lukewarm response by young people to the statement that 'young people are just not interested in politics in Northern Ireland' (Table 9.6). Half of all young people disagree with the statement while just over one quarter agree (26 per cent). The adult responses are similar to those of the young people. Slightly more males than females agree that young people are just not interested in politics (29 per cent and 25 per cent respectively). There is little variation across religious groups, with Catholic respondents least likely to agree and most likely to disagree that young people are not interested in politics.

This strong endorsement for the idea that young people are keen to be heard and would welcome the opportunity to influence contemporary politics is undermined by the finding that only half of them believe that young people are interested in politics.

Table 9.6 Young people are just not interested in politics (%)

|  | Strongly agree/agree | Neither agree nor disagree | Strongly disagree/disagree | Don't know |
|---|---|---|---|---|
| *Age* | | | | |
| 12–17 years | 26 | 16 | 50 | 8 |
| 18 years and over | 27 | 22 | 47 | 4 |
| *Gender* | | | | |
| Male | 29 | 20 | 46 | 5 |
| Female | 25 | 20 | 50 | 6 |
| *Religion* | | | | |
| Catholic | 26 | 17 | 52 | 6 |
| Protestant | 27 | 23 | 45 | 5 |
| No religion | 30 | 21 | 45 | 5 |

*Young People and Their Rights*

In the area of rights awareness, a key question for children and young people around the world is 'have you ever heard of the UN Convention on the Rights of the Child?' Responses from most young people are mainly negative (72 per cent), with only one quarter (25 per cent) replying in the affirmative. The remaining 4 per cent don't know (Table 9.7). The adult response is a bit more positive, with over one third (36 per cent) saying they have heard of the Convention. Thirty-four per cent of males and 31 per cent of females have heard of the Convention, while Catholics are most likely (34 per cent), and those with no religion least likely (29 per cent), to have heard of it.

Table 9.7 Have you ever heard of the UN Convention on the Rights of the Child? (%)

|  | Yes | No | Don't know |
|---|---|---|---|
| *Age* | | | |
| 12–17 years | 25 | 72 | 4 |
| 18 years and over | 36 | 60 | 4 |
| *Gender* | | | |
| Male | 34 | 63 | 4 |
| Female | 31 | 65 | 4 |
| *Religion* | | | |
| Catholic | 34 | 62 | 4 |
| Protestant | 32 | 65 | 3 |
| No religion | 29 | 71 | 1 |

The Life and Times survey explored the attitudes of respondents towards the rights and opportunities of children in Northern Ireland to express their views. When asked 'should young people have more opportunity to express their views, less opportunity, or is it about right the way it is now?', Table 9.8 shows that the vast majority of young people believe more opportunities are required (84 per cent). Only 9 per cent consider that it is about right, a tiny minority think they should have less opportunity (1 per cent) while 5 per cent don't know. The adults have a different view with around one third (31 per cent) believing that the current opportunities are about right, 61 per cent that more opportunities should be provided and a small minority (4 per cent) believing that fewer opportunities should be available. More women than men (72 per cent and 64 per cent respectively) and many more Catholics (76 per cent) than Protestants (62 per cent) believe that young people should have more opportunities to express their views.

Table 9.8 Should young people have more opportunity to express their views? (%)

|  | More opportunity | Less opportunity | About right | Don't know |
|---|---|---|---|---|
| *Age* | | | | |
| 12–17 years | 84 | 1 | 9 | 5 |
| 18 years and over | 61 | 4 | 31 | 5 |
| *Gender* | | | | |
| Male | 64 | 3 | 26 | 6 |
| Female | 72 | 3 | 21 | 4 |
| *Religion* | | | | |
| Catholic | 76 | 3 | 18 | 4 |
| Protestant | 62 | 3 | 27 | 6 |
| No religion | 69 | 2 | 28 | 2 |

In response to the question 'do you think that young people in Northern Ireland today have more opportunity to express their views than young people 20 years ago, less opportunity or about the same?', 80 per cent of teenagers affirm the view that more opportunities are now available (Table 9.9), a view that is even stronger among adults (88 per cent).

The difference in findings between these questions and the earlier questions is interesting. It would seem that despite a willingness to express their views, together with greater opportunities and encouragement to do so, young people are not receiving or are not assimilating the rights information necessary to inform those views.

Table 9.9 Do young people have more opportunity to express their views today than 20 years ago? (%)

| | More opportunity | Less opportunity | About right | Don't know |
|---|---|---|---|---|
| *Age* | | | | |
| 12–17 years | 80 | 6 | 0 | 13 |
| 18 years and over | 88 | 2 | 7 | 3 |
| *Gender* | | | | |
| Male | 86 | 3 | 4 | 7 |
| Female | 86 | 4 | 5 | 5 |
| *Religion* | | | | |
| Catholic | 85 | 4 | 6 | 5 |
| Protestant | 86 | 3 | 5 | 7 |
| No religion | 89 | 5 | 2 | 4 |

## Young People and Drugs

Drugs are widely acknowledged to be a problem affecting today's youth, both in Northern Ireland and in other areas of the UK. It is therefore unsurprising that three questions in the Life and Times survey were devoted to exploring attitudes to drugs. In response to the assertion that 'the drug problem in Northern Ireland isn't nearly as bad as some people make out', Table 9.10 shows that more than half (54 per cent) of all young people disagree, only 21 per cent agree, while around one quarter either don't know (14 per cent) or have no view on the matter (11 per cent). The adult response is more unequivocal with 73 per cent disagreeing and only 12 per cent agreeing that the drug problem in Northern Ireland isn't nearly as bad as some people make out. Fewer males than females disagree (64 per cent and 70 per cent respectively) while respondents who have no religion are more likely to agree than Catholics or Protestants (23 per cent as opposed to 13 per cent of Catholics and 15 per cent of Protestants).

Table 9.10 The drug problem in Northern Ireland isn't nearly as bad as some people make out (%)

|  | Strongly agree/agree | Neither agree nor disagree | Strongly disagree/disagree | Don't know |
|---|---|---|---|---|
| *Age* |  |  |  |  |
| 12–17 years | 21 | 11 | 54 | 14 |
| 18 years and over | 12 | 7 | 73 | 8 |
| *Gender* |  |  |  |  |
| Male | 17 | 10 | 64 | 9 |
| Female | 12 | 7 | 70 | 11 |
| *Religion* |  |  |  |  |
| Catholic | 13 | 7 | 69 | 11 |
| Protestant | 15 | 10 | 67 | 8 |
| No religion | 23 | 7 | 63 | 6 |

More than half (54 per cent) of all young people agree with the statement that 'it's not hard to get hold of drugs in most schools if you really want to', 25 per cent disagree, 14 per cent don't know and the remaining 7 per cent neither agree nor disagree (Table 9.11). The adult response is more affirmative, with the proportion in agreement reaching almost two thirds (65 per cent) and only a small minority disagreeing (9 per cent). There are no marked variations across gender or religious groups.

Table 9.11 It is not hard to get hold of drugs in most schools (%)

|  | Strongly agree/agree | Neither agree nor disagree | Strongly disagree/disagree | Don't know |
|---|---|---|---|---|
| *Age* |  |  |  |  |
| 12–17 years | 54 | 7 | 25 | 14 |
| 18 years and over | 65 | 10 | 9 | 16 |
| *Gender* |  |  |  |  |
| Male | 60 | 10 | 13 | 16 |
| Female | 63 | 8 | 14 | 15 |
| *Religion* |  |  |  |  |
| Catholic | 61 | 10 | 14 | 16 |
| Protestant | 64 | 9 | 13 | 15 |
| No religion | 63 | 9 | 16 | 12 |

The majority (72 per cent) of young people agree with the statement that 'the best people to educate teenagers about drugs are other young people themselves', a small minority (14 per cent) disagree while the same proportion has no view on the matter (Table 9.12). This is broadly endorsed by the adult response, although fewer adults than young people agree with the statement (61 per cent). Females are more likely than males to agree (69 per cent and 61 per cent respectively) and there is marked variation across the religious groups with more Catholics (71 per cent) than Protestants (60 per cent) or those with no religion (66 per cent) agreeing that the best people to educate teenagers about drugs are other young people.

Table 9.12 The best people to educate teenagers about drugs are other young people themselves (%)

|  | Strongly agree/agree | Neither agree nor disagree | Strongly disagree/disagree | Don't know |
|---|---|---|---|---|
| *Age* | | | | |
| 12–17 years | 72 | 6 | 14 | 8 |
| 18 years and over | 61 | 13 | 20 | 5 |
| *Gender* | | | | |
| Male | 61 | 13 | 22 | 5 |
| Female | 69 | 9 | 15 | 7 |
| *Religion* | | | | |
| Catholic | 71 | 9 | 15 | 5 |
| Protestant | 60 | 13 | 21 | 6 |
| No religion | 66 | 9 | 21 | 5 |

These findings are unsurprising, though they might have been more interesting if the questions had unpicked the term 'drugs' to define and discriminate between different types.[11] Again, a significant finding is the perception that teenagers themselves provide the best potential educational resource.

*Facilities for Young People*

The module on the Rights of the Child concludes with three questions exploring attitudes towards the availability of facilities for teenagers. As Table 9.13 shows, a very large majority (84 per cent) of young people endorse the question 'do you think there should be more facilities, fewer or are there about the right amount?' Only a tiny minority (1 per cent) think there should be fewer facilities for young people, 11 per cent think that the number of facilities is about right and 4 per cent don't know. Three quarters of adult respondents believe there should be more facilities for young people while 18 per cent believe there are about the right amount. Fewer males than females think more facilities are needed for young people (75 per cent and 80 per cent respectively) while respondents with no religion (83 per cent) and Catholic respondents (81 per cent) are more likely than Protestant respondents (74 per cent) to think that more facilities should be provided.

Table 9.13 Do you think there should be more facilities, fewer or are there about the right amount? (%)

|  | More | Fewer | About the right amount | Don't know |
|---|---|---|---|---|
| *Age* | | | | |
| 12–17 years | 84 | 1 | 11 | 4 |
| 18 years and over | 75 | 1 | 18 | 6 |
| *Gender* | | | | |
| Male | 75 | 1 | 18 | 7 |
| Female | 80 | 2 | 14 | 4 |
| *Religion* | | | | |
| Catholic | 81 | 1 | 14 | 5 |
| Protestant | 74 | 2 | 18 | 6 |
| No religion | 83 | 0 | 14 | 3 |

Respondents were then presented with a list of facilities and asked to choose which one they believe is most needed. The list provided was rather conservative, with no reference to venues such as cyber cafes, video arcades, skateboard parks, etc. More than one quarter (28 per cent) of teenage respondents picked more leisure centres, 20 per cent more youth clubs, 15 per cent more cinemas, 8 per cent chose later and more frequent public transport, 9 per cent more concerts while the remainder were spread over other options with very few opting for more libraries (Table 9.14). There are some noticeable differences in the adult responses, one of which is that more adults (31 per cent) than young people believe there should be more youth clubs. This may be a reflection of the belief among many adults that youth clubs provide a safer environment for young people than cinemas or concert venues. Also, it is interesting to note that more adults than young people would like public transport to run more often and later than it does at present.

Table 9.14 Which of these facilities would you like to see more of? (%)

|  | 12–17 years | 18 years and over |
|---|---|---|
| More leisure centres | 28 | 25 |
| More youth clubs | 20 | 31 |
| More cinemas | 15 | 8 |
| More concerts | 9 | 6 |
| More and later public transport | 8 | 15 |
| Something else | 8 | 3 |
| Cheaper public transport | 6 | 6 |
| Don't know | 3 | 1 |
| More parks | 1 | 4 |
| More libraries | 1 | 1 |

The concluding question asked 'would you like to see the schools opened up during the summer?' Perhaps unsurprisingly, the response from the young people was equivocal with 40 per cent replying in the affirmative, 52 per cent in the negative and some 8 per cent not knowing (Table 9.15). The adult response is a good deal stronger with almost two thirds (65 per cent) replying in the affirmative and only 28 per cent disagreeing. There is no appreciable difference in responses across gender, although there is variation across religious groups: a large majority of those with no religion considered that the schools should be open in the summer (79 per cent as opposed to 52 per cent of Catholics and 60 per cent of Protestants).

It is somewhat surprising that the strong findings relating to the inadequacy of facilities for young people were not even stronger. There is a real need in Northern Ireland for more age appropriate, non-denominational, locally based, modern recreational facilities for children and young people. The interest in keeping schools open during the summer may well reflect disenchantment with the alternatives.

Table 9.15 Would you like to see the schools opened up during the summer? (%)

|  | Yes | No | Don't know |
| --- | --- | --- | --- |
| *Age* | | | |
| 12–17 years | 40 | 52 | 8 |
| 18 years and over | 65 | 28 | 7 |
| *Gender* | | | |
| Male | 56 | 36 | 8 |
| Female | 58 | 35 | 7 |
| *Religion* | | | |
| Catholic | 52 | 41 | 7 |
| Protestant | 60 | 33 | 7 |
| No religion | 79 | 18 | 4 |

### The Findings from the Rights of the Child Module

The findings from the module are rather worrying if not surprising. It was a low profile enquiry with no challenging propositions. It was not possible to explore the thorny issues which might be regarded as of more pressing concern for young people of this age group wherever they are resident, for example issues concerned with sexual relations, health, environment and financial independence. It conspicuously ignores the issues which are more distinctively characteristic of this age group in Northern Ireland. Attitudes to joy riding, violence and intimidation, cross-community relationships, bereavement, suicide and so on, which impact directly upon very many young people in this jurisdiction, were not seen as appropriate subjects in a survey of this kind. (For those interested in these subjects, please see Smyth and Scott, 2000.)

Yet, the findings are important because they reveal such a weak knowledge of rights and a poor appreciation of the opportunities in which they might be exercised. Despite the very real legal advances made in recent years in Northern Ireland in relation to the rights of children and others, it is salutary to reflect on how little this has impacted upon the awareness and attitudes of our young people. It is particularly disappointing that adults were unable to demonstrate a greater level of interest in children's rights.

Perhaps the survey also points to a possible strategy for improving young people's awareness of their rights? Given the strong endorsement for schools as the medium for articulating views and for young people as a self-learning resource, it may be that a specific information dissemination programme, targeted at schools and using a team of trained teenagers, might promote a greater general knowledge and appreciation of children's rights.

### Conclusion

In Northern Ireland, as elsewhere in Western society, the rights of children have now acquired a much greater legal salience than was ever available to any previous generation.[12] This is largely due to the influence of initiatives taken outside the jurisdiction, particularly the conventions and their attendant case law together with the example set by the Children Act 1989. Within this jurisdiction, the Children (NI) Order 1995 marked an enormously important step forward in the recognition of children's legal interests, both as regards their welfare and their rights, but much more needs to be done.

The findings from the Rights of the Child module graphically reveal one particular area where improvement is urgently required. The respondents' level of awareness of children's rights was surprisingly poor. Undoubtedly, in the intervening period, bodies such as the Children's Law Centre and the Northern Ireland Guardian ad Litem Agency have done a lot to raise that level. However, given the singular cultural/political context of this jurisdiction with 30 years of violence as testimony to its difficulty in accommodating the rights of minority groups, it is perhaps time to consider more radical and structural initiatives to ensure equitable civic space for all minorities. A Bill of Rights may now be necessary to address the position of children and young people as well as that of other minority groups and ensure that an awareness of the rights of children is fully embedded in our society

(Foster and Freed, 1972). Additionally, the assertive leadership now required to mainstream children's rights in education, health and social services and throughout our social infrastructure can probably only be satisfactorily progressed by a regionally based Children's Commissioner.

## Notes

1. Other important obligations include: Article 12 which gives children the right to be heard in all decisions taken which affect their interests; Article 18 which requires the state to render appropriate assistance to parents and legal guardians to facilitate the upbringing and development of their children; Article 19 which requires the state to take all appropriate legislative, administrative, social and educational measures to protect a child from all forms of physical or mental violence, injury or abuse, neglect or negligent treatment, maltreatment or exploitation, including sexual abuse, while in the care of parent, legal guardian or other person; and Article 27 which requires the state to recognise the right of every child to a standard of living adequate for that child's physical, mental, spiritual, moral and social development.
2. Subject to the exception that where to do so is: (a) in accordance with the law; and (b) is necessary in a democratic society (i) in the interests of national security, public safety or the economic wellbeing of the country, (ii) for the prevention of crime and disorder, (iii) for the protection of health or morals or (iv) for the protection of the rights and freedom of others.
3. See, for example, the judgment of Gillen J in *Re T (A Child) (Article 16(1)(b)(I) Adoption (NI) Order 1987 and the Inherent Jurisdiction*, unreported, the High Court (9.03.01) where he refers to *McMichael v UK* [1995], 20 EHRR 205 and *Johansen v Norway* [1996], 23 EHRR 33 for illustrative authority to substantiate his compliance with Articles 2, 8 and 6(1) of the 1998 Act.
4. See, further, Northern Ireland Human Rights Commission, *Making a Bill of Rights for Northern Ireland*, Belfast, 2001 (Chapter 10), 'The rights of children'. The Commission makes a strong case for including special protection for children's rights in a proposed Bill of Rights which would strengthen the position of a Children's Commissioner which also has its support.
5. A principle established in *Gillick v West Norfolk and Wisbech Area Health Authority* [1986] 1 AC 112, [1985] 3 All ER 402 HL; a decision which radically altered the law relating to the consent of a mature minor.

6. For example, the role and weighting given to the welfare interests of a child differs according to whether the issue arises in criminal or civil proceedings and, if the latter, whether in adoption or in other family proceedings, and according to whether a decision on the issue is made by the judiciary or by others.

7. The 1995 Order repealed legislation which had long gone from the statute books of England and Wales, including: the Custody of Infants Act 1873, the Guardianship of Infants Act 1886, the Custody of Children Act 1891 and the Illegitimate Children (Affiliation Orders) Act (NI) 1924. The 1995 Order thus did much more to advance the rights of children in Northern Ireland than the equivalent legislation – the Children Act 1989 – did for their counterparts in England and Wales.

8. This new structure is important for children's rights because it enables issues of public and private law to be consolidated and ensures that the child's interests are given a paramount weighting when such issues are being determined.

9. This twin-track approach to welfare and rights is restricted to family proceedings; there is no role for a *guardian ad litem* in criminal proceedings.

10. The 1995 Order has recently been supplemented by provisions in other legislation such as the Family Homes and Domestic Violence (NI) Order 1998 and the Family Law Bill 2001, which consolidate the rights approach.

11. The Centre for Child Care Research (School of Social Work, Queen's University Belfast) is concluding its regional study of adolescents and drug abuse. The findings provide evidence that this is now a significant problem in Northern Ireland. However, to appreciate the nature, extent and long-term implications of the problem it is necessary to distinguish between 'hard' and 'soft' drugs.

12. As an indicator of progress, it should be remembered that it is less than a century since the death penalty was abolished in respect of children (by the Children Act 1908) and slightly more than 50 years since the abolition of penal servitude, hard labour and whipping (by the Criminal Justice Act 1948).

### References

Eekelaar, J. (1986) 'The emergence of children's rights', *Oxford Journal of Legal Studies*, Vol. 161.

Flekkoy, M. (1991) *A Voice for Children* (London: Jessica Kingsley).

Fortin, J. (1998) *Children's Rights and the Developing Law* (London: Butterworths).

Foster, H. and Freed, D. (1972) 'A Bill of Rights for children', *Family Law Quarterly*, Vol. 343.

Freeman, M. (1996) 'Children's rights, a comparative perspective' in M. Freeman (ed.) *Issues in Law and Society* (London: Ashgate).

Freeman, M. and Veerman, P. (1992) *The Ideologies of Children's Rights* (Dordrecht: Martinus Nijhoff, Kluwer Academic Publishers Group).

Goldstein, J., Freud, A. and Solnit, A.H. (1973) *Beyond the Best Interests of the Child* (New York: Free Press new edition 1979).

Goldstein, J., Freud, A. and Solnit, A.H. (1986) *In the Best Interests of the Child* (London: Free Press, Collier Macmillan Publishers).

HMSO (1994) *The United Kingdom's First Report to the UN Committee on the Rights of the Child* (London: HMSO).

HMSO (1999) *The United Kingdom's Second Report to the UN Committee on the Rights of the Child* (London: HMSO).

Kilkelly, U. (1999) *The Child and the European Convention on Human Rights* (Aldershot: Ashgate).

Mnookin, R.H. (1985) *In the Interests of Children* (London: Chatto & Windus).

O'Halloran, K. (1999) *The Welfare of the Child: The Principle and the Law* (Aldershot: Arena/Ashgate Publications).

Smyth, M. and Scott, M. (2000) *The Youthquest 2000 Survey* (Derry/Londonderry: INCORE).

Veerman, P.E. (1991) *The Rights of the Child and the Changing Images of Childhood* (Dordrecht: Martinus Nijhoff, Kluwer Academic Publishers Group).

# 10 Pensions and Pensioners in Northern Ireland

*Eileen Evason*

The 1999 Northern Ireland Life and Times survey contained a sub-stantial module relating to pension provision and the circumstances of pensioners in Northern Ireland. The aim of this chapter is to present the data and place it within a fuller discussion of the policy context and allied matters. Therefore, the chapter begins by summarising the policy background to the research, followed by an outline of the gaps in data for Northern Ireland which prompted the work. The main findings from the survey are then considered and their implications for current policy discussed.

## *Policy Background*

Pensions policy in the postwar period has been characterised by frequent change, much uncertainty and growing complexity (Evason, 1999). The basic flat rate state pension (£72.50 in 2001) was introduced in 1948. During the 1950s, as living standards rose, and other countries developed earnings-related provision, the British model appeared increasingly ungenerous and outdated. Additionally, as more employers started to provide occupational pensions, two classes of pensioners emerged. Firstly, those with the basic state pension and a pension from their employment. Secondly, those reliant on the basic state pension and – if they were willing to claim it – a top-up from means-tested National Assistance. After much discussion, and some false starts, a radical shift in British pensions policy finally occurred in 1975 with the enactment of the Castle scheme.

Under the new arrangements the basic flat rate pension would continue, but would be increased annually in line with prices or wages, whichever were higher. This uprating formula would ensure that the base moved in line with the living standards of the general population. Alongside the flat rate pension, the Castle scheme also provided for the introduction of the State Earnings Related Pension

Scheme (SERPS). This would deliver a second state pension based on earnings to those not in occupational pension schemes. The formula used for the calculation of entitlement favoured women and the lower paid and, as is usual in state provision, the entire scheme was to be financed on a pay-as-you-go basis, rather than the type of funding whereby contributions are invested and outcome depends on performance.

The Castle scheme was introduced with all-party support and it appeared that a consensus had finally been reached. This consensus did not last long however. In 1980 the newly elected Conservative government amended the annual uprating formula so that the basic pension would rise in line with prices only. In consequence, the basic pension has fallen steadily as a percentage of average earnings and, in today's terms, will be worth £31 by the year 2050 (Social Security Committee, 2000, paragraph 65). In 1986, the formula for calculating SERPS entitlement was altered so that from 1999, the additional pension paid under the scheme would be steadily reduced. Uniquely, within the European Union context, the overall intention of government was to privatise second tier provision by promoting reliance on personal and occupational pensions. Throughout the 1990s, the Conservative government persisted with this strategy, despite the Maxwell scandal which tarnished occupational pension schemes, and the mis-selling of personal pensions, which undermined public confidence in this financial product.

The election of a Labour government in 1997 has resulted in yet another shift in pensions policy. The new strategy that is emerging (Department of Social Security (DSS), 1998; 2000) appears to have three main strands. Firstly, the basic state pension will continue to wither away. Secondly, the state will continue its withdrawal from second tier provision. Thus SERPS will be wound down, and rights will not be accrued under this scheme after 2002. There will be a new State Second Pension for some – those on very low wages, carers and persons whose employment is substantially disrupted by sickness – but this will not mature until the year 2050. By and large, therefore, it is assumed that people will make their own provision via occupational pensions, personal pensions and the new stakeholder pensions, which are a repackaged form of personal pensions. Thirdly, means-tested Income Support for pensioners has been relabelled the Minimum Income Guarantee and has moved sharply ahead of the basic state pension. Thus, while the basic state pension is currently £72.50 and, in the main, receipt of this amount is contingent upon contributions being paid or credited for 90 per cent of working life, the Minimum Income Guarantee for a single pensioner, who may have paid no contributions at all, is £92.15.

## Pensions Policy and the Northern Ireland Context

As a consequence of the principle of parity, pensions policy in Northern Ireland has followed that of Britain to the letter. This has not, however, been accompanied by an equivalent growth in our knowledge of pension provision and the circumstances of pensioners here. Northern Ireland has no counterparts to the Family Resources Survey (although this gap may soon be closed), or to the major research efforts on pensions conducted in Britain during the 1990s (for example, Disney, Grundy and Johnson, 1997; Hedges, 1998; McKay, Heaver and Walker, 2000). As a result, at a general level, by the mid-1990s we lacked the most basic data on obvious matters relating to post-retirement arrangements and the financial circumstances of pensioners here. At a more specific level, it was clear that, although the concerns being raised about the overall direction of British policy (Piachaud, 1999; Social Security Committee, 2000) might be of particular significance in Northern Ireland, we lacked the data to assess this possibility.

The first set of concerns related to those under retirement age. Current strategy generally requires people, particularly those in younger age groups, to be actively engaged with – and thinking about – their provision for retirement. Building up an adequate personal pension requires people to make an early start and, for example, the stakeholder pension of £74 a week cited as an illustration in the Green Paper (DSS, 1998) was based on contributions of £50 a month for 33 years. There is a general concern that encouraging people in younger age groups to think about pensions may be difficult. At this point in their lives people have the more immediate and pressing financial costs of buying a home and raising a family. For Northern Ireland, the capacity for self provision may be further depressed by, for example, lower wages and the more limited participation of women in the labour market.

A second set of issues, raised in particular by the Social Security Committee of the House of Commons (2000), related to older workers. The cuts in SERPS (which are now coming into effect), and the continuing decline of the basic pension will produce a cohort of workers who will receive less than they may have expected from the state when they retire. They have little time, and may well not have the capacity, to make additional provision. Again, by virtue of the distinct socio-economic profile of Northern Ireland, it may be surmised that this will be a particular problem in this part of the United Kingdom.

The third set of issues related to the increasingly generous means-tested Minimum Income Guarantee to be renamed and repackaged as the Pension Credit in 2003. Here we are back to the problems traditionally associated with means-testing: incentives and take-up. There is the difficulty of encouraging people to make their own provision if it becomes known that there is a reasonable safety net in place for those who do not. More immediately, this policy is based on the argument that more generous means-tested help, rather than improvements to the basic state pension, is the most appropriate way of assisting pensioners, as resources are concentrated on those with lower incomes. However, the argument only makes sense if those entitled to means-tested help actually claim it. In Britain it appeared that take-up was the core weakness of this part of the total strategy (Social Security Committee, 2000). For Northern Ireland, we had no empirical data from which to make any assessment of the position.

In sum, while pensions policy raised many questions of particular interest here, we did not have the information to address them. To do so we needed to know, for example, what arrangements people under retirement age were actually making, how much thought they were giving to pensions, and their general grasp of the subject. With regard to those over retirement age, we needed information comparable to that provided by the British Family Resources Survey and recent research (Corden, Costigan and Whitfield, 1999; Costigan, Finch, Jackson, Legard and Ritchie, 1999) on the extent of failure to claim the Minimum Income Guarantee, and the barriers to take-up. Additionally, to fill other obvious gaps in knowledge, we required data on health and issues relating to long-term care. The Life and Times survey has helped to fill these and other gaps in our knowledge.

The Pensions and Pensioners module consisted of three parts. The first section focused on thinking about retirement and the provision that people below pensionable age (60 years for women and 65 years for men) had made for retirement. The second section concentrated on the employment status and history of respondents who are aged 50 years and over, but are under pensionable age and are not in full-time employment. Finally, the third section related to respondents of pensionable age. To ensure that there were adequate numbers for analysis, a booster sample was drawn. Full details on the sampling methodology can be found in Appendix I of this volume.

The analysis and discussion in this chapter will focus on the first and third sections. Part of the data has been summarised elsewhere (Evason, Dowds and Devine, 2001; Evason, Dowds and Devine, forthcoming).

## Persons under Retirement Age

### Thoughts and Expectations of Retirement

The findings produced from this section are a series of puzzles and causes for concern. In line with other research (Hedges, 1998), Table

10.1 indicates that only a minority of our interviewees have given a lot of thought to how they would manage financially on retirement. There is some variation by gender, employment status and age but, across all groups, those who have given a lot of thought to the matter are in the minority. Interestingly, given the policy directions discussed above, 63 per cent of males in the 18 to 34 years age group have given not much or no thought at all to the matter, with the figure for women in this age group being 67 per cent.

Table 10.1 Thought given to financial management on retirement (%)

|  | Male | Female | All |
| --- | --- | --- | --- |
| A lot of thought | 16 | 10 | 13 |
| Some thought | 33 | 33 | 33 |
| Not much thought | 20 | 21 | 21 |
| No thought at all | 30 | 36 | 33 |
| Don't know | <1 | 1 | <1 |
| No answer | 1 | 1 | 1 |

Reluctance to engage with the issue of retirement until it is an imminent prospect is hardly surprising and, indeed, this is one of the main reasons for government involvement in this field. What is of more interest is the fact that, despite their having given little thought to how they would manage, few respondents under retirement age (7 per cent) expect to be quite badly off or very badly off. As Table 10.2 indicates, regardless of employment status, the majority of those who feel able to answer this question think that they would at least be able to manage.

In part, these expectations may be well founded, if they are based on what provision respondents are actually making. However, they may also derive from incorrect assumptions about state provision. One of the most significant findings is the widespread confusion about state pensions. Only 33 per cent of adults are actually aware of the existence of SERPS, and the majority (58 per cent) are unable to select the correct amount of the basic state pension at the time of the interview ($£66.75$). Most importantly, the majority of interviewees (77 per cent) appear to think that the basic state pension is a universal pension paid to everyone on retirement, rather than being a National Insurance pension with entitlement largely determined by the individual's National Insurance contributions record. This view is most prevalent among married women (79 per cent) and may help to account for the confidence of those engaged in full-time home care shown in Table 10.2.

The pattern emerging is of an adult population giving little close thought to retirement, assuming to a large extent that they will be

Table 10.2 Expected standard of living on retirement by employment status (%)

| | Working full time | Working part time | Looking after the home | Sick/disabled | Unemployed | Full time education | Other | All |
|---|---|---|---|---|---|---|---|---|
| Comfortably off | 16 | 16 | 13 | 2 | 8 | 20 | 13 | 15 |
| Quite well off | 24 | 14 | 12 | 5 | 11 | 13 | 20 | 18 |
| Able to manage | 48 | 51 | 57 | 59 | 53 | 22 | 47 | 48 |
| Quite badly off | 3 | 11 | 7 | 19 | 11 | – | 6 | 6 |
| Very badly off | <1 | 1 | 1 | 1 | 2 | – | 1 | 1 |
| Don't know | 8 | 4 | 9 | 14 | 14 | 43 | 10 | 11 |
| No answer | 1 | 2 | 1 | – | 1 | 2 | 3 | 1 |

able to manage, but doing so with unsound assumptions about state provision.

### Provision Being Made

Individuals may reach retirement age with a patchwork of entitlement: years spent in one or more occupational pension schemes, periods as full members of SERPS, periods of contributions to personal pensions, and periods covered by credited contributions or the home responsibilities protection provisions which give some assistance to persons not in employment.

Assessing the provision being made is therefore a complex task. First of all, the arrangements people had in place at the time of the interview will be considered. An attempt will then be made to chart the general pattern of provision among those interviewed, and to identify possible problems.

### Occupational Pensions

Just over one third of employees (38 per cent) are members of occupational pension schemes, and the majority of these (85 per cent) are in the more advantageous final salary arrangements. This raises a number of issues. Firstly, there is a gender variation as 32 per cent of female employees are members of an occupational pension scheme, compared with 45 per cent of males. This is a sharper differential than that for Britain as a whole (Office for National Statistics (ONS), 2000), and the particular features of Northern Ireland described above have clearly impacted on the prospects of women here securing adequate private provision in their own right. The consequent and particular significance for women here of the winding down of the SERPS safety net should also be noted. Secondly, there is a good deal of confusion among those in occupational pension schemes about particular aspects of the schemes they are in. For example, 38 per cent of members do not know what provisions their scheme makes for post-retirement increases.

During the 1980s and 1990s there has been heavy support from government for personal pensions, which have been viewed as being more in tune with the new ethos of individuals freeing themselves from dependence on the state and old fashioned corporate welfare (Evason, 1999). However, among respondents, there is general support for occupational pensions, as opposed to personal pensions. Only 7 per cent of interviewees support the statement 'I am not happy with relying on a works pension as I would rather manage my own affairs'. Surprisingly, this more individualistic perspective enjoyed less support

(5 per cent) among those under the age of 35 years, than among those aged 50 years and over, for whom the comparable figure was 9 per cent. The vast majority (81 per cent) of interviewees in occupational pensions endorse the statement that 'the advantage of a works pension is that you don't have to think about it'. In summary, it would appear that a pattern of provision which is in decline enjoys a good deal of support. In addition, there is little evidence that what people would really prefer is the self-management and self-provision which is at the core of current strategy.

Finally, the extent of membership widens when account is taken of past membership of schemes where rights had not been cashed in. The proportion of employees with some entitlement rises to 52 per cent, and accounts for 26 per cent of all respondents below pensionable age. Table 10.3 indicates that among older members, three quarters (74 per cent) have membership records of more than ten years and many will retire with a sound addition to state provision. This group may be considered to be a fortunate minority. As employment patterns continue to change, and fewer employers provide pensions (with those who do moving to money purchase schemes), this cohort could be the last sizeable group to benefit from a form of provision that has played a significant role in raising the living standards of pensioners over the past 20 years.

Table 10.3 Years of membership of occupational pension scheme by age (%)

|  | 18–34 | 35–49 | 50–64 | All |
|---|---|---|---|---|
| <1–2 | 31 | 4 | 6 | 12 |
| 3–5 | 32 | 13 | 9 | 17 |
| 6–10 | 19 | 25 | 4 | 18 |
| 11–15 | 16 | 15 | 17 | 16 |
| 16–20 | 2 | 20 | 25 | 16 |
| 21–25 | – | 15 | 10 | 9 |
| 26–30 | – | 4 | 9 | 4 |
| 31–35 | – | <1 | 8 | 2 |
| 36 and over | – | – | 6 | 1 |
| Don't know | 1 | 5 | 4 | 4 |
| Not answered | – | – | 1 | <1 |

*Personal Pensions*

Respondents were asked if they are currently contributing to a personal pension, and 16 per cent are. This is slightly lower than the figure recently reported for Britain of 20 per cent (ONS, 2000), and is worrying for a number of reasons. Firstly, given the exclusion of the self-employed from SERPS, government (DSS, 1998) has been particularly concerned that this group should take out personal pensions. However, only 45 per cent of respondents who are self-employed are actually doing so, and this figure is slightly below that for Britain (DSS, 1998). Secondly, there is a degree of ambivalence about the arrangements being made. Thus 64 per cent of those with personal pensions agree or strongly agree with the statement 'I prefer a personal pension as you are managing your own affairs to suit yourself'. At the same time, 51 per cent support the statement 'I would prefer a good state or company pension so that I didn't have all of the hassle'. The third, and major, concern about this group relates to the amounts of the monthly contributions reported.

Discussions of outcomes with regard to personal pensions are hazardous. Annuity rates have fallen sharply in recent years and may, or may not, rise in the future. Roughly speaking, at the time of writing, a fund of £10,000 is required to purchase a weekly income of £15, and this, when added to the basic state pension, would still leave a pensioner below the means-tested Minimum Income Guarantee. Substantial contributions over a long period are therefore required, and the conventional benchmark used for contributions is £50 a month. Among respondents currently contributing to a personal pension, 53 per cent make monthly contributions of £50 or under. The contributions being made by women are particularly low, with 59 per cent making monthly contributions of £50 or under, compared to 49 per cent of men.

### State Pensions

Out of the 1,695 respondents under retirement age, 1,032 are not members of an occupational or personal pensions scheme, that is, they are reliant on state provision. There has been a tendency in recent years to depict this group as neglectful of both the future and of their duty to make pension arrangements. This is only one perspective. An alternative viewpoint is that many of those in this group have been making provision – via the payment of substantial contributions to the National Insurance scheme. On this basis, the difficulties this group may face may be said to relate to the diminishing entitlement these contributions will deliver.

Over three quarters (78 per cent) of this group have paid at least some National Insurance contributions, with the majority (70 per cent) reporting a record of contributions for most of their working lives to date. There has been much recent debate about the contributory principle and whether or not this can be viewed as constituting some form of contract between the state and the individual (Social

Security Committee, 1999). Regardless of the conclusion which may be reached on this, in line with other work (Hedges, 1998), our data suggest that people place much emphasis on payments made to the state and expect to benefit accordingly. Two thirds (66 per cent) of those relying on state provision agree or strongly agree that 'I have paid my tax and National Insurance so I assume I will be all right'. This figure rises to 80 per cent among those who appear to have fairly complete contribution records. The assumption that people should not rely on the state, despite the National Insurance contributions they have paid, appears to have had little impact on the thinking of the general population.

The final point to emerge from this section has already been discussed, but deserves further emphasis. For all of the efforts throughout the past 20 years to move people into private second tier provision, the state is still a major player in the field. This is clearly shown in Table 10.4, which presents current arrangements cumulatively. It can be seen that 29 per cent of adults in Northern Ireland have occupational and/or private pensions, but the proportion with provision more than doubles when those with fairly complete National Insurance records – who will have entitlement under SERPS – are added in.

Table 10.4 Cumulative arrangements for pension provision by gender (%)

|  | Male | Female | All |
|---|---|---|---|
| In an occupational pension scheme | 18 | 15 | 16 |
| In an occupational and/or personal pension scheme | 35 | 23 | 29 |
| In occupational and/or personal pension scheme, or has paid National Insurance for most of working life | 68 | 57 | 62 |
| None of the above | 33 | 43 | 39 |

*Overall Patterns of Provision*

Less than one third of the respondents under pensionable age (29 per cent) is making private second tier provision (that is, occupation and/or personal pension schemes), although some of this provision is of doubtful quality. Exactly one third (33 per cent) have strong records as full members of the National Insurance scheme. However, the structure they are reliant upon is being dismantled. Finally, 39 per cent of adults have no current second tier arrangements in place.

There is, therefore, some cause for concern, but account needs to be taken of age, as well as past and current provision. The Social

Security Committee (2000) has drawn attention to the particular problems that may be posed for those in older age groups who will receive less than they might have expected, and have little time to make alternative provision. In Northern Ireland this problem may be particularly acute. Our data indicate that among males over 50 years, 40 per cent have some private provision but the most common (42 per cent) form of provision made is the payment of National Insurance contributions for most of the working life. A further 17 per cent of these older males have neither this – though they will have some National Insurance record – nor any current or past history of private provision. Among older women the position is rather worse, with only 26 per cent having full National Insurance records, and 49 per cent having neither this nor private provision.

Turning to those in younger age groups it would appear that there may be substantial difficulties with current policy at this end of the spectrum as well. Among men under 35 years, only 30 per cent report that they have made some form of private provision for their retirement. The comparable figure for women is 22 per cent. Current policy assumes that the bulk of this age group will support themselves in retirement via non-statutory provision. The size of the shift required, as indicated by findings from the Life and Times survey, suggests that the task of achieving current policy objectives is a formidable one.

## Attitudes and Preferences with Regard to Pensions

Finally, one further reason why current policy may not succeed is indicated by results from a series of attitudinal questions asked of those respondents below pensionable age. In line with other data (Hedges, 1998) our findings suggest that current policy is simply out of step with the general views of the population on pensions policy. Interviewees were presented with statements reflecting, roughly speaking, three different approaches to the role of the state with regard to pensions. Table 10.5 indicates little support for the first statement

Table 10.5 Preferred approach to state pension provision (%)

| | |
|---|---|
| The state continues to provide a very modest basic pension and helps the poorest with a means-tested top-up | 19 |
| The state provides a modest pension which is sufficient to live on without hardship or having to claim Income Support. If people want more they have to provide it themselves | 38 |
| The state provides a pension based on earnings which is sufficient to live on with a few luxuries and means that people's living standards do not fall substantially when they retire | 36 |
| Don't know/other response | 8 |

that 'the state continues to provide a very modest basic pension and helps the poorest with a means-tested top-up', which approximates to the British model. There is broader, but evenly divided, support for the second and third statements, which relate to the Scandinavian and West European models respectively .

## Pensioners in Northern Ireland

An important aspect of the Pensions and Pensioners module was the focus on respondents over pensionable age, which examined their living standards and financial situation.

### Sources and Levels of Incomes

Table 10.6 details the sources of income of pensioners in Northern Ireland. It can be noted that, with a predictable variation by gender, the proportion of interviewees reporting income from occupational pensions is rather lower than that for Britain (ONS, 2000). Two other aspects of the table should be noted. Firstly, there is the heavy dependence on benefits intended to assist with the extra costs of disability. This is a reflection of the relatively high level of disability among adults in Northern Ireland generally (McCoy and Smith, 1992). Secondly, only 19 per cent of interviewees report that they are in receipt of Income Support, but in Northern Ireland as a whole 27 per cent of the population aged 60 years and over are in receipt of this benefit. It should be noted that the analysis based on the Life and Times survey data excludes men aged between 60 and 64 years, and further analysis suggests that the main reason for this discrepancy is claimant confusion on which benefits they were actually getting from the state. This is a common problem and, for example, in consequence, the Pensioners Income Series (produced by the Department of Work and Pensions) reports benefit income as a unified category. For the purposes of current policy, however, there is the obvious difficulty of encouraging claimants to claim means-tested help when so many seem unclear about what they are actually already in receipt of.

Table 10.7 indicates that a substantial proportion of pensioner households in Northern Ireland can be described as financially hard pressed. Recent research (Parker, 2000) suggests that the minimum income required by a single pensioner at the time of the survey was £90, after housing costs and disregarding additions to cover the costs of disability. The corresponding figure for married couples was £135. Table 10.7 indicates that the majority (66 per cent) of single pensioners are either on Income Support, and by definition below the

£90 threshold, or report weekly incomes below this level. The figure for married couples is lower at 50 per cent. These low incomes are ameliorated in a proportion of cases by savings or other assets. A minority of those on lower incomes (19 per cent) report savings and assets of £8,000 plus. More typically, in 59 per cent of cases, savings are under £1,000.

Table 10.6 Sources of income of pensioners (%)

|  | Pensioner couples | Single males | Single females | All |
|---|---|---|---|---|
| State retirement /widows pension | 96 | 97 | 94 | 95 |
| Employers pension | 38 | 30 | 18 | 29 |
| Income Support | 8 | 15 | 32 | 19 |
| Attendance Allowance * | 11 | 12 | 21 | 15 |
| Disability Living Allowance (DLA) – care component | 11 | 6 | 8 | 9 |
| Earnings | 20 | 7 | 4 | 6 |
| Personal pension | 3 | 6 | 2 | 3 |
| Invalid Care Allowance | 4 | 6 | 2 | 3 |

* Includes Constant Attendance Allowance

Table 10.7 Weekly income of pensioners (%)

|  | Single | Couples |
|---|---|---|
| Under £90 | 35 | 14 |
| £90–£99 | 3 | 2 |
| £100–£124 | 8 | 15 |
| £125–£134 | 4 | 7 |
| £135+ | 20 | 50 |
| On Income Support | 31 | 12 |

### Income Support (now Minimum Income Guarantee)

One aim of the Pensions and Pensioners module was to identify entitlement to Income Support (now Minimum Income Guarantee), as well as to other benefits. A special computer programme was written which identified apparent entitlement, and advised respondents of the weekly figure involved. Clearly, given the low levels of weekly income previously highlighted, pensioners in Northern Ireland have much to gain from the substantial improvements in means-tested help being put in place. Actually securing these gains, however, requires that they are already claiming this benefit and secure the increases automatically, or can be persuaded to claim if they are not doing so. In the light of the high proportion of persons already claiming Income Support, it was hypothesised that the latter group would be very small in size, and that take-up would not prove to be a major problem in this part of the UK. The hypothesis was proved to be wrong.

From Table 10.8 it can be seen that 13 per cent of pensioners appear to be entitled to, but not claiming, Income Support. In 89 per cent of cases, the amount apparently unclaimed is £5 or more. The extent of non take-up noted here is broadly in line with calculations made by the Department for Social Development and the estimates for Britain (DSS, 1999).

Table 10.8 Apparent entitlement of pensioners to Income Support (%)

|  | Pensioner couples | Single males | Single females | All |
|---|---|---|---|---|
| No entitlement | 64 | 54 | 41 | 54 |
| Already claiming | 10 | 15 | 32 | 18 |
| Appears entitled | 10 | 16 | 15 | 13 |
| Appears entitled with successful AA/DLA claim | – | 2 | 1 | 1 |
| Insufficient information | 16 | 14 | 11 | 14 |

Where persons with apparent entitlement were identified, they were asked if they wished to receive the forms and information required to claim this benefit. If so, information packs were sent out with further offers of assistance. However, we have no way of knowing whether or not eligible respondents actually submitted claims and/or what the outcomes were. There may well therefore be a problem of continuing reluctance to claim which is cloaked by apparent willingness to take further action. Beyond this, there is the clear and evident problem of those who were informed of their possible entitlement, but who did not wish to proceed any further. These account for nearly half (47 per cent) of all of those identified as having grounds for a claim.

This significant finding bears out the concerns expressed earlier in this chapter about reliance on more generous means-tested help (rather than an increase in the basic state pension) to assist existing pensioners. Research on the problem of take-up, which now extends back over 30 years, indicates that a reluctance to claim entitlement is a consequence of structural features of the benefits themselves, as well as of individual attitudes and behaviour (Corden, 1999). The reluctance of some Life and Times survey respondents to pursue their entitlement fits in clearly with this analysis. By definition, applications for means-tested benefits involve the completion of lengthy and complex forms. At the same time, the volume of personal information which has to be disclosed may offend an individual's sense of privacy. This mix of structural and attitudinal factors appears to be of most significance in the thinking of those Life and Times respondents reluctant to claim. Hence, 56 per cent agree or strongly agree with the statement 'I am not happy about having to disclose so much information about my affairs' and 49 per cent support the statement 'I don't want the bother of filling in forms'. Lesser reasons contributing to a reluctance to claim include 'it's not the same as the pension that you've contributed for' (38 per cent) and 'it's a bit like taking charity' (29 per cent).

*Disability, the Need for Care and the Funding of Care*

Forty-five per cent of pensioners interviewed report a longstanding illness or disability. Respondents were asked about their need for personal care, as well as their ability to carry out a set of tasks (such as making a cup of tea). Only 31 per cent of respondents require no help at all, while 27 per cent need substantial assistance. For a fuller discussion, see Evason, Dowds and Devine (2000). For many pensioners, therefore, the possibility of admission to a nursing home or residential care is not a remote possibility. The funding of long-term care for elderly persons has been the subject of as much debate and controversy in Northern Ireland as elsewhere (Evason, 1998), and so was a pertinent topic to be considered within the Pensions and Pensioners module.

Results from the 1994 Northern Ireland Social Attitudes survey indicated little public support generally for the provisions in place in this sphere (Evason and Robinson, 1996). Results from the Life and Times survey build on that by demonstrating considerable confusion among the elderly about charges for nursing home and residential care. Again, the direction of policy appears to be out of step with the general views of the population most likely to be affected.

Exactly half of the pensioners interviewed indicate that they are worried that they might require nursing or residential home accommodation at some point. The aspects of going into such care which are of most concern are 'loss of independence' (37 per cent) and 'leaving one's own home and things' (28 per cent). Cost played only a small part (10 per cent) in the concerns expressed. In part, however, this may be due to the confusion which surrounded this subject. As elsewhere, the current position is that where persons are placed in such care, an assessment of means is conducted to determine the contribution the person can make to the charges levied. Unless the home is occupied by a spouse, an elderly or disabled relative, or such other person that it would be appropriate to take into account, the value of the house will be assessed. This will normally mean that the person cared for has capital of £18,500 plus and is deemed able to meet the full cost of care. There are no provisions whereby people can protect their assets by transfer. Nevertheless, 51 per cent of pensioners in Northern Ireland believe that they can do so by, for example, signing over the property at least seven years in advance of their needing care. Forty-one per cent of respondents do not know whether or not this is possible, and only 9 per cent know that it is not. There is clearly a need to address the confusion and misunderstanding among pensioners about the current charging policy.

Turning to attitudes on the funding of long-term care, the arguments for and against the current arrangements are complex, but some of the most commonly rehearsed positions are set out in Table 10.9. There is some support for the view that taxpayers, who may be on low incomes themselves, should not have to pay for the care of those with substantial means. There is, however, a very clear endorsement of the view that charging for care is asking pensioners to pay twice over and a strong belief that parents needing care should be able to hand their property on to their children.

These data are relevant as, at the time of writing, Northern Ireland is considering its future policy in this area. Many organisations and individuals made representations to the Royal Commission (Sutherland, 1999) and the recommendation that both nursing and personal care should be free was welcomed widely. There is much interest in the Scottish example, which has followed Sutherland, and awareness of the narrower approach – free nursing care only – adopted in England. The adoption of the minimalist English position seems unlikely to secure broad support here.

In sum, our data on pensioners reflect the legacy of past years of high unemployment and the other particular features of the region noted in the introduction. The picture to emerge is of a population of retirement age which is heavily dependent on statutory and particularly means-tested support. There is the predictable prevalence of low incomes and it is also evident that, despite the relative strength of Northern Ireland's networks for providing benefits advice, the take-up problem is as acute here as elsewhere. Additionally, the data indicate a substantial level of ill health and need for care combined with confusion about aspects of current policy relating to the provision of long-term care.

## Conclusion

Taken as a whole our data cast some doubt over many aspects of current policy. With regard to those under retirement age the core

Table 10.9 Attitudes of pensioners towards paying for residential care (%)

| | Strongly agree | Agree | Neither agree nor disagree | Disagree | Strongly disagree | Don't know |
|---|---|---|---|---|---|---|
| It is not fair to ask taxpayers, many of whom are on low incomes, to pay for the care of people who may have substantial savings and assets | 11 | 36 | 10 | 15 | 6 | 22 |
| Elderly people, who have paid tax and National Insurance, are being charged twice if they have to pay for care | 35 | 43 | 7 | 2 | <1 | 13 |
| Elderly people who need care should be able to leave their homes to their children | 37 | 42 | 5 | 2 | 1 | 12 |
| Grown up children should not expect taxpayers to pay more so that they can inherit their parents' property | 6 | 24 | 16 | 26 | 7 | 21 |
| There should be a cut off point so that the house is only taken into account if it's worth a great deal | 10 | 34 | 10 | 12 | 5 | 29 |

issues to emerge are lack of engagement with post-retirement provision, confusion, private pensions of questionable quality and a cohort of older workers whose main form of provision consists of reliance on a structure that will deliver less and less over the coming decade. With regard to those over retirement age, it is clear that a central plank of current policy – the Minimum Income Guarantee for pensioners – will be as difficult to implement fully and effectively in Northern Ireland as elsewhere. There is also, for example, evidence of confusion with regard to charges for long-term care.

Most importantly, perhaps, what stands out from the data is the lack of support among the general population for core and major social policies. The changes of the 1980s and 1990s with regard to pensions and allied areas are simply not in tune with popular views and attitudes. The task of getting people to voluntarily make their own arrangements to ensure that they have adequate incomes and access to long-term care in their old age would be difficult at the best of times. Doing so within a context where there is limited sympathy with, or support for, the policies being pursued will be challenging indeed.

I am grateful to the editors of *Benefits* and the *Journal of Social Policy and Administration* for permission to draw on material published in completing this chapter.

## References

Corden, A. (1999) 'Claiming entitlement: take-up of benefits' in J. Ditch (ed.) *Introduction to Social Security* (London: Routledge) pp. 134–54.

Corden, N., Costigan, P. and Whitfield, G. (1999) *Helping Pensioners: Evaluation of the Income Support Pilots*, Social Security Research Report No. 105 (Leeds: Corporate Document Services).

Costigan, P., Finch, H., Jackson, B., Legard, R. and Ritchie, J. (1999) *Overcoming Barriers – Older People and Income Support*, Social Security Research Report No. 100 (Leeds: Corporate Document Services).

Department of Social Security (DSS) (1998) *A New Contract for Welfare: Partnerships in Pension* Cm. 4179 (London: The Stationery Office Limited).

Department of Social Security (DSS) (1999) *Income Related Benefits – Estimates of Take-Up in 1996/97 (Revised) and 1997/98* (London: Government Statistical Service).

Department of Social Security (DSS) (2000) *The Pension Credit: A Consultation Paper*, Cm 4900 (London: The Stationery Office Limited).

Disney, R., Grundy, E. and Johnson, P. (eds) (1997) *The Dynamics of Retirement*, Department of Social Security, Research Report No. 72 (London: HMSO).

Evason, E. (1998) 'The Funding of Long-Term Care', Report to Royal Commission prepared for Unison (NI).

Evason, E. (1999) 'British pensions policies: evolution, outcomes and options' in J. Ditch (ed.), *Introduction to Social Security* (London: Routledge).

Evason, E., Dowds, L. and Devine, P. (2000) *Pensions and Pensioners in Northern Ireland*, Report to the Nuffield Foundation, Department for Social Development and Training and Employment Agency (Jordanstown: University of Ulster).

Evason, E., Dowds, L. and Devine, P. (2001) 'Pensions: provision, perceptions and preferences amongst persons under pensionable age', *Benefits*, Issue 31, pp. 14–19.

Evason, E., Dowds, L. and Devine, P. (forthcoming) 'Pensioners and the Minimum Income Guarantee: observations from recent research', *Journal of Social Policy and Administration*.

Evason, E. and Robinson, G. (1996) 'Informal care in Northern Ireland' in R. Breen, P. Devine and L. Dowds (eds), *Social Attitudes in Northern Ireland: The Fifth Report, 1995–1996* (Belfast: Appletree Press) pp. 49–69.

Hedges, A. (1998) *Pensions and Retirement Planning*, Department of Social Security Report No. 83 (Leeds: Corporate Documents Services).

McCoy, D. and Smith, M. (1992) *The Prevalence of Disability in Northern Ireland* (Belfast: Policy, Planning and Research Unit).

McKay, S., Heaver, C. and Walker, R. (2000) *Building Up Pension Rights*, Department of Social Security Research Report No. 114 (Leeds: Corporate Document Services).

Office for National Statistics (ONS) (2000) *Family Resources Survey Statistical Report, 1998–9* (Leeds: Corporate Document Services).

Parker, H. (2000) *Low Cost but Acceptable Incomes for Older People* (Bristol: Policy Press).

Piachaud, D. (1999) 'Security for old age', *Benefits*, Issue 26, pp. 1–7.

Social Security Committee (1999) Fifth Report, *The Contributory Principle* (London: The Stationery Office Limited).

Social Security Committee (2000) Seventh Report, *Pensioner Poverty* (London: The Stationery Office Limited).

Sutherland, S. (1999) *With Respect to Old Age*, Report by the Royal Commission on Long Term Care (London: The Stationery Office Limited).

# 11 Social Inequality

*Robert Miller*

The Northern Ireland Life and Times survey is a participant in the International Social Survey Programme (ISSP), an annual survey of attitudes to social and economic policy issues that is carried out in more than 35 countries. The data from the surveys are deposited at the Zentralarchiv für Empirische Sozialforschung (Central Archive for Empirical Social Research) at the University of Cologne, Germany. The ISSP addresses a different topic each year, which in 1999 was social inequality. Consequently, this module was included in the 1999 Life and Times survey.

The concept of social inequality as operationalised in the ISSP module has a focus that is both specific and diffuse, and centres around the inequality of income and wealth. Other types of inequality that might be relevant across all ISSP participating countries – such as gender inequality – or that are highly relevant to Northern Ireland specifically – that is, religious/ethnic inequality – were not covered in the 1999 ISSP module. Rather than using any doctrinaire theory of class-based inequality, the ISSP employed a general commonsensical concern with material difference in its operationalisation of economic inequality. The module contains an extensive series of questions that can tell us much about views on economic inequality in Northern Ireland.

This chapter begins by establishing the relative importance of class, religion, gender and age in their effects upon attitudes to material social inequality. After that, the chapter will present the findings of the ISSP module with particular recourse to social class. As such, it can be considered a companion piece to other chapters in this volume that deal with alternative types of inequality; specifically Hughes and Donnelly on community relations and Heenan and Lloyd on housing and social exclusion.

## The Relative Importance of Class, Religion, Gender and Age

The Social Inequality module contains over 50 questions. Dealing with issues of material inequality, one could expect direct associations between the responses to these questions and people's social class. At the same time, however, one could argue that other means of categorising the respondents could be just as relevant. Religion, in terms of Protestant/Catholic, is known to constitute a fundamental watershed of opinion on many issues in Northern Ireland. Furthermore, one of the central features of religious discrimination in Northern Ireland of course has been its material dimension. A legacy of this could be that religion, independent of social class, might prove significant in determining people's attitudes to questions of social inequality. Gender is also an important watershed of opinion and it is well documented that any material disadvantages or discrimination suffered by Catholics in present-day Northern Ireland pale in comparison to those suffered by women (see, for example, Kremer and Montgomery, 1993; Miller, 2001). So, a person's gender potentially could be as salient as their social class for determining their attitudes to material inequality. In an analogous manner, age constitutes yet another influence on attitudes and the elderly are also an often-ignored materially deprived category.

Attempting to depict the totality of potential relationships between the whole of the set of variables in the Social Inequality module with class, religion, gender and age is untenable. Space considerations rule this out and, more importantly, such a long drawn out approach could end by establishing that several of these variables are of little relevance. Hence, one needs to establish, overall, which of the above variables are fundamental in their effects upon attitudes to social inequality.

As a first step, a 'left/right wing' scale was constructed based upon the additive responses to 17 questions (Table 11.1). The values of the scale range from 28 to 79 and, as Figure 11.1 shows, their distribution approximates closely to a normal distribution. Low scores indicate left wing views and high scores indicate right wing views.

The left/right wing scale was then used as the dependent variable in a regression analysis in which social class, age, gender, and whether respondents were Catholic or Protestant were entered as independent variables. As shown in Table 11.2, social class is the only variable that significantly affected respondents' scores on the left/right wing scale; the higher the social class, the more conservative the responses. While the coefficients imply that Catholics have more left wing scores and Protestants more right wing scores, neither coefficient is statistically significant, and both age and gender show virtually no association with the scale values. Hence, while religion, gender and age may be salient for other types of opinion, their unique effect upon attitudes to *material* inequality can be ruled out. Consequently, subsequent analyses will focus upon social class.

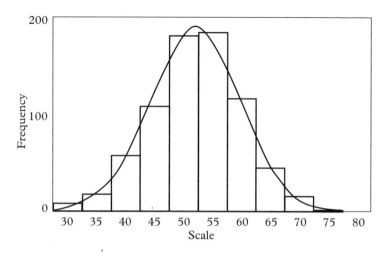

Figure 11.1 Distribution of 'left/right wing scale' values

Table 11.1 Statements and questions used in construction of 'left/right wing' scale*

---

There is one law for the rich and one for the poor.
Inequality continues to exist because it benefits the rich and powerful.
To get all the way to the top in Northern Ireland today, you have to be corrupt.
In Northern Ireland people get rewarded for their effort.
In Northern Ireland people get rewarded for their intelligence and skills.
Large differences in income are necessary for Northern Ireland's prosperity.
Ordinary working people get their fair share of the nation's wealth.
Differences in income in Northern Ireland are too large.
It is the responsibility of the government to reduce the differences in income
  between people with high incomes and those with low incomes.
Inequality continues to exist because ordinary people don't join together to get
  rid of it.
Present economic differences between rich and poor countries are too large.
People in wealthy countries should make an additional tax contribution to
  help people in poor countries.
How important is coming from a wealthy family?
How important is knowing the right people?
Is it right or wrong that people with higher incomes can buy better health care
  than people with lower incomes?
Is it right or wrong that people with higher incomes can buy better education
  than people with lower incomes?
In your opinion, in Northern Ireland how much conflict is there between poor
  people and rich people?

---

* Cronbach's *Alpha* internal consistency reliability measure = 0.7138.

Table 11.2 Regression on 'left/right wing' scale

| Variable | Standardised coefficient |
| --- | --- |
| Social class* | 0.205 |
| Age | 0.012 |
| Gender (0 = female, 1 = male) | 0.001 |
| Catholic (0 = others, 1 = Catholic) | −0.088 |
| Protestant (0 = others, 1 = Protestant) | 0.094 |
| $r^2$ | 0.068 |

* The effect of social class on the respondent's score is highly significant ($p < 0.001$, $b = 0.205$). All other variables are not significant.

Table 11.3 displays the mean scores on the left/right wing scale for each of the six social class categories. The differences between classes are statistically significant and the pattern is as one might expect – the higher the social class, the more conservative a respondent is likely to be. The mean for the professional category shows the greatest separation from the rest, being over five units above that for managerial/technical but there is no abrupt break between the non-manual and manual categories. Social class will not always have a significant effect upon response but, when social class is found to make a difference, these patterns will reappear: a steady gradient towards more conservative responses as one moves up the social class hierarchy; a more extreme shift for the highest professional group; but no abrupt change in opinions at the manual/non-manual divide.

Table 11.3 Mean score on 'left/right wing' scale by social class

| Social class* | Mean score |
| --- | --- |
| Professional | 58.8 |
| Managerial/technical | 53.7 |
| Non-manual | 52.4 |
| Skilled manual | 51.4 |
| Partly skilled | 50.2 |
| Unskilled | 50.4 |

* Significance of differences in mean scores (analysis of variance): $p < 0.001$

## Attitudes to Social Inequality

In order to test attitudes to general social inequality issues, respondents were asked to indicate how much they agreed or disagreed with a set of 13 statements (Table 11.4). In general, respondents tend towards moderation in their opinions, avoiding strong agreement or strong disagreement, and tend to be neutral or only to agree or disagree with statements.

The ISSP Social Inequality module was also asked in the 1999 British Social Attitudes survey (Jowell, Curtice, Park, Thomson, Jarvis, Bromley and Stratford, 2000), so it is possible to compare the Northern Irish responses with those for Britain. There is an almost exact correspondence between the two surveys in the distribution of responses for the vast majority of questions. The rare instances when the British pattern of responses differs from that for Northern Ireland will be discussed later in this chapter.

Significant proportions of Northern Irish respondents are fairly cynical about the general fairness of social stratification, with over half of the sample agreeing with both the statements 'inequality continues to exist because it benefits the rich and powerful' and 'there is one law for the rich and one law for the poor'. In contrast to the other social classes, nearly half (47 per cent) of respondents within the highest social class stratum, the professionals, disagree with the latter statement.

The cynicism evident in the responses to these first two questions is moderated somewhat in that less than 20 per cent of the sample agree that 'to get all the way to the top in Northern Ireland today you have to be corrupt'. Again, perhaps it is not surprising that over three quarters of those closest to the top, the professionals, disagree with this statement. 'Meritocracy' can be expressed in the formula: Ability + Effort = Reward. The general support for a meritocratic view of society continues with more respondents agreeing or strongly agreeing than disagreeing or strongly disagreeing with the statements that 'people get rewarded for their effort' and 'people get rewarded for their intelligence and skills'. However, this meritocratic view is tempered by instrumentality: almost three quarters of respondents agree or strongly agree that 'no one would study unless they expected to earn more than ordinary workers'.

There is little support for the current level of inequalities in income and wealth, and this is uniform across class lines. Three times as many people disagree/strongly disagree rather than agree/strongly agree that 'large differences in income are necessary for Northern Ireland's prosperity' and that 'ordinary working people get their fair share of the nation's wealth'. Similarly, almost two thirds of respondents agree that 'differences in income in Northern Ireland are too large'. One in six respondents (16 per cent) strongly agree with this statement, compared with 31 per cent of British respondents who strongly agree with the equivalent statement for Britain. There is also general agreement by almost two thirds of Northern Irish respondents that 'it is the government's responsibility to reduce differences in income'.

Table 11.4 Agreement/disagreement with equality statements (%)

| | Strongly agree | Agree | Neutral | Disagree | Strongly disagree |
|---|---|---|---|---|---|
| One law for rich, one for poor*** | 23 | 46 | 17 | 14 | 1 |
| Inequality benefits rich and powerful*** | 10 | 46 | 27 | 16 | 1 |
| You have to be corrupt to get to the top** | 5 | 14 | 29 | 35 | 18 |
| People are rewarded for effort*** | 4 | 39 | 33 | 20 | 4 |
| People are rewarded for intelligence and skills[ns] | 5 | 49 | 27 | 16 | 3 |
| Only reason to study is higher earnings*** | 24 | 48 | 14 | 12 | 2 |
| Prosperity requires a large income differential[ns] | 2 | 14 | 34 | 40 | 10 |
| Ordinary people get a fair share of wealth[ns] | 2 | 17 | 19 | 49 | 13 |
| Income differential in NI is too large[ns] | 16 | 48 | 27 | 8 | 1 |
| Government should reduce income differentials*** | 17 | 45 | 24 | 12 | 1 |
| Ordinary people don't fight inequality*** | 7 | 38 | 33 | 20 | 3 |
| Gap between rich and poor countries is too large* | 26 | 54 | 17 | 3 | <1 |
| More tax on wealthy to help poor nations[ns] | 18 | 39 | 26 | 15 | 3 |

Significance of association (Kendall's $Tau^b$) with social class:
[ns] Not significant
* p<0.05
** p<0.01
*** p<0.001

Here, however, support is not uniform across classes. In contrast to all other groups, the comparatively high income professionals, who would lose out if income differentials were reduced, are more likely to disagree rather than agree with this statement. Neither is there much support for the idea that the solidarity of average people combats inequality; only one fifth of the sample disagree with the statement 'inequality continues to exist because ordinary people don't join together to get rid of it'.

In keeping with its cross-national comparative bent, the ISSP Social Inequality module contains two statements about social inequality between nations: 'present economic differences between rich and poor countries are too large' and 'people in wealthy countries should make an additional tax contribution to help people in poor countries'. Large proportions of the sample agree that the economic differential is too large (80 per cent) and claim they would be in favour of paying additional tax to reduce it (55 per cent).

While there is agreement with the principle of meritocracy, large proportions of respondents also see 'connections' as being significant for who actually gets ahead. Over half of respondents feel that 'coming from a wealthy family' is important, with almost 20 per cent stating it is very important and a further 5 per cent saying essential (Table 11.5). The proportion believing that 'knowing the right people' is important is even higher, with less than a quarter saying these type of connections are not significant. Proportionately more of the professionals than any other strata see connections as being not very important.

Table 11.5 Attitudes towards the importance of connections (%)

| | Essential | Very important | Fairly important | Not very important | Not at all important |
|---|---|---|---|---|---|
| Coming from a wealthy family[ns] | 5 | 19 | 29 | 31 | 16 |
| Knowing the right people*** | 10 | 29 | 38 | 18 | 5 |

Significance of association (Kendall's $Tau^b$) with social class:
[ns] Not significant
*** $p < 0.001$

One might have expected that few would support the obvious inequalities of rich people having the right to use their wealth to purchase better health care or educational opportunities than those available to the general population, but this is in fact not the case. Somewhat more of the respondents say that it is right that 'people with higher incomes can buy better health care' and 'people with higher incomes can buy better education' than the proportions who say it is wrong (Table 11.6). Furthermore, these views are general across all class strata and do not just reflect the self-interest of the upper groups. Just as many respondents in the upper non-manual strata as in the lower manual strata believe that using their wealth in this manner is wrong. Similarly, the proportions of the lower manual strata that say purchasing better health care or education is definitely or somewhat right are just as large as for the rest of the sample. In contrast to Northern Ireland, a higher proportion of respondents in Britain say that the use of wealth to secure better health care or education is definitely right.

Table 11.6 Attitudes towards the use of wealth (%)

|  | Definitely right | Somewhat right | Neutral | Somewhat wrong | Definitely wrong |
|---|---|---|---|---|---|
| Buying better health care[ns] | 15 | 26 | 22 | 18 | 19 |
| Buying better education[ns] | 16 | 25 | 21 | 18 | 20 |

Significance of association (Kendall's $Tau^b$) with social class:
[ns] Not significant

The high level of support for the statement 'it is the government's responsibility to reduce differences in income' implies support for increased taxation. This is confirmed by a direct question. Three quarters of respondents say people with high incomes should shoulder a larger or much larger share of the tax burden (Table 11.7). While there is a statistically significant association with social class, this significance is largely due to a somewhat higher proportion of the partly skilled manual strata supporting a much larger share of the tax burden being placed on the rich. In general, a majority of all strata support a more steeply gradated income tax, and even two thirds of the upper non-manual strata support raised taxes on the wealthy.

Table 11.7 Tax share of people with high income should be ...** (%)

| Much larger | Larger | Same as now | Smaller |
|---|---|---|---|
| 26 | 47 | 27 | 1 |

Significance of association (Kendall's $Tau^b$) with social class:
** $p<0.01$

## Perceptions of Extent of Conflict in Society

Respondents were asked five questions about their perceptions of the extent of conflict between groups in Northern Ireland. In effect, these

questions are assessing the prevalence of different views of social stratification among the sample, since four of the pairs contrasted are all
different ways of conceiving of the top and the bottom of society. The
fifth pair is an age-based contrast between the young and the old.
Unfortunately, the survey does not ask the extent of conflict between
groups defined by religion or gender, so an opportunity to compare the
relative salience in people's minds of different types of social stratification has been lost.

Table 11.8 shows that the results are remarkably congruent across
all five pairs. Typically, one in five respondents say that there is no
conflict between the groups named for four of the five pairs. The
modal answer for all pairs is that the extent of conflict is not very
strong. The proportions in Northern Ireland who see no conflict are
considerably higher than those for Britain.

Table 11.8 Perceptions of extent of conflict in Northern Ireland between
different groups (%)

| | Very strong | Strong | Not very strong | No conflict |
|---|---|---|---|---|
| Poor and rich* | 5 | 29 | 49 | 17 |
| Working and middle class* | 3 | 22 | 54 | 21 |
| Workers and management[ns] | 6 | 40 | 45 | 9 |
| Bottom and top of society[ns] | 10 | 37 | 38 | 15 |
| Young and old[ns] | 6 | 27 | 46 | 22 |

Significance of association (Kendall's $Tau^b$) with social class:
[ns] Not significant
* $p < 0.05$

The pair 'top and bottom of society' has somewhat more who state
that conflict is very strong. The extent of difference between classes
is minimal, only barely reaching statistical significance for the contrasts
between 'poor and rich people' and 'the working and middle classes'.
In these instances the upper non-manual professional and
managerial/technical strata are less likely to claim that conflict is strong,
in contrast to the unskilled strata in which more do claim conflict is
strong. Hence, there is only weak evidence of support for an hypothesis
of people in Northern Ireland having a view of class-based conflict
that is informed by any doctrinaire roots.

## Pay

The Social Inequality module contains a broad collection of items that
relate to pay and level of remuneration. Respondents were asked about

the importance of a set of factors for deciding the level of pay: 1) 'time spent in education/training'; 2) 'how well the job is done'; 3) 'how hard the person works'; 4) 'the amount of responsibility'; 5) 'whether the job requires supervising others'; 6) 'what is needed to support a family'; 7) 'whether the person has children to support'. Table 11.9 shows that an overwhelming majority of respondents rate all factors at least fairly important. The significance of the meritocratic viewpoint comes through clearly via response to education/training, how well a job is done and how hard one works all being rated highly. These factors are rated higher than responses to the same questions on the British Social Attitudes survey. The factor attracting the most support among Life and Times survey respondents is how well a job is done, with over 80 per cent rating it as very important or essential. Levels of responsibility and supervision also are seen by most respondents as important for pay. The significant association of level of responsibility with social class is due to more of the managerial/technical strata – perhaps not surprisingly – rating this factor as essential, and more of the unskilled rating it as not very important.

Table 11.9 Attitudes towards the importance of different factors in deciding pay (%)

|  | Essential | Very important | Fairly important | Not very important | Not at all important |
|---|---|---|---|---|---|
| Education/training* | 17 | 44 | 33 | 6 | <1 |
| How well job is done[ns] | 31 | 50 | 18 | 2 | <1 |
| How hard one works* | 28 | 48 | 21 | 2 | <1 |
| Amount of responsibility** | 25 | 54 | 21 | 1 | <1 |
| Supervising others[ns] | 11 | 51 | 34 | 3 | <1 |
| Need to support a family*** | 17 | 38 | 30 | 11 | 4 |
| Children to support*** | 15 | 29 | 29 | 18 | 9 |

Significance of association (Kendall's $Tau^b$) with social class:
[ns] Not significant
* $p<0.05$
** $p<0.01$
*** $p<0.001$

Opinions about the significance of family responsibilities for deciding the level of remuneration are less unanimous. While these are still seen as important, differences between social strata become more significant. Probably reflecting different levels of financial constraint, the upper non-manual strata are more likely than the rest to rate family responsibilities as not very important or not at all important. The lower manual strata, in contrast, are more likely to rate family responsibilities as essential or very important for setting pay. Northern Irish respondents rate the two family responsibility options higher than the British.

Respondents were also asked to estimate how much people in nine different occupations earn and then to say how much they think people in those same occupations should earn. Table 11.10 shows the resulting averages contrasted with the self-reported earnings of the working respondents themselves, and their statement of what they think they should earn. The nine specified occupations unfortunately concentrate upon six high-level occupations which are contrasted with three fairly low-level occupations, thereby missing out the majority of employed people who would fall somewhere in between. Nevertheless, the results are enlightening. When the respondents' estimates of actual earnings are contrasted with their feelings about what certain occupations should earn, the pattern is clear. With the exception of general practitioners (GPs), respondents feel that the highly paid are overpaid and that the lowly paid deserve more. The overpayment differences range from £8,230 too much for solicitors to £41,650 for chairmen. In contrast, the amounts of underpayment for the less well paid occupations are all similar, averaging out at £2,680. There are no clear-cut differences between social class categories in terms of their estimates of what occupations are paid, what they should be paid or the difference between the two. All class strata, including the higher strata, see the higher occupations as being overpaid and the lower occupations as underpaid.

Table 11.10 Respondents' estimate of levels of pay of selected occupations (£)

| Occupation | Estimate of pay | Should be paid | Difference |
|---|---|---|---|
| Chairman | 111,310 | 69,990 | 41,650 |
| Judge | 77,400 | 56,660 | 20,740 |
| Cabinet minister | 70,220 | 46,820 | 19,510 |
| Factory manager | 66,330 | 55,950 | 10,380 |
| Solicitor | 50,030 | 41,800 | 8,230 |
| GP | 40,690 | 41,160 | −470 |
| Factory worker | 13,660 | 16,310 | −2,650 |
| Unskilled worker | 9,580 | 12,110 | −2,530 |
| Shop assistant | 8,740 | 11,600 | −2,860 |
| Respondent's own earnings | 15,110 | 18,560 | −3,450 |

On average, respondents see their incomes as closer to that of the lowly paid; the average of £15,110 for all working respondents is just £1,450 above that of the highest of the low, factory worker. However, it is important to note that the income figure is for *working* respondents only. If the incomes of non-working respondents were included, the average would drop. The average amount they feel they should be paid – £18,560 – is £3,450 above their actual pay. Hence, as with their view of the three lowly paid occupations, respondents in general feel themselves to be underpaid. This was confirmed when they were asked about their opinions of their earnings (Table 11.11).

Table 11.11 Does the respondent think his/her pay is fair?[ns] (%)

| Much less than fair | A little less than fair | About fair | A little more than fair | Much more than fair |
| --- | --- | --- | --- | --- |
| 16 | 39 | 42 | 2 | 1 |

Significance of association (Kendall's $Tau^b$) with social class:
[ns] Not significant

Just over 40 per cent of respondents feel that their pay is 'about fair for me', and a similar proportion feel that their earnings are 'what I deserve' (Table 11.2). However, almost no one feels they are overpaid and the majority feel underpaid, including 16 per cent who feel their pay is much less than what is fair and 16 per cent who feel it is much less than they deserve. In particular, it is the partly skilled strata that feels it is paid 'much less than I deserve'.

Table 11.12 Respondents' assessment of their own earnings*** (%)

| Much less than deserved | Less than deserved | What I deserve | More than deserved | Much more than deserved |
| --- | --- | --- | --- | --- |
| 16 | 40 | 42 | 1 | <1 |

Significance of association (Kendall's $Tau^b$) with social class:
*** p<0.001

While implementing the respondents' feelings about appropriate levels of pay would result in a narrowing of pay differentials between the lowest and highest paid, the respondents' views on the amount of pay that different occupations deserve does not constitute an attack on income differentials. Even if the respondents' views could be put into effect and the differential between the highest paid and lowest paid occupations halved from a factor of almost 13 to a factor of 6, this differential still would be substantial.

### Changes in Social Status

Respondents were asked to rank themselves on a scale of social status ranging from one to ten (where ten was high status) and then to repeat the operation for where they feel they would have been ranked ten years earlier. The majority of respondents put themselves at the middle of the scales both for the present and ten years ago – on each ten point scale, over half the respondents place themselves at points 5 or 6. While minorities of respondents in each social class category rank themselves high or low, most opt for the centre (Figure 11.2). Respondents in the lower class categories tend to self-assign themselves somewhat lower rankings and there is a significant correlation between social class level (as determined by coding respondents' job) and their self-assigned status level.

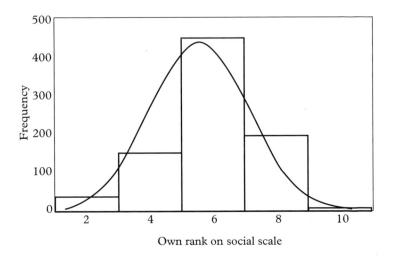

Figure 11.2 Self-ranking on social scale

While the rankings that respondents give themselves in the present and those they give themselves for ten years ago are highly correlated, the correlation is not perfect and there is a noteworthy amount of change (Figure 11.3). Half of the respondents give themselves a different ranking now compared to that of ten years ago. While the general trend is up, the overall mean rises by only a quarter of a unit, and 18 per cent rank themselves *lower* than ten years ago.

A regression analysis of the effects of social class, religion, gender and age upon change in self-ranking was carried out to establish which factor was most important in causing a change in self-perceived status. The results, as shown in Table 11.13 indicate that age is by far the most important: being older is highly significantly associated with giving oneself a lower rank in comparison to ten years ago. Probably as a reflection of improving chances of upward mobility for Catholics

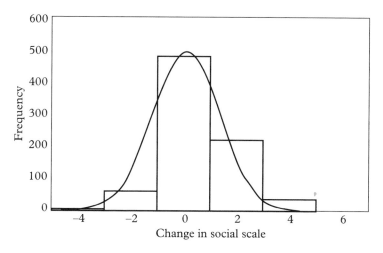

Figure 11.3 Change in ranking over last ten years

(Breen, 2000; Miller, 2001), after taking account of the effect of age, being Roman Catholic is associated with giving oneself a higher rank now. Similarly, the regression results indicate that those currently in higher social class positions are more likely to report an improvement in social standing. Presumably, the reason for this is that at least some of those presently in higher strata moved up into them during the last ten years, as well as some of those in lower strata having fallen down over the same period. Neither being Protestant nor one's gender is found to exert a significant independent effect upon change in self-ranked status.

Table 11.13 Regression on change in social standing

| Variable | Standardised coefficient |
| --- | --- |
| Social class | 0.094** |
| Age | −0.248*** |
| Gender (0 = female, 1 = male) | 0.066[ns] |
| Catholic (0 = others, 1 = Catholic) | 0.147** |
| Protestant (0 = others, 1 = Protestant) | 0.029[ns] |
| $r^2$ | 0.089 |

[ns] Not significant
** p<0.01
*** p<0.001

Table 11.14 shows the actual amount of change for the variables that were found to be significant. The professional social class category shows the greatest rise of any in the table, an increase of +0.77 unit. After that, the amount of rise gradually tails off as one goes down the strata until the unskilled category shows no net increase. While the non-Catholic religion category shows a moderate increase, the increase in status reported by Catholics is three times greater. The mean changes for age categories shows a combination of ageing and life/career course effects. The youngest age category reports a relatively large increase in self-assigned status (which is hardly surprising since these respondents are comparing themselves to ten years previously when they were still children or young adolescents). Respondents aged between 25 and 34 years are those who are moving into what will be the peak earning years for many and this is reflected in the large increase in comparative status that they report. After that, the size of the increase in status gradually tails off until the oldest age group of those still of working age, aged between 55 and 64 years, actually reports a net drop in status in comparison to a decade before. This presumably reflects the drop in earning potential that many suffer from in their latter working years along with chronic long-term unemployment forcing some into what in effect is an early retirement. Finally, the greatest drop in status is reported by respondents aged 65 years and over, reflecting the drops in living standards to which many of the elderly and retired fall victim.

Table 11.14 Mean change in social standing scale over last 10 years

| Social class | Professional | 0.77 |
|---|---|---|
| | Managerial/technical | 0.35 |
| | Non-manual | 0.38 |
| | Skilled manual | 0.25 |
| | Partly skilled | 0.13 |
| | Unskilled | −0.01 |
| Religion | Catholic | 0.47 |
| | Non-Catholic | 0.13 |
| Age | 18–24 | 0.53 |
| | 25–34 | 0.72 |
| | 35–44 | 0.31 |
| | 45–54 | 0.14 |
| | 55–64 | −0.15 |
| | 65 years and older | −0.24 |
| Overall | | 0.251 |

Respondents were also asked to compare the status of their job with that held by their father when they were 16 years old. Reflecting the general trend of upward social mobility in Northern Ireland over the last generation, over half assess their present status as being higher than that of their father, with only one in five saying it is lower (Table 11.15). As one would expect, more of the upper non-manual strata than the rest of the sample feel that their status was higher. More of the unskilled manual strata than the others feel that their current status is lower, but even in this group more report a net improvement (36 per cent say their status is higher, in contrast with 32 per cent who said it is lower or much lower).

Table 11.15 Job status of respondent compared to father (%)

|  | Much higher than father | Higher than father | About the same | Lower than father | Much lower than father |
|---|---|---|---|---|---|
| Professional | 23 | 62 | 8 | 8 | – |
| Managerial/Technical | 20 | 44 | 20 | 13 | 3 |
| Non-manual | 16 | 30 | 29 | 20 | 5 |
| Skilled manual | 12 | 39 | 36 | 12 | 1 |
| Partly skilled | 10 | 38 | 33 | 13 | 6 |
| Unskilled | 10 | 26 | 32 | 31 | 1 |
| Overall | 15 | 37 | 29 | 16 | 4 |

Significance of Kendall's $tau^b$ p<0.001

## Conclusion

The political landscape in Northern Ireland remains warped by the sectarian divide so that people only have the realistic option of voting for parties that are more or less extreme in their unionism or nationalism. The normal option of choosing a party on the left or the right of the political spectrum in effect is not available. Options are theoretically available such as the Conservative Party, the Women's Coalition or the Green Party, but these very definitely are minority parties with even less of a prospect than the mainstream Northern Irish parties of wielding real power in government. Even the Alliance Party, the party of the centre, draws its sole rationale for existence from (anti-)sectarianism. This means that debate around issues such as the extent of material inequality and government intervention in people's lives that inform normal politics elsewhere receive short shrift in Northern Ireland. In most countries, elections provide the acid test of people's true political beliefs along a continuum from left to right. However, in Northern Ireland where all politics, whatever its hue of orange or green, is basically reactionary, this corrective is not possible. In such a context, the findings of the ISSP Social Inequality module provide a valuable insight into public opinion about real politics.

The patterns of responses to questions on inequality for Northern Ireland match those for Britain almost exactly. The differences that can be found between the two are not that the Northern Irish are more conservative, but rather that the Northern Irish tend to be somewhat more likely to favour meritocratic opinions. At the same time, however, there is no apparent evidence that those who hold left wing opinions in Northern Ireland also cleave to any particular doctrine. Hence, the sphere of non-sectarian political opinion in Northern Ireland can be characterised by generalised support for left-oriented redistributive social policies that transcend class boundaries with this generalised support existing independent of any class-based ideology.

Seen in this light, the results from the Social Inequality module are very interesting. The dominance of unionism in Protestant politics and the litany that 'the Northern Irish are at heart a conservative people' do not seem to fit with the drift of empirical findings here. Majorities of respondents favour policies and express opinions that, if implemented, would have the effect of redistributing wealth through higher levels of taxation, particularly taxation of the better off. Those in jobs receiving higher levels of pay are generally seen as being overpaid and those in low-paid jobs are seen as under-remunerated. Furthermore, while there clearly are links between opinions and class position with respondents located in the higher strata holding somewhat more right wing views, this association with class is not overarching. Many, often a majority, of those in the upper strata *also* favour redistributive social policies and voice left wing opinions. At the same time, there is no apparent evidence that those who hold left wing opinions also cleave to any particular doctrine. Hence, the sphere of non-sectarian political opinion in Northern Ireland can be characterised by generalised support for left-oriented redistributive social policies that transcends class boundaries and, interestingly, this generalised support seems to exist independent of any class-based political ideology.

### References

Breen, Richard (2000) 'Class inequality and social mobility', *American Sociological Review*, Vol. 65, No. 3.

Jowell, Roger, Curtice, John, Park, Alison, Thomson, Katarina, Jarvis, Lindsey, Bromley, Catherine and Stratford, Nina (eds) (2000) *British Social Attitudes: The 17th Report – Focusing on Diversity* (London: Sage Publications/National Centre for Social Research).

Kremer, John and Montgomery, Pamela (eds) (1993) *Women's Working Lives* (Belfast: HMSO).

Miller, Robert (2001) *Social Mobility in Northern Ireland – Patterns by Religion and Gender* (Belfast: Equality Commission for Northern Ireland).

# Appendix I
# Technical Details of the Survey

*Paula Devine*

The chapters within this book primarily use data from the 1998 and 1999 Northern Ireland Life and Times surveys. However, some chapters also refer to data from the Northern Ireland Social Attitudes survey series which ran from 1989 to 1996 (Stringer and Robinson, 1991; 1992; 1993; Breen, Devine and Robinson, 1995; Breen, Devine and Dowds, 1996; Dowds, Devine and Breen, 1997; Robinson, Heenan, Gray and Thompson, 1998), as well as to other attitudes surveys, such as the British Social Attitudes survey.

## *The Overall Design*

The Life and Times survey involves face-to-face interviews with adults aged 18 years and over. The main part of the interview is carried out using computer assisted personal interviewing (CAPI) and the respondent is also asked to complete a self-completion questionnaire. The Young Life and Times survey, which runs alongside the adult version, includes interviews with young people aged 12 to 17 years. This involves a paper questionnaire containing a sub-set of questions from the adult survey, and one complete module of particular relevance to young people. In 1998 this was Rights of the Child, with Education being the focus in 1999.

## *Survey Content*

The survey consists of a set of modules which varies between years, although most modules are designed to be carried out on a regular basis, so that time-series data can be built up in years to come. However, two modules – Political Attitudes and Community Relations – are undertaken annually.

Not all modules are asked of the full adult sample. Where a smaller sample size is sufficient for a module, the sample is split, such that only half the respondents are asked those questions. For example, the structure of the 1999 survey allowed for half the sample to be asked the questions within the Attitudes to Genetics Research module, while the other half were asked questions within the Transport module. The modules included in the 1998 and 1999 surveys are shown in Table A1.1.

The questions asked as part of the International Social Survey Programme (ISSP) are included in the self-completion questionnaires. In 1998 this module focused on Religious Observance, and on Social Inequality in 1999.

Table A1.1 Survey content by year

|      | Version A | Version B |
|------|-----------|-----------|
| 1998 | Background | Background |
|      | Rights of the Child | Public Understanding of Science |
|      | Political Attitudes | Political Attitudes |
|      | Crime and Fear of Crime | Gender and Family Roles |
|      | Community Relations | Community Relations |
|      | Housing | Housing |
|      | Religious Observance (ISSP) | |
| 1999 | Background | Background |
|      | Attitudes to Genetics Research | Transport |
|      | Political Attitudes | Political Attitudes |
|      | Education | Education |
|      | Community Relations | Community Relations |
|      | Pensions and Pensioners | Pensions and Pensioners |
|      | Social Inequality (ISSP) | |

### Sampling Methodology

The Postcode Address File (PAF) is used as the survey sampling frame, and is a comprehensive database of addresses in Northern Ireland. The sampling process begins by stratifying Northern Ireland into three geographic regions – Belfast, east of the Bann and west of the Bann – based on an amalgamation of District Council Areas. This stratification is undertaken to ensure that areas of lower population density, such as those west of the Bann, are adequately represented, and is standard practice in Northern Ireland social surveys. A random sample of addresses is then taken from each stratum, with probability proportionate to the number of addresses within it.

The next stage involves randomly selecting one adult to be interviewed from each household, which is achieved by the interviewer carrying out a Kish grid procedure. In this way, one adult is randomly selected from a household, which itself is randomly selected. However, this introduces a bias, as an adult living in a household with a large number of adults is less likely to be asked to take part than adults living in small or single adult households. To compensate for this, the data are weighted by a weight factor (WTFACTOR) which is based on the number of adults within the household.

During the interview with the selected adult, information is collected on the age and sex of every member of the household, as well as their relationship to the respondent. The CAPI programme identifies any 12 to 17 year olds, all of whom are eligible to participate in the Young Life and Times survey. Their parent or guardian is asked to sign a formal consent form, giving permission for them to be interviewed. Thus, all young people aged 12 to 17 years in that household are interviewed, unless they are unavailable or unwilling to take part. No weighting procedure is required when analysing the data from the Young Life and Times survey.

During the fieldwork for the 1998 survey, it was apparent that the number of interviews achieved with young people was likely to be lower than expected. For this reason, it was decided to initiate a booster sample at the mid-point of the fieldwork to make up for the shortfall. A separate random sample of addresses was taken from the PAF. When interviewers called at these addresses, they established whether any young people aged 12 to 17 years were normally resident there. If so, permission was sought in the normal way to interview all such young people and interviews proceeded as described above.

The 1999 Life and Times survey included a module on Pensions and Pensioners, part of which focused solely on respondents of pensionable age (that is, women aged 60 years and over, and men aged 65 years and over). In order to yield a large enough number of respondents to enable in-depth analysis, a booster sample was taken, in consultation with the funding bodies. This additional sampling frame consisted of recipients of state retirement pension, and those of pensionable age who received any of six other benefits (including relevant disability benefits and Income Support). Interviews were achieved with 818 pensioners – 505 identifed from the main sample, and 313 from the booster sample.

### Fieldwork

Households identified in the sample were sent an advance letter which explained the purpose of the survey, outlined the method by which an individual respondent would be selected from the household, and requested cooperation with the project. The letter provided households with contact details for the project team and the fieldwork company, and also confirmed that a donation of £1 would be made to Action Cancer on behalf of each respondent.

For each year of the survey, fieldwork took place during October to December, although this was extended to mid-January 2000 for the 1999 survey. Interviewing was carried out by social survey interviewers employed by Research and Evaluation Services (RES). Every fieldworker attended a briefing session conducted jointly by RES and members of the Life and Times survey project team.

All interviews were conducted in the respondents' homes. Interviewers made up to a maximum of five calls before the person identified in the sample was deemed to be non-obtainable. Table A1.2 shows the status of addresses, and the number of addresses identified as 'in scope'. The self-completion form was either completed and handed back to the interviewer at the time of the main interview, or the interviewer called back at a later stage to collect it.

Table A1.2 Status of addresses

| Year | Addresses issued | Vacant /Derelict /Commercial | Total in scope |
|------|------------------|------------------------------|----------------|
| 1998 | 2,806 | 158 | 2,648 |
| 1999 | 3,337 | 189 | 3,148 |

## Response Rates

Table A1.3 shows the reason for non-achievement of interviews with adults drawn in the sample. Table A1.4 shows the response rate for versions A and B of the main stage interviews, as well as for the self-completion questionnaires. Table A1.5 shows the response rates for the Young Life and Times survey.

Table A1.3 Breakdown of response for adults

| | 1998 | | 1999 | |
|---|---|---|---|---|
| | Number | % | Number | % |
| Achieved | 1,800 | 68 | 2,200 | 70 |
| Refused | 497 | 19 | 551 | 17 |
| Non-contact | 325 | 12 | 337 | 11 |
| Other | 26 | 1 | 60 | 2 |
| Total | 2,648 | 100 | 3,148 | 100 |

Table A1.4 Completion of versions A and B

|                                          | 1998 | | 1999 | |
|                                          | Version A | Version B | Version A | Version B |
|------------------------------------------|-----------|-----------|-----------|-----------|
| Number of main stage interviews          | 910       | 890       | 1,076     | 1,124     |
| Number of self-completion achieved       | 812       | 813       | 830       | 902       |
| % of self-completion achieved            | 89        | 91        | 77        | 80        |

Table A1.5 Breakdown of response for young people

|                                                      | 1998 | 1999 |
|------------------------------------------------------|------|------|
| Total number of young people identified              | 482  | 608  |
| Total number of young people interviewed             | 356  | 449  |
| Response rate for Young Life and Times survey (%)    | 74   | 74   |

## Sampling Errors and Confidence Intervals

Since no sample ever entirely represents the characteristics of the population from which it is drawn, it is necessary to estimate the amount of error due to the sampling methodology. The Life and Times survey uses a simple random sample design, whereby each member of the population has an equal chance of being included in the sample. For such a design, the sampling error of any percentage ($p$) can be calculated using the following formula, where $n$ is the number of respondents upon which $p$ is formulated:

*Sampling error (s.e.) of $p = \sqrt{(p(100 - p)/n)}$*

The 95 per cent confidence interval for the population percentage can be calculated, using the following formula:

*95 per cent confidence interval = $p \pm 1.96 \times s.e.$ ($p$)*

Table A1.6 displays the sampling errors and confidence intervals for key variables from the 1998 and 1999 Life and Times survey. The margin of error for all sample estimates is within the parameters of $\pm 3\%$

Table A1.6 Sampling errors and confidence intervals for key variables by year

| | | %(p) | Standard Error of p (%) | 95% confidence intervals |
|---|---|---|---|---|
| 1998 | *Age* | | | |
| | 18–24 | 10.3 | 0.7 | 8.9–11.7 |
| | 25–44 | 40.8 | 1.2 | 38.5–43.1 |
| | 45–64 | 30.0 | 1.1 | 27.9–32.1 |
| | 65–74 | 11.4 | 0.8 | 9.9–12.9 |
| | 75 years and over | 7.4 | 0.6 | 6.2–8.61 |
| | *Gender* | | | |
| | Male | 43.3 | 1.2 | 41.0–45.6 |
| | Female | 56.7 | 1.2 | 54.4–59.0 |
| | *Marital status* | | | |
| | Married/cohabiting | 53.4 | 1.2 | 51.0–55.7 |
| | Single | 25.2 | 1.0 | 23.2–27.2 |
| | Widowed/divorced/separated | 21.4 | 1.0 | 19.5–23.3 |
| | *Religion* | | | |
| | Catholic | 35.1 | 1.1 | 32.9–37.3 |
| | Protestant | 52.6 | 1.2 | 50.3–54.9 |
| | No religion | 9.9 | 0.7 | 8.5–11.3 |
| | Other | 1.3 | 0.3 | 0.8–1.8 |
| | Refused | 2.1 | 0.3 | 1.4–2.8 |
| 1999 | *Age* | | | |
| | 18–24 | 11.0 | 0.7 | 9.7–12.3 |
| | 25–44 | 40.2 | 1.1 | 38.2–42.3 |
| | 45–64 | 29.2 | 1.0 | 27.3–31.1 |
| | 65–74 | 10.4 | 0.7 | 9.1–11.7 |
| | 75 years and over | 8.6 | 0.6 | 7.4–9.8 |
| | *Gender* | | | |
| | Male | 42.7 | 1.1 | 40.6–44.8 |
| | Female | 57.3 | 1.1 | 55.2–59.4 |
| | *Marital status* | | | |
| | Married/cohabiting | 50.6 | 1.1 | 48.5–52.7 |
| | Single | 27.6 | 1.0 | 25.7–29.5 |
| | Widowed/divorced/separated | 21.7 | 0.9 | 20.0–23.4 |
| | *Religion* | | | |
| | Catholic | 37.7 | 1.0 | 35.7–39.7 |
| | Protestant | 48.6 | 1.1 | 46.5–50.7 |
| | No religion | 10.1 | 0.6 | 8.8–11.4 |
| | Other | 0.1 | 0.1 | 0–0.1 |
| | Refused | 3.5 | 0.4 | 2.7–4.3 |

### *Data Preparation*

Data from the main stage of the survey were collected by CAPI using Surveycraft software. These were then converted to SPSS format to facilitate analysis. All paper-based data (self-completion questionnaires and the young person's survey) were entered via the SPSS data entry system. The data files from the CAPI and self-completion questionnaires were then merged and were subject to an extensive range of inter- and intra-variable logic checks.

Occupational variables were derived using the Computer Assisted Standard Occupational Coding (CASOC) software. This programme enables a match to be made between the text describing the respondent's occupation and the most similar occupational description taken from the Registrar General's Standard Classification of Occupations. When a match is made, the system automatically assigns the official three digit code from the Standard Classification of Occupations to this case. This three digit code is the direct basis for the derivation of related information on a social class grouping.

### Dissemination

Survey results are put on the Life and Times web site <http://www.ark.ac.uk/nilt> six months after the end of fieldwork, providing frequency tables for every question, along with a breakdown by age, gender and religion. Users can also download the actual SPSS data files from the web site if they wish to undertake their own secondary analysis. Technical reports are produced for each year in Portable Document Format (PDF) and are posted at <http://www.ark.ac.uk/nilt/techinfo.html>. The web site also includes publications and online resources relevant to the survey topics.

The datasets for each year are also lodged with the UK Data Archive at the University of Essex <http://www.data-archive.ac.uk>. Data relating to the ISSP module are lodged in the Zentralarchiv für Empirische Sozialforschung (Central Archive for Empirical Social Research) at the University of Cologne <http://www.gesis.org/en/za/index.htm>.

The survey team has also set up a helpline for those who need additional tables or have any query about the survey. A leaflet advertising the existence of the data and how to access them is also sent to schools, voluntary groups, civil servants, journalists and assembly members. The funders of the survey receive the dataset somewhat earlier than the public (three months after the end of fieldwork). However, funders also agree to one of the guiding principles of the survey, that the information is made available to all and that no one person or organisation has ownership of the results.

### Comparison with Other Surveys

Another issue pertinent to social surveys is that of non-response bias, whereby the characteristics of non-respondents differ from those of respondents. In order to estimate non-response bias, the characteristics of the sample are compared with the same variables in the population at the time of sampling. Although the 1991 Census of Population provides population-wide data, it is somewhat out of date for this purpose. For this reason, the Continuous Household Survey (CHS) is often used for comparison, as it has a larger sample than most social surveys, has a similar simple random sample design, and is carried out annually.

Tables A1.7 to A1.9 provide a comparison of Life and Times data with results from the 1998/99 CHS and Census of Population.

Table A1.7 Comparison of individual characteristics (%)

|  | Life and Times 1998 | Life and Times 1999 | CHS 1998/99 | Census 1991 |
|---|---|---|---|---|
| *Age* |  |  |  |  |
| 18–24 | 13 | 15 | 13 | 16 |
| 25–34 | 19 | 19 | 19 | 21 |
| 35–44 | 20 | 20 | 19 | 18 |
| 45–54 | 20 | 18 | 17 | 15 |
| 55–59 | 7 | 7 | 7 | 6 |
| 60–64 | 6 | 6 | 6 | 6 |
| 65 years and over | 15 | 15 | 18 | 18 |
| Refused | <1 | – | – | – |
| *Marital Status* |  |  |  |  |
| Single | 26 | 27 | 27 | 28 |
| Married/cohabiting | 61 | 60 | 58 | 59 |
| Widowed | 7 | 7 | 9 | 9 |
| Divorced/separated | 6 | 7 | 7 | 6 |
| Base = 100% | 1,800 | 2,200 | 5,390 | 1,117,221 |
| *Economic activity* |  |  |  |  |
| Working | 51** | 50** | 50 | 49* |
| Unemployed | 5 | 5 | 5 | 9 |
| Economically inactive | 43 | 40 | 40 | 42 |
| Refused/missing | 1 | 5 | 5 | 0 |
| Base = 100% | 1,800 | 2,200 | 5,390 | 1,167,938 |

* Based on total population aged 16 and over
** Includes schemes and employment training etc

Table A1.8 Comparison of tenure (%)

|  | Life and Times 1998* | Life and Times 1999* | CHS 1998/99 | Census 1991 |
|---|---|---|---|---|
| Owner occupied | 66 | 66 | 73 | 62 |
| Rented, NIHE | 25 | 22 | 19 | 29 |
| Rented, other** | 8 | 9 | 6 | 8 |
| Other (e.g. rent free) | 1 | 3 | 1 | 1 |
| Base = 100% | 1,800 | 2,200 | 5,390 | 530,369 |

* Household characteristics are based on unweighted data from the Life and Times survey
** Includes rented from a housing association and rented privately

Table A1.9 Comparison of stated religious denomination (%)

|  | Life and Times 1998 | Life and Times 1999 | CHS 1998/99 | Census 1991 |
|---|---|---|---|---|
| Protestant | 51 | 48 | 46 | 50 |
| Catholic | 38 | 39 | 31 | 38 |
| Other religion | <1 | <1 | <1 | – |
| No religion | 9 | 10 | 2 | 4 |
| Unwilling to say/don't know | 2 | 3 | 19 | 7 |
| Base = 100% | 1,800 | 2,200 | 5,390 | 1,577,836 |

### References

Breen, R., Devine, P. and Robinson, G. (eds) (1995) *Social Attitudes in Northern Ireland: The Fourth Report, 1994–1995* (Belfast: Appletree Press).

Breen, R., Devine, P. and Dowds, L. (eds) (1996) *Social Attitudes in Northern Ireland: The Fifth Report, 1995–1996* (Belfast: Appletree Press).

Dowds, L., Devine, P. and Breen, R. (eds) (1997) *Social Attitudes in Northern Ireland: The Sixth Report, 1996–1997* (Belfast: Appletree Press).

Robinson, G., Heenan, D., Gray, A.M. and Thompson, K. (eds) (1998) *Social Attitudes in Northern Ireland: The Seventh Report* (Aldershot: Ashgate).

Stringer, P. and Robinson, G. (eds) (1991) *Social Attitudes in Northern Ireland, 1990–91 Edition* (Belfast: Blackstaff Press).

Stringer, P. and Robinson, G. (eds) (1992) *Social Attitudes in Northern Ireland: The Second Report, 1991–92* (Belfast: Blackstaff Press).

Stringer, P. and Robinson, G. (eds) (1993) *Social Attitudes in Northern Ireland: The Third Report, 1992–1993* (Belfast: Blackstaff Press).

# Appendix II
# Notes on the Tabulations

1 Figures in the tables are from the 1998 or 1999 Northern Ireland Life and Times survey, unless otherwise indicated.

2 Tables are percentaged as indicated.

3 In tables, '<1' indicates less than 0.5 per cent, but greater than zero; '–' indicates zero.

4 When findings based on the responses of fewer than 100 respondents are reported in the text, reference is generally made to the small base size.

5 Percentages equal to or greater than 0.5 have been rounded up in all tables (for example, 0.5 per cent = 1 per cent, 36.5 per cent = 37 per cent).

6 In many tables the proportions of respondents answering don't know or not giving an answer are omitted. This, together with the effects of rounding and weighting, means that percentages will not always add to 100 per cent.

7 The self-completion questionnaire was not completed by all respondents to the main questionnaire (see Appendix I). Percentage responses to the self-completion questionnaire are based on all those who completed it.

# Appendix III
# Using Life and Times Survey Data

Tables of results for every question asked within the 1998 and 1999 Northern Ireland Life and Times surveys are available on the Life and Times survey web site <http://www.ark.ac.uk/nilt>. Results are available in the form of a frequency table, as well as cross-tabulations by age, sex and religion grouping (Catholic, Protestant and no religion).

While this book provides in-depth analysis on a variety of topics, and basic tables of results can be found on the web site, users may wish to undertake their own analysis of the data. For this reason, datasets are available from the Life and Times survey web site <http://www.ark.ac.uk/nilt> in SPSS portable file format. These can be downloaded and used for secondary analysis. The datasets are also deposited, and can be obtained from the UK Data Archive at the University of Essex <http://www.data-archive.ac.uk>. Datasets for all years of the Northern Ireland Social Attitudes survey, which ran from 1989 to 1996, are also deposited at the UK Data Archive. Data for modules included as part of the International Social Survey Programme (ISSP) are deposited at the Central Archive for Empirical Social Research at the University of Cologne <http://www.gesis.org/en/za/index.htm>.

Each year, the Life and Times survey includes modules on Political Attitudes and Community Relations. The following table identifies the modules fielded in all years of the Northern Ireland Social Attitudes survey, as well as the Life and Times survey, and indicates which modules were asked as part of the International Social Survey Programme. Excluded are standard classification items such as economic activity, religious denomination and party identification, all of which are asked every year.

Table A3.1 Modules by year of survey

| | Northern Ireland Social Attitudes survey | | | | | | | Life and Times survey | | | |
| | 1989 | 1990 | 1991 | 1993 | 1994 | 1995 | 1996 | 1998 | 1999 | 2000 | 2001 |
|---|---|---|---|---|---|---|---|---|---|---|---|
| AIDS | ✓ | | | | | | ✓ | | | | |
| Attitudes to work | ✓ | | | | | | | | | | |
| | | ISSP | | | | | | | | ✓ | |
| Charitable giving | | | ✓ | ✓ | | | | | | | |
| Childcare | | | | | ✓ | ✓ | | | | | |
| Civil liberties | | | ✓ | | ✓ | | | | | | |
| Community relations | ✓ | | ✓ | ✓ | ✓ | ✓ | ✓ | ✓ | ✓ | ✓ | ✓ |
| Countryside and the environment | | ✓ | | ✓ | ✓ | ✓ | ✓ | | | ✓ | |
| | | | | | | | | | | ISSP | |
| Culture and arts | | | | | | | | | | | ✓ |
| Crime and the police | | ✓ | | | | | | ✓ | | | |
| Diet and health | ✓ | | | | | | | | | | |
| Drugs | | | | | | | ✓ | | | | |
| Economic prospects | ✓ | ✓ | ✓ | ✓ | | ✓ | ✓ | | | | |
| Education | | | | ✓ | | ✓ | | | ✓ | | ✓ |
| Family networks | | | | | | | ✓ | | | | ✓ |
| | | | | | | | | | | | ISSP |
| Gender issues at the workplace | | | ✓ | | ✓ | | | | | | |
| Gender roles | | | ✓ | | ✓ | | | ✓ | | ✓ | |
| | | | | | ISSP | | | | | | |
| Genetics research | | | | | | | | | ✓ | | |
| Global environmental issues | | | | ✓ | | | | | | ✓ | |
| | | | | | | | | | | ISSP | |
| Health and lifestyle | | | ✓ | | | | | | | | ✓ |
| Housing | | ✓ | | | | | ✓ | ✓ | | | |
| Informal carers | | | | | | ✓ | | | | | |
| National Health Service | ✓ | ✓ | ✓ | ✓ | ✓ | ✓ | ✓ | | | | |
| National identity | | | | | | | ✓ | | | | |
| Pensions and pensioners | | | | | | | | | ✓ | | |
| Policy and the public | | ✓ | | | | | | | | | |
| Political trust | | | | | ✓ | | ✓ | ✓ | ✓ | ✓ | ✓ |
| Poverty | ✓ | | | | | ✓ | | | | | |
| Public understanding of science | | | | | | | | ✓ | | | |

Table A3.1 *continued*

| | Northern Ireland Social Attitudes survey | | | | | | | Life and Times survey | | | |
| --- | --- | --- | --- | --- | --- | --- | --- | --- | --- | --- | --- |
| | 1989 | 1990 | 1991 | 1993 | 1994 | 1995 | 1996 | 1998 | 1999 | 2000 | 2001 |
| Race and immigration | | | | | | ✓ | | | | | |
| Religious beliefs | | | ✓ | | | | | ✓ ISSP | | | |
| Rights of the child | | | | | | | | ✓ | | | |
| Role of government | | | ✓ | | | | ✓ | | | | |
| Sexual morality | ✓ | ✓ | | | | | | | | | |
| Single parenthood and child support | | | | ✓ | ✓ | ✓ | | | | | |
| Social capital | | | | | | | | | | ✓ | |
| Social class | ✓ | ✓ | | | ✓ | | | | | | |
| Social inequality | | | | | | | | | | ✓ ISSP | |
| Taxation and public spending | | | | | | ✓ | ✓ | | | | |
| Transport | | | | | | ✓ | | ✓ | | | |
| UK's relations with Europe/other countries | ✓ | ✓ | ✓ | ✓ | ✓ | ✓ | ✓ | | | | |
| Welfare reform | | | | | | | | | | ✓ | |
| Welfare state | | | | ✓ | | ✓ | ✓ | | | | |

# Contributors

**Owen Barr**
Health Research Board (Dublin) Nursing and Midwifery Research Fellowship, School of Nursing, University of Ulster

**John D. Brewer**
Professor of Sociology, School of Sociology and Social Policy, Queen's University Belfast

**Paula Devine**
Research Director of ARK (Northern Ireland Social and Political Archive), Institute of Governance, Public Policy and Social Research, Queen's University Belfast

**Caitlin Donnelly**
Lecturer, School of Policy Studies, University of Ulster

**Eileen Evason**
Professor in Social Administration and Policy, University of Ulster

**Liz Fawcett**
Lecturer, School of Communication, University of Ulster

**Tony Gallagher**
Professor of Education, Graduate School of Education, Queen's University Belfast

**Ann Marie Gray**
Lecturer, School of Policy Studies, University of Ulster, and Policy Director of ARK

**Bernie Hannigan**
Professor, Dean of Faculty of Life and Health Sciences, University of Ulster

**Deirdre Heenan**
Lecturer, School of Policy Studies, University of Ulster

**Joanne Hughes**
Lecturer, School of Policy Studies, University of Ulster

**Katrina Lloyd**
Research Director of ARK, Institute of Governance, Public Policy and Social Research, Queen's University Belfast

**Roger MacGinty**
Lecturer, Department of Politics, University of York

**Robert Miller**
Senior Lecturer, School of Sociology and Social Policy, Queen's University Belfast

**Kerry O'Halloran**
Senior Research Fellow, School of Policy Studies, Assistant Director (Research), Centre for Voluntary Action Studies, University of Ulster

**Gillian Robinson**
Senior Lecturer, School of Policy Studies, University of Ulster and Director, ARK

**Alan Smith**
Professor, School of Education, University of Ulster

**Kate Thompson**
Research Officer, School of Nursing, University of Ulster

**Rick Wilford**
Reader, School of Politics, Queen's University Belfast

# Index

*Compiled by Sue Carlton*

210